SAVING JENNY

Better to reign in Hell than to serve in Heaven. Mammon with his industrious crew set to build, Pandemonium, the high capital of Satan and his peers. . . . Long is the way and hard, that out of Hell leads up to Light.

—John Milton, *Paradise Lost*

SAVING JENNY

Rescuing Our Youth from America's Opioid and Suicide Epidemic

Vivian Percy
In collaboration with Anna Badini, PhD

Radius Book Group
New York

Distributed by Radius Book Group
A Division of Diversion Publishing Corp.
443 Park Avenue South, Suite 1004
New York, NY 10016
www.RadiusBookGroup.com

The author writes under the *nom de plume* Vivian Percy. She holds a JD, passed the bar, and is an attorney in good standing in the State of New York.

For information, email info@diversionbooks.com.

First edition: June 2018
Hardcover ISBN: 978-1-68230-999-5
Trade Paperback ISBN: 978-1-63576-521-2
eBook ISBN: 978-1-63576-423-9

Cover design by Marina Drukman, Marina Drukman Design Studio
Interior design by Scribe Inc.
Cover illustrations: "Close up of a girl crying" used by permission from Rebecca Nelson © Arcangel Images; "A broken and cracked window" used by permission from M. Brodie © Alamy Stock Photo

DISCLAIMER

I have tried to recreate events, locales, and conversations from my memories of them. In order to maintain their anonymity, in all instances I have changed the names of individuals, institutions, and places. I may have changed some identifying characteristics and details, such as physical properties, occupations, genders, locales, places of residence, and employment. Any resemblance to real people or places is coincidental. This book is designed to provide information and motivation to its readers and is not intended as a substitute for the medical advice of physicians. It is sold with the understanding that in all cases individuals should seek their own personal legal and medical advice.

The main character in this book is a composite character representing all the young people who have suffered from opioid addiction and suicidality in today's America. This is their story.

—Vivian Percy, July 28, 2017

In loving memory of all the young people
who have died in this atrocity
And with a call to save those still battling against it

And to Jenny, my daughter and my heroine, whose courage, honesty, and love inspire me every single day

CONTENTS

ACKNOWLEDGMENTS

I wrote *Saving Jenny* with the goal of saving lives. Reflecting, researching, and writing a book with this broad of a scope was very demanding, and it would have been impossible to bring *Saving Jenny* to light without the assistance of many people. I chose to write under the *nom de plume*, Vivian Percy, to protect the anonymity of all who were involved, due to the sensitivity of the material and the unfortunate fact that women, and even men, are still blamed and sometimes persecuted for being victimized and traumatized in our world. This incredible injustice and the lack of charity need to change.

First, I want to thank Dr. Anna Badini, a wonderful and brilliant psychoanalyst and friend, for her generous collaboration from the very beginning and throughout. This was especially helpful as we reviewed the accuracy of my descriptions of therapeutic practices within psychiatric/rehab facilities.

In addition, I am extraordinarily grateful to Mark Fretz, of Radius Book Group, who first had faith in *Saving Jenny* and in what the book was trying to achieve—to give validation to suffering individuals and families and empower everyone in society to call for the therapeutic, institutional, educational, political, economic, social, and cultural reforms necessary to defeat this scourge. It is thanks to Mark and his indefatigable devotion, guidance, and vision that *Saving Jenny* will have the opportunity to assist in the rescue of others afflicted by addiction and suicidality. And as Mark has told me so many times, "This country is full of millions of Jennies." Special thanks also to Christine Saunders for sharing with me that she read the entire manuscript in one sitting, and her heartfelt sympathy for its story. I am so appreciative, as well, that I was blessed to work with David Aretha, editor extraordinaire and encourager, who gave so generously of his time and caring. David restructured the raw chapters, bringing them into a cohesive whole, and confronted me (in a good way!) with constant important suggestions, constructive intellectual challenges, determination, and rigor. Then it was the wonderfully talented Marina Drukman who distilled the horrors of the epidemic that our young people face in her brilliant conception and artwork, giving us our compelling book cover. And S. A. "Sam" Jernigan of Renaissance Consultations—thank you so much for your empathy, amazing creativity, and passionate commitment to the message of *Saving Jenny.*

I must also express my deep gratitude to all of Jenny's friends who came forth as outstanding Good Samaritans and saviors. On so many occasions, they went above and beyond the normal call of duty to aid me in safeguarding Jenny. And thank you, Cora, Ivan, Maria, Rob, and Sharon, for your true friendship and support. Also, many thanks to Dr. G and Dr. L for their insights and humanity and to the countless therapists, physicians, pastors, counselors, members of law enforcement, and others whom I have never met but whom I know are battling this epidemic, in the trenches, with their total dedication.

In retrospect, I would like to thank my grandmother, Vivian, a sincere believer, who taught me that when something is wrong, you never give up fighting against it and you never give in. And with my deepest love and admiration for my own Jenny, thank you for all your love, faith, caring, strength, and generosity of spirit and for teaching me the meaning of true bravery of heart. Thank you for just being you, and I am so proud that you are my daughter.

Finally, there is no way that Jenny and I would have survived this all on our own, and I give thanks to God for saving us and bringing us through this tremendous ordeal with His infinite compassion and mercy and the power of prayer.

PART I

"Their Children's Cries Unheard"

First Moloch, horrid King,
Besmeared with blood of human sacrifice,
and parent's tears;
Though, for the noise of
drums and timbrels loud,
Their children's cries unheard
That passed through fire
To his grim idol.

—John Milton, *Paradise Lost*

introduction

EVERYBODY FEELS THE EVIL

> If Society is tranquil, it is not because of its strength and its well-being, but because it fears its weakness and infirmities. . . . Everybody feels the evil, but no one has courage or energy enough to seek the cure.
>
> —Alexis de Tocqueville, *Democracy in America*, 1835–40

It is 10 o'clock on a muggy July morning in 2017. I am slowly suffocating under the stifling suburban splendor of Round Bridge, New York, when I receive a heartrending text from my daughter Jenny's friend Emily that pierces my senses:

"I can't believe no one found Mikey for days. . . . The neglect is atrocious. . . . Like they all killed him. . . . They all used him up until he died!"

I immediately telephone Emily, as she is clearly very distressed and wants to talk to me. The first thing she needs to tell me is that her friend Mikey, a sweet-looking boy with childlike, sad blue eyes, overdosed on OxyContin one week ago. She feels especially aggrieved because he always seemed to be all alone and looking for love. Emily informs me that she is furious because, since the age of seventeen, he had been preyed upon by less affluent parasites in their late twenties who brought him lots of drugs—which he paid for, both his and theirs. And after they partied with him, they mocked him behind his back.

Sensing his fragility and lack of confidence, they domineered him. But he let them in because he needed to feel a sense of belonging, part of a group, liked, or wanted. Emily rages:

> He paid so much financially. . . . He paid with his life. . . . He was molded by these horrible bullies! . . . They took control. . . . They made him believe that getting messed up every day was the coolest thing a person could achieve with their lives. . . . But they had friends and school and jobs and a life. . . . He had no other friends, . . . no job, no school. . . . And they were secretly jealous of what he had materially, and he was needy. . . . So they could take advantage of him. . . . They just tailored him to be their feeding machine! . . . They just used him up!

Emily tells me she is suspicious about his demise: "But as usual around here, the 'recorded' truth about his passing will be nothing like the 'real' truth of his death." She also vows that from now on she is calling and texting all her friends at least twice a day, "because you never know what someone is going through." Good for Emily.

Last week the cops arrested an OxyContin dealer, "Ryan," right underneath my second-story kitchen window, located over the graveled, stately drive of our Gothic-style apartment building. The dealer, the son of an opulent local family, was let out of jail on only a few thousand dollars' bail. Why not also give him a ticket to fly? And Jenny, I later discover, also knew Mikey, as they had attended the same "alternative" high school. She was deeply disturbed by his passing, as she has lost so many friends and acquaintances over the past two years to this same scourge. And this makes her feel marked, as if something is very wrong with her.

I mention Mikey's tragic end to a neighbor, who replies, "Well, no one put the drugs in his hand and made him take them. No one *made* him do it!" That is the reaction of many people who don't want to hear about the drug epidemic and who feel like these kids had it coming for indulging in a vice and a corrupt lifestyle.

What they don't understand is that these deaths do not end the plague, and what drives these children to the brink is not a habit, which can be stopped with reasonable effort, but an addiction—a disease of physical/psychic enslavement that is compulsive and cannot be blocked easily at will.

Not every drug user is perilously hooked, but those who commit suicide most certainly are. And the path goes from drug use for fun and "relief," to abuse for a better reprieve from preexisting pain of all kinds, to overwhelming dependence. Only a few (the healthier ones) realize when it is time to stop and can manage the extent of their self-medication.

The truth of the matter is that an out-of-control craving for drugs is oftentimes only the surface symptom of underlying serious conditions such as brain injury, fixed reliance on prescribed opioid medication, trauma, and/or other psychological, emotional, and social afflictions that are not being treated and breed inner suffering and ill health. Then the compelling nature of addiction leads to overdose and suicide. Reportedly, drug overdoses now kill more souls in the US than car crashes (in excess of 63,000 lethal overdoses in 2016)[1], and suicide is cited as the second leading cause of death for ten- to twenty-four-year-olds, with 5,178 fatalities in this group in 2012 (likely higher in 2017).[2] Furthermore, US life expectancy fell in 2016 for the second year running for the first time since 1962–63 and, before that, in the 1920s. The BBC quotes Robert Anderson, chief of mortality statistics at the National Center for Health Statistics, who calls the two-year drop "shocking."[3] If one considers that most overdoses are suicides, then we are facing a pandemic of the self-murder of our children that outstrips the opioid epidemic itself.

One might ask, If that is so, then why isn't anything being done about it? Aren't there rehab/detox and psychiatric centers?

And that is the exact predicament.

First, many of these establishments are grossly ineffective, and worse, they are often damaging. Although announced as between 40 percent to 60 percent by the National Institute on

Drug Abuse,[4] the recidivism rate at most rehab facilities, based on our own experiences, the self-admission of even vaunted rehab centers, and the many addicts I have spoken to, it is in excess of 90 percent.

Second, a large number of the so-called mentally ill youth are, in fact, victims of early trauma and abuse who have been labeled as "bi-polar," "borderline," "schizophrenic," "ADHD," "OCD," "ODD," subject to inherited "substance abuse disorder," and/or "chronically depressed." These mainly "genetic/neurological disorder" diagnoses fit the mechanical and ultimately noncurative, but financially remunerative, insurance-driven Big-Pharma pill solution employed by almost all facilities. Although some of the medications may provide a lessening of distressing symptoms for certain individuals, quite often the true source of the psychic affliction, personal and family trauma, remains unexamined, untreated, and unhealed. And nearly all antipsychotic medications could have potentially serious side effects, in particular on a developing brain.

Third, compounding the problem, insurance companies approve only 3 percent to 4 percent of the inpatient treatment time needed for genuine recovery (psychiatric "cure" and/or sobriety), were an effective program in place (see chapter 6).

Fourth, the extraordinary sums of money charged are prohibitive except for the very few super-wealthy, who can afford to pay out of pocket.

Then the view zooms out to include pressing family, financial, community, cultural/societal, and spiritual matters that come into play, which will be addressed.

And isn't something being done about all that?

I began this book in early 2015 after learning of so many of Jenny's friends who had recently died from drug overdoses or suicides, not knowing at the time that these clusters of fatalities would continue in even greater numbers over the next three years. I had often felt that the passage of Jenny and her peers into the lost world of addiction and depression was a fall into hell and that many aspects of their baleful wanderings were aptly described in John Milton's prodigious *Paradise Lost*, as referenced in part 1 herein. But I also believed in my heart that there must be a way out of their Pandemonium—a "Paradise Regained," a liberating path up to the light, as set forth in part 2 of this book.

My single goal in writing this tale was to help find a way to save lives. It was my purpose to disclose what Jenny and her fellow travelers had experienced and witnessed, in memoir form (part 1), as a vehicle to diagnose the exact causes of our present inability to halt the pandemic, and then, most importantly, to discover the true remedy and practical solutions for stemming and ultimately defeating it (part 2). And this country is full of millions of Jennies and Johnnies.

As I progressed in my work, I realized that I was writing for everyone in American society, not a specific micro-readership, inasmuch as this crisis imperils all of us. And this is because our drug-addicted/mentally injured youth are the canaries in the coal mine of a nation falling apart from within due to its lack of human values. This is a reality that must be confronted and remedied forthwith if we are to save our children and ourselves.

It became clear that there are inseparable factors involved that need to be dealt with. The issue of trauma and what would constitute truly effective therapy are of primary importance. A huge area that needs to be exposed is the *mis*treatment we (and others) received at the different facilities established for the explicit purpose of solving the problems. So too is the way in which insurance companies and hospital protocols—or the disregard thereof—undercut the securing of adequate treatment. Moreover, of great concern is their approach to dealing with the patient's parents, who are too often mishandled, destroying the parent-child bond and any chance of a healthy family relationship, growth, and love.

What is absent in the addiction/psychiatric treatment paradigm conclusively revealed itself. Almost all therapeutic organizations (hospitals, rehabs, specialized schools) seem to be financially driven corporations that function for the sole purpose of perpetuating their own existence and not of ensuring that the best and most effective methods of healing are delivered. This is obvious on its face, as no addict or person suffering from trauma and mental affliction is going to be cured in three to five days (the limit of most insurance coverage). Yet the hospitals and rehabs have not protested this spurious protocol, while their coffers are filled by it—and amply. David Armstrong and Evan Allen of the *Boston Globe* cite how many rehab facilities seem to be mere profit centers that allegedly have no care for the amelioration of those who come to them in one last hopeful attempt to save their lives. One recovery CEO states "it's nothing more than puppy mills for insurance billing. . . . There is no investment in helping them get better."[5]

Nor can confronting addiction/mental health issues be separated from an examination of the current state of the institution of the nuclear family, the dissolution of the extended family, and our culture in which addiction flourishes, the illness is seen or avoided, and humanity has been turned on its head. All the former moral, kinship, and community frameworks that served as barriers to destructive and self-destructive activities, as well as available outside sources of help and positive encouragement—like religion, God, or a higher power—have either severely contracted, collapsed, or been abolished.

This has reduced our public environment to a malignant, material-engulfing, amorphous glob with no sense of good and evil, right and wrong, or beneficent direction as to what constitutes a truly meaningful, worthy, healthy, and bright life or uplifting ideals. Instead, it has become an acrid place where money, power, social standing, and cosmetic perfection are the only measures of a human being. Our young people are offered too little love; scant trustworthy, compassionate relationships; and few transcendent beliefs or aspirations that feed the soul. But at the same time, they are surrounded by a social milieu that promotes the (false) notion that it is justified and "good" to pursue any instinct, urge, or seduction. In addition, so many of them were deprived of the nurturance, affection, guidance, protection, and focused attention of traditional, relaxed stay-at-home parenting—now made nearly impossible due to the antifamily government, cultural stance, and tax structure of the last fifty years.

All this has robbed our children of a loving and healthy attachment to their parents, their innocence, and their authentic selves; they feel the unrelenting absence and grieve its devastating loss. Therefore, it is not surprising that our disoriented, despairing, and pain-ridden sons and daughters try to find solace and forgetfulness in drugs, self-harming behaviors, and, finally, in death.

Ultimately, undergoing manifold aspects of this tribulation—the agony of so many other parents—has led me to propose and set forth the suggested elements of new individually personal, professionally therapeutic, and sociocultural paradigms of healing based on spirituality, love, and virtue.

In part 1, we travel—sometimes with ironic humor—from the elite private schools of Upper Manhattan, to the gangs of New York City, to underground raves and human sex trafficking, on and off the venal (and even life-threatening) rehab-hospital-relapse "scary-go-round," and through the feckless court system. As a single mother, I use myself as Jenny's human shield, engaging in countless rescue missions. In my efforts to protect her, I eventually see this deadly disease for what it is while uncovering and analyzing the harms inflicted by our addiction/mental health care facilities and our society.

As my battle to save Jenny reaches a crisis point, I come to believe (as proposed in detail in part 2) that personal and collective restoration can be achieved (1) through the incorporation of spirituality, love, and virtue into the individual, familial, community, educational, and health care/government systems and on a societal and national-leadership basis and (2) by adopting a soul-centered therapeutic model in which spirituality, altruistic love, and psychodynamic treatment are synonymous.

Chapter 11 sets forth specific policy and cultural changes needed to bring about the crucial political, social and economic reforms vital to combatting this plague. In addition, I propose a twenty-point program for the successful inpatient treatment of those suffering from drug addiction.

1

SEEING IN A MIRROR DIMLY

It is April 2016, and after a very harsh winter, we expect a delayed spring—sometime in June. Looking in the mirror, I see a ravaged ghost of my former self and reflect that never, ever could I have imagined that my life and that of my twenty-year-old only child would have come to this.

Jenny has traveled from New York City to visit me in my "classy" flat in the sprawling tri-state suburbs, which I have been trying to sell since she was banished from the premises four months ago by my country-club-minded co-op board. She had created a "noise alert" when she screamed with anguish and rage, while in the grips of a nervous breakdown, the day after she had been brutally attacked and first-stage human trafficked. The unsympathetic board did not take this into consideration and held the reason for her outcry against her. Officially disabled with post-traumatic stress disorder (PTSD) for the past seven years, she has been fatherless since that tragic early Thanksgiving morning of 2006, when her dad died in her arms of a massive heart attack. Jenny has suffered deeply because I was an "elsewhere" mother when she was very young, and over the past decade, I have striven, with all my heart and soul, to be there for her and rescue and protect her in this world. Childhood is supposed to be a love story, but I am only too aware that (as with so many of her peers) Jenny's was, in so many respects, an absence-of-love story.

Today I have sneaked Jenny into my apartment, as I can sense she is in peril. Ragged and thin, she is sitting silently opposite me at the kitchen table. I can feel that she is desperate to talk, and there is something very important that she wants to tell me. Finally, looking straight at me with wide eyes filled with terror, she trembles as she speaks in a low and somber voice charged with alarm:

"Eight of my friends have died in the past week of overdoses or they have killed themselves. Everyone is dying; too many people are dying all around me. We are losing a lot of people this month."

Jenny is panic stricken and scared to the bone, and something eerie and ominous hangs in the air. Implicit in her comment is a plea: *You are an adult, and you adults are not doing anything to stop this sacrificing of your children.*

She continues: "I've been using lots of drugs, lots of Molly." The friendly name belies how powerful MDMA, also known as Ecstasy, is—a synthetic drug that drastically alters mood and perception, causing a surge in euphoria, energy, and activity, widely used in the "rave" scene. "Look at my eyes. I have such dark circles under my eyes, and they're getting worse and worse, and I can't stop it. I don't feel well; I've been feeling like I'm going under."

Jenny looks at me again, the light in her enormous amber-gold eyes dulled by the large, ashy patches beneath them and by the exhaustive battle she is not sure she can win.

"I have been feeling that death has been stalking me for a long time now. For weeks, I have been feeling death stalking me."

She and I have been through every treatment center we can find. Today, I hold her hands tight and tell her how much I love her, that she is everything to me, and that we will get through this together. We have a good talk. Jenny then says (again) that she has to stop using drugs, that she *is* going to stop, and that after speaking with me, she does not feel death stalking her anymore.

Where "It" Must Be Kept a Secret

I knew one of the students to whom Jenny referred. The photos in the news articles about her passing show a lovely, talented young lady radiating beams of sunshine. The parents in exclusive Hudson Valley Round Bridge speak in hushed tones about her and the other graduates of one high school class who have recently taken their own lives. They do not want this report to get out to the wider public, or else property values (today's *real* values and social prominence) may go downhill. Denial is the name of this game.

And unhappily, here the sole "family" or community guidance that many receive from stressed-out, high-achiever parents and upscale residents is the pressured obligation to pursue high-status careers that their children hate or may not be equipped to attain. Being able to succeed in vaunted worldly terms is the only allowance of personal worth they will be accorded. But the closeted truth is that some of the adults also cannot live up to these harsh, Draconian valuations of a person, as there has been a rash of parent suicides in Round Bridge as well.

Now that this book is almost finished, it is April 2017, and many more youngsters have succumbed to overdoses or suicides in and around our town. Denial and pretense should be much less acceptable, because they have become almost impossible to sustain. But still the baneful behaviors are worsening, and teachers must deal with mental and emotional disturbances and pugilism formerly observed only occasionally in high school, now being acted out on a wide scale by students in the first grade. Students are kicking, pushing, punching, and throwing against the walls the other girls and boys in their classes and subjecting them to haughty verbal diatribes. Some instructors feel physically ill having to write incident reports on a daily basis for six-year-olds just out of kindergarten.

"Why is this happening?" one teacher asks me. "What can I do? I wish I could see what is going on inside their homes."

These young ones are being primed for drug use, and at a much earlier age.

There is no intervention, there is no therapy for the student or the family, and human values are not permitted to be taught at any educational level, save perhaps for "good sportsmanship" in gym class.

But even those (from all layers of society, as we will detail herein) who have owned up to their problems and are grappling with the nightmare of drug addiction and suicidal depression feel nearly hopeless—because there is little help.

The "Treatments" Are Not Working

I recall a discussion with Jenny's New York City psychoanalyst in August 2011. This kind, highly trained, and intelligent lady was visibly pained as I recounted Jenny's experiences at various mental health centers, therapeutic schools, and rehabs while we attempted to do everything possible to find help for Jenny in her struggle with complex, chronic, and what I would also term "compound" PTSD and secondary substance abuse. That was six years and fourteen diagnoses ago. Jenny's therapist was especially shocked, as it became critically clear that *the same "at-risk" children flock to the same institutions, year after year, just as sick or sicker, and never improve.*

With wincing honesty, she said,

"This shows that what these places are doing is not working.

No one is getting well.

You need to write a book about this."

Traumatized and Addicted Youth throughout Our Society

> People were created to be loved. Things were created to be used. The reason why the world is in chaos is because things are being loved and people are being used.
>
> —His Holiness the 14th Dalai Lama

Jenny's friends tell me how they hate the pervasive desensitization around them and in the wider culture. They lament, "We are losing a whole generation of young people, just gone, and nobody cares or stops it. Doesn't anybody see what is going on?" It may come as a shock to the reader that despite their often untoward antics, these youths overtly bemoan the moral turpitude that envelops them. They shake their heads, indicating their helplessness to find their way out of Pandemonium, because the ancient signposts have either rotted away or been removed, and the old structures they could have grabbed onto to lift themselves out have broken down.

Many of our desperate children engage in perilous activities, such as punching one another in hardcore heavy-metal mosh pits and shuffling at raves in hazardous underground warehouses where "anything goes" while numbing out on Ecstasy and ketamine. This is not just a Saturday night—it is a way of antilife, and it is permitted. Jenny recounts saving a fellow raver from dying by puncturing him in the chest with her EpiPen, a la *Pulp Fiction*, and rape is commonplace when girls and young women are drugged out and defenseless.

Jenny tells me that she and her fellow ravers are like the characters on "the island of misfit toys": they do not belong anywhere else. It is relevant that most are from single-parent households, about 30 percent seem to be young veterans enduring the ravages of PTSD, some are battling cancer or other medical ailments, and quite a few are the victims of ostracization who felt unwanted by their communities and families. All these young people—many formerly middle class—have been unlucky in life, on their own *Logan's Run* through the streets. They are forced to make money in unhealthy ways, as they are too mentally and/or physically ill to function and too odd in appearance to obtain even minimum-wage legitimate employment, let alone have the capability to pursue an education and a career. There is no help for them in the way they need to be helped, and as "decent" society has rejected them, they commiserate with the raver "family" of the people of PLUR (peace, love, unity, respect). Unfortunately, this "family" most often serves up contaminated drugs for breakfast, lunch, and dinner, with the promoters and the "talent" taking their cuts the way that vultures feed off the wounded and the dying.

Jenny's Facebook cover page shows a malevolently grimacing, blackhearted, demonic skull version of *Alice in Wonderland*'s March Hare. This is a popular theme for most of the ravers, who feel they have fallen down the rabbit hole. She thinks it is "cool," while I believe it is a subconscious cry for help. The problem is that I am on the other side of the looking glass, and I cannot reach her. She hears my calls, only faintly, and she repeatedly tells me, "You do not see me" and that I see only myself in the mirror. I know she is telling me that I do not yet love her in the way that she needs to be loved, and I feel paralyzed, stupid, and wanting.

I have tried and tried, but I do not yet know how to pull Jenny back to the safe side. *I have paid a fortune for the experts to "fix" this, so why has no one helped her in the way she needs to be helped? What don't I get? What is it exactly that I do not see?* But I refuse to give up.

Another cautionary children's tale comes to mind as I reflect on these young people. They remind me of Pinocchio in the land of the donkeys, and we, the parents, are like Geppetto. I look at Jenny's empty bed and anxiously wonder, Where is she? And where is the Blue Fairy? Then I think back to how this all began.

2

FROM ORPHANED WITH PARENTS TO TRAGEDY, PTSD, AND ADDICTION

It is March 2009, and the two years following the death of my husband, Armand, have been very painful for Jenny. He was a brilliant professor of psychology and a larger-than-life figure always filled with optimism, fun, and vigor. Nobody could rain on his parade, which was why his students and his patients loved him so much—that and the fact that he was totally dedicated to them. Although fifteen years older than me and suffering from a congenital heart condition, he often looked younger. A dashing Hungarian, with golden eyes like Jenny's, he loved to bet on horses, play tennis, eat at the local diner, and cry at movies. I have not dealt with my grief, and Jenny has not processed what Armand's passing means to her.

Armand and I had tried to conceive a child for many years prior to Jenny's birth. When, in that fifth year of our marriage, a nurse practitioner came to tell me that I could no longer care for my Alzheimer's-affected mother in her Upper East Side apartment, Armand arranged to have her placed in an excellent nursing home in Manhattan. He was so good to my mother, which was another reason I loved him so much. Within one month thereafter, not having fully realized the severe stress I had been under in being the sole caretaker of an Alzheimer's patient, I became pregnant with Jenny. As a young woman, I had always said that I was afraid I would never have a child, and more than anything in the world, I wanted a little girl. God answered my prayers at the age of thirty-five.

In the New York City real estate downturn of 1995, we scraped together the down-payment money to purchase a one-bedroom apartment in which to begin our lives together as a family, and I decorated Jenny's room (a converted dining room) in chintz, white wicker, and Peter Rabbit. I was painting the kitchen yellow when my water broke on that hot summer afternoon. Unexpectedly, Jenny and I both almost died several times, during and immediately after Jenny's birth, and I fought for our survival over and over again.

This was how our lives together began. Do the incidents of your birth set the tone and the slate for the rest of your life? Are they a sign of the challenges that you will be fated to meet in the years to come? It would seem so. I do not yet know why Jenny and I have been bound together, at sea in this constant voyage around the obstacles of life-and-death encounters, but we have spent the last twenty years, just like Odysseus, trying to find our way home.

Jenny and the Nannies Arrive

After five days in the ICU, I bring our beautiful baby, Jennifer, out of the hospital on my birthday. Jenny is a miracle, enchanting and highly responsive, and she smiles at the end of one week. Armand has hired one of the last German, post–World War II, hospital-trained overnight baby nurses on the Upper East and West Sides. "Schotzie" (Edelheid Schotz) loves Armand and Jenny, but she seems to dislike almost all mothers. She jokes that she fires out "shots." (She reminds me of Ms. Trunchbull from *Matilda*). Schotzie demands that we purchase the "Silver Star" pram from London and shop for Jenny at deluxe Gallic children's clothing stores like Jacadi and Au Chat Botté. We buy Schotzie the pastries she requests from the finest French pastry shop in Manhattan. She informs me and Armand of the allotted times when we are allowed to eat, sleep, come out of our bedroom, retire to our bedroom, watch TV, and go outside. That said, she is so faithful, spotless, organized, and devoted to Jenny that we allow her to run our lives. Schotzie is an Upper Manhattan legend who is famous for telling one father (in front of his daughter's pediatrician as they began the three-month baby checkup), "You shut uppp uuunt let me shpeeek to ze doctor, becuz you do not know anyzeng about ze baby!" and for scolding and standing in front of the NYPD, showing them how to direct traffic properly when children need to cross to the other side.

Every woman needs the support of her own family when she becomes a mother for the first time, but I have no siblings, my father is deceased, and my mother does not know who I am anymore, so I am domineered by Schotzie and defer to her expertise. Then, after a blissful year at home with my beloved Jenny, Armand tells me that he needs for me to go to law school so that I can help him financially. I am stricken, because he really means it. I feel that I owe him for all we have expended on my mother's care.

I have no one to turn to for advice or help. My own mother was never home with me, and I had vowed to be with my child as she grows up, but that is not going to take place. It is an example of "repetition-compulsion." Armand told me Freud was pretty much right about everything, and it looks as though Freud is correct again, but do I have to personally be one of the proofs of his great insights?

When Jenny is one and a half years old, I look at her new nanny, Fatima, who is a wonderful Egyptian lady, and I hand Jenny to her as the wind of awful foreboding howls through my soul. I have no idea why, but I say, "I feel that I have lost her already."

"Oh, no," Fatima answers. "Please don't say that. That is so sad." However, there it is, and I sense that forces I cannot see have set down a penal sentence. In ancient China, execution was not death but separation from one's family.

Fatima is about to move with her husband to New Hampshire, and during the next ten years of Jenny's life, she will have thirty-two nannies, including assorted day, overnight, weekday, and weekend nannies. Some stay for several years at a time, some of them are temporary caregivers hired in emergencies, and some leave when they are intercepted by super rich mothers in Central Park who outbid me by $300 per week and extra days off.

Absent Mother: A Tale of Catastrophes

Armand's office is now in a new, modest, duplex, two-and-a-half-bedroom apartment we have moved into, but he is mainly a missing father, as he works very hard. He is unavailable most of the time and exhausted in the evenings. On an early Sunday afternoon in August, when Jenny is just two years of age, I return from a Princeton Review LSAT prep session and discover Jenny breathing in an odd and rapid manner. Both Jenny's nanny and Armand explain to me that Jenny was playing, and that is why her chest is rising and falling so quickly. However, this has the appearance of something totally different to me, and I feel that I must take Jenny to the pediatrician immediately. When we arrive, the doctor examines Jenny and says, "You have great instincts as a mother; she has no air in her lungs." Jenny is about five minutes away from going into an asthmatic coma and is rushed to Gideon Hospital, where she is placed in intensive care for one week. They lock Jenny in a thick metal cage that is elevated off the hospital room floor and anchored to the ceiling and the tiles by a strong lacquered pole. The nurses and doctors work around the clock for days trying to raise Jenny's oxygen saturation level, giving her nebulizer treatments every two hours, and more if needed. I stay with Jenny 24/7, sleeping in a chair, having our nanny relieve me for just one hour when I need to go home to shower and change my clothes, and then coming right back again. In the next eighteen years, Jenny will undergo at least another thirty emergency-room visits or hospital admissions pursuant to asthma attacks. All the signs are clearly screaming "Cassandra" forewarnings that

I should not go to law school and that I should stay home with Jenny.

After this incident, I start to sleep in Jenny's room regularly, oftentimes administering emergency albuterol-sulfate applications throughout the night and filling the bathroom with steam by running hot water in the shower and tub to ease Jenny's breathing as she sits on my lap. Every evening, we play Chopin's impromptus, the Nutcracker, and Christmas carols on a series of swirling CDs, and this is the music that Jenny falls asleep to. We perform and sing all the songs from the recent Disney movies. She twirls in my arms with her hands outstretched and her soft face upturned to me, her "Mozzarella cheek" pressed next to mine. She trills, "Can you . . . paint with all . . . the colorrrsss . . . of the winnnnddddd" from *Pocahontas*, which is our favorite. Like all children, she is sprinkled with stardust. Jenny's nanny bemoans, "I keep trying to get her to playact with me, but she will not do this with anyone but you."

When Jenny is two and a half, Armand and I are watching an orchestra play a lively Scottish symphony on PBS. Jenny enters the room with confident bravura and twinkling eyes, takes off Armand's tie with a flourish, wraps it from her shoulder to her hip with certain determination, and starts to dance a jig. We look up at the painting of my perfectly featured ancestor (why didn't I get her nose?) Mary Fraser MacLaren, which hangs in the front hall, and whose daughter Mary-Jane helped run the underground railway between Kentucky and Indiana. Jenny looks so like the lady in the portrait, with her shiny and cascading auburn hair, flawless skin, wide high cheekbones, and determined chin. Jenny also inherited my mother's sparkling smile and rakish dimples. (Thank goodness for alteration of generations!) Armand and I are stunned and exchange knowing glances as we watch Jenny doing her spritely version of the Highland fling. We both feel something spooky at the exact same moment, as Armand, regarding me purposefully, says, "You did not teach that to her, did you?" I look at him, grasping his meaning, and answer, "No, I did not teach her that." However, I think this was her innate gift for dance and theater showing through.

Within three months afterward, I start abdicating as a mother. I pray to God to put a halt to this, but I do not know how to stop abdicating, and it is all slipping through my fingers. While attending to my mother, preparing for law school, helping Armand with his practice, and caring for Jenny and the home, I am spreading myself too thin. I feel rotten to the core and inadequate while trying to give Jenny the superlative of everything by way of payment for my absence. I am the behind-the-scenes puppeteer, the "Phantom of the Opera." I enroll Jenny in a highly regarded music school and a choice private preschool, but my time with her becomes less and less as I start to compete in one of the top legal programs—when Jenny is three years old. I am one of four women who are married with a child out of some twelve hundred students. I tell myself that I am doing this for my family, as Armand's health is potentially fragile, and I might require a lucrative profession with which to support my daughter and even my husband for many years to come, but it will turn out to be the opposite. Jenny needs me more than my career, and we will all pay a horrendous price for this seemingly correct but ultimately destructive decision. Jenny desperately wishes for and is so worthy for me to be home with her to give her love, to nurture her soul, to be her teacher, and to share precious moments that cannot be captured in a squeezed-in half hour of "quality time," a misnomer if ever there was one. We are both missing out on miraculous experiences and forever memories that we will never have together. My better instincts are overridden by the Arbeit-Geist of the "Barbarians at the Gate," which tells me that I cannot rest and that I am worthless if I am not somebody in the world. Just being Jenny's mother will be considered "lame." I have accepted the lie that women can (and should) do it all. The devil must be laughing.

Jenny longs for me more than I know, especially as we have no extended family, and I imagine that she feels so acutely and soul splittingly alone. She cannot articulate her pain at such an early age, but her symptoms will speak volumes in the years to come. She will feel rejected, lost, and not good enough. She will be ill treated by other children, she will be abused by nannies because I am not there to protect her, and she will be lacking the self-assurance with which to defend herself and progress in this world. Her pediatrician and the experts advised me that "the research shows" that I only need to stay with Jenny until the age of three, but they are so misinformed and misinforming, and I really screw up.

I have bought into the Manhattan social/corporate rat race, thinking that I am giving Jenny the "very best" when all she wants is me. Instead, she feels the "very worst" without me being home with her, because no matter how wonderful the surrogate caregiver, all children passionately love their parents and ardently desire their own mothers to be with them when they are growing up. I recall meeting with my friend Hua, a fellow attorney from an illustrious Chinese family who resigned her position as a partner in a top New York City law firm. She noticed that her six-year-old daughter was not learning to read even though she was attending a well-known private girls school, where she was a "legacy" student. Hua told me that she came home one evening and found her daughter cowering in a corner, crying, "Please don't let her hit me," speaking about their trusted nanny. Evidently, the peltings had been going on for years, and on a daily basis. After that incident, Hua stayed home full time, and her daughter's reading level normalized. Why did I not heed this foretokening?

Years later, I will learn that Jenny was sexually molested and abused around the age of six by two nannies who were friends of one another and recommended to me by mothers at Jenny's "select" school. I had fired both within one month for their overt disrespect but was to discover, subsequently, that their surliness had been an expression of deep-seated evil and envy. As a result of their wickedness, Jenny will suffer inner psychic torment for years to come.

Working eighteen-hour weekdays and twelve-hour weekends, as a forty-year-old competing with twenty-five-year-olds, I am stressed out and morphing into a soulless automaton. There is cut-throat competition in the post-9/11, dot-com-bust, economic slump of 2001, and the attorneys in my firm work even harder and longer to secure their positions. The prevailing wisdom is that there is no "in between" on the island of Manhattan. You are a failed parent if you do not send your children to an elite private school, for they will then not get into Harvard or a comparable Ivy League college, and the alternative is a public school where you must drop them off with a crash helmet, a machete, and a bulletproof vest. This is the environment that we live in and what is expected of us. Where are all the "normal" kids that I grew up with, whose parents, like mine, paid five dollars per month for a local "parochial" education?

Manhattan's Ongoing Private Schools: Fierce Competition

Jenny's ongoing school, the Van der Weiden Academy, located on the Upper West Side, is arguably one of the top private educational domains in Manhattan. The cost is $25,000 per year (by 2016, this will have risen to $50,000 per annum), and the competition for admission is legendary—"more difficult than Yale Law School" is the standard comparison. But sending Jenny to one of these schools, thinking I was giving her the finest opportunities in life, was a drastic mistake. Her experiences there almost totally and permanently decimated her self-confidence and sense of self-regard and belonging anywhere. Everything that follows is by way of explication.

The snobbish mothers in Jenny's preschool never dared to exercise their usual discriminatory tactics against other parents or children, as they would then not receive the recommendation of the headmistress for their own children's admission to an elite K–12 lyceum. Therefore, Jenny was well treated. However, there is no reining in the attack-moms once their children enter the prestigious continuing braineries. They have arrived, and their hefty yearly donations, combined with their relentless event-hosting and fundraising activities, give them tremendous clout.

Jenny and I are optimistically outgoing, and we hope that we will make many new friends with whom we will remain close for the rest of our lives. However, as a mother who must work, not one who simply wants to work, I am a human breach of social etiquette among the "one percenters" who surround us in this neighborhood. These women do not see any point in making playdates with the daughter of an "odd mom out." Therefore, Jenny's only two friends in her class of thirty students are her best friend from preschool, Sarah, who is kindness itself, and a lovely scholarship student named Alisha. The mothers whisper about some women they know whose sons or daughters had to go to public (!) preschools and who now cannot get into private schools because they and their children are considered "tainted." Their blatant biases are unpleasant and offensive.

Jenny's real bleakness starts in first grade, as lovely Sarah and her family have moved overseas, where her mother and father are on assignment for a major bank. Increasingly, Jenny comes home reporting that she is being taunted, insulted, and physically bullied. Finally, one day, a group of girls asks Jenny to meet them for a student's birthday celebration in one of the recreation areas of the school. Jenny is happy, feeling that she is finally being included. But when she arrives at the location, all the girls holler "Let's get Jenny" and start to beat her up. Perhaps they are doing this because Jenny is one year younger than her classmates (having skipped a year of preschool), the smallest girl in her class, and already considered an outsider. Furthermore, she is isolated, as her only friend, Alisha, has been placed in the other class section, and they perceive that her mother is never around. The students push Jenny to the ground, punch her, jump on her, and savagely kick her in the stomach with their Oxford uniform shoes until she starts to throw up. Thankfully, an older boy enters the room and runs to get an adult. *Where were the teachers?*

That night, I listen to Jenny cry out for help in her sleep, and the next day I confront the principal and the head of the lower school, demanding an apology from these vicious little thugs and accountability for their actions. Armand warns me that I am mistaken to do this because there are hundreds of applicants for every spot in this stratospherically exclusive educational enclave, and he counsels, "They will come after us." Nonetheless, I respond, "What kind of mother would I be if I did not stand up for Jenny and for what is right?" Jenny has no idea why she is being so cruelly singled out. She feels bad about herself and her mom, who is supposed to make her happy. However, Armand, with his keen, realistic, and practical view of things, is correct as usual. After this scandalous incident, the principal hounds our family. This has happened on his watch, so he must protect himself by blaming the victim rather than admitting that they have a large number of awful students in their school acting out the boardroom aggressions of their corporate-raider parents (who pay $25,000 per year in tuition, not including the expected additional yearly donations of some $5,000 to $20,000 more) and their minions.

I do my best to participate in Jenny's key activities as often as possible: I leave my office to take her to birthday parties, to all school performances and functions, and to her rehearsals at her dance center and a well-known acting institute. When I have the available hours, I coach her in the performing arts, and she enjoys our time together. She joins the children's chorus of a New York City opera company and tap dances in the "Broadway Kids" benefit shows for the homeless.

Every Saturday (which is my only day off), desperate to make up for my absence during the week, I try to cheer Jenny up by taking her to FAO Schwarz, the Disney Store, the Warner Bros. Studio Store, pottery making at a ceramics workshop, and the Metropolitan Museum of Art, where we join in mommy/child art classes. We "take tea" at the dining room of American Girl Place, where we also attend the musical/theatrical performance *The American Girl's Review* and have Jenny's dolls beautified at the dolls' hair salon. Wow! A truly privileged childhood, one might think.

However, it all starts to seem pointless, for as Jenny turns eight and starts heading toward puberty, her resentment of me and her rage are becoming hard-fixed, and we both feel a palpable estrangement. In her heart, I am no longer her mother, whom she, as a very young child, so longed for and hoped to be. That time is past, and it is too late. Jenny now sees me as a betrayer who handed her over, undefended, to the unimaginable experience of sexual predation at the hands of two depraved women, leaving her isolated to deal with her confusion and pain and thinking she could not confide in anyone. She later told me that she believed she would neither be listened to nor protected if she told the truth, because Armand and I were engaged in nonstop work and never around, and her abusers seemed to have all the power. She felt that she was all on her own. As far as Jenny is concerned, I am just someone who swoops in, buys her stuff, and leaves. Jenny feels like an orphan with parents.

I know that I buy her too many things, but I feel that she rarely sees me, so in those moments during the week and on Sundays when I am not there, at least Jenny can hold onto the presents I have given her and say to herself, "My mommy gave me this," "My mommy loves me," because she has nothing else. I am a hamster on a wheel, and I no longer know what I am doing. We are being run over by the tyranny of not enough money in New York City and relentless social pressure. This is not what I want, and it is certainly not what any of us need, and it is not me. I am a simple girl who went to the Catholic school around the corner from my humble abode in a middle-class suburb of Gotham. I was a tomboy, sent there for discipline, and the religious principal warned my mother that I would "suffer greatly" in life because I refused to conform. And they were worried about my health because I was so thin that my uniform knee socks never ceased to pool around my ankles. When I was a mere five years of age and much older boys grabbed a sensitive young lad and bullied him, I threw myself into the middle of the gang and, pretending to be crazy, hurled myself around while swinging fiercely and wildly. I was incensed and screamed at them to "let him go!" as I grasped his hand, pulling him away from his torturers. My mother, who had told me not to interfere, was shocked—but it worked. I took my refuge in painting landscapes, reading Charles Dickens, and listening to the great composers. After watching the actor Cornel Wilde play the role of Chopin in *A Song to Remember* (shown over and over on TV on *Million Dollar Movie*), I decided I wanted to be a classical pianist. I spent all my allowance money on "mission babies" (the name given to poor children in foreign lands for whom Catholic school students during the 1950s and 1960s were encouraged to give donations) and jaw breakers, and I sneaked food from the nuns' kitchen to feed to homeless mother cats and kittens. They nicknamed me "cat woman." Today, I would be locked in a room with four shrinks and charged with theft. What is going on? What have I allowed to happen? *I do not fit in here, and what is more—they all know it.* How can I extricate myself from this sticky spider's web?

One day, I have a dreadful epiphany. I walk into FAO Schwarz, look around, and realize I have to leave. I have to leave because I no longer belong there. There is nothing left for me to purchase in the store because basically I have already purchased something of everything in the store. I turn around and walk out feeling like I have been hit in the face with a brick. I am a dead mother walking.

Armand wanted me to work as an attorney but ironically my so-called achievement of landing a job at a prestigious law firm is putting a strain on our marriage. Nothing is turning out as we thought it would. My nonpresence is terrible for Jenny and bad for him. There is a growing lack of communication, and we are like ships passing in the night because of my grueling schedule. We both feel trapped because I now need to keep that job to pay my $100,000 in law school loans, all the life insurance policies, Jenny's now $30,000-per-year school, her summer camp, and her extracurricular classes, clothes, medical coverage and pharmaceuticals, and nannies. In addition, I pass ample amounts of cash monthly under the table to the staff in the nursing home to ensure that my mother receives special care. (These secret payments probably keep my mother alive much longer than without them.) And there are many other expenses involved in my mother's good keeping. Personally, I have not bought myself any new clothes for nine years.

I want to follow my heart's dictate, which tells me to find a way to stay home with Jenny. Every second that I am at work is dripping with toxic guilt because of my separation from her, but Armand tells me that we need my position more than I realize.

The whole situation takes a tremendous toll on my health, as I undergo several medical crises. First, after collapsing in my office, my blood pressure is dangerously low, and I am rushed into uterine surgery. Then I am hospitalized for two weeks with a life-threatening histamine reaction and, later, with severe bouts of pneumonia. Armand has a minor diabetic stroke in 2004, which does not affect him cognitively but leaves him unable to function at his prior pace. My mother passes away in 2005. Then I am diagnosed with a massive dermoid tumor attached to my ovary in early 2006. Throughout all this, Jenny is becoming more and more traumatized and terrified, but I keep working because there does not seem to be a choice, especially as I have become the main support of the family.

Tragedy Strikes at Thanksgiving 2006

Finally, I decide to leave my job, having calculated that I have enough money in my retirement fund and legal associate life insurance policy to draw upon for one year.

My surgeon informs me that I must go into laparoscopic surgery immediately to remove both ovaries and fallopian tubes as well as the giant dermoid because it is now cutting off the blood flow to my heart and sometimes, in frightening and gripping episodes, I am doubled over, even in public. I beg her to do a good job because I cannot leave my daughter an orphan. I don't know why I say this.

Two weeks later, at 11 p.m. on Thanksgiving Eve, I am still partially recovering from my operation in another room when eleven-year-old Jenny finds Armand in extremis and calls the ambulance. His doctor had given him Avandia for diabetes, and it is subsequently alleged that Avandia causes heart attacks and strokes in half the patients who take it.

They transport Armand to the one hospital I know will be the kiss of death, but EMS refuses to drive him anywhere else. They intubate him.

For several months' prior, there were premonitions that this was going to happen. Only a few weeks ago, Armand told me that he had dreamt of seeing all the stars shining so brightly in Bermuda, where we had spent our honeymoon, and that he thought that meant that he was going to die. On this day, the movies on TV are all about daughters who have lost their fathers, and I recall to Armand that Thanksgiving was my mother's birthday, and I miss her so much. I have purchased a multicolored-light LED Christmas tree, and Armand comments with childlike sweetness that it is so beautiful, and he apologizes to me for his being ill. My heart is breaking, but I tell him that no, I am so sorry that he is not feeling well, but we will get him better. Death always seems to be preceded by a big neon sign, but coming on the day it does, it is excessively cruel to us, especially to Jenny.

In the hospital, the doctor tells me, "It is all over. We have done all that we can do, and he is not going to make it."

I reply, "I do not care what you say; I want to see my husband."

"No, he has tubes in him, and it is not pretty. No, you can't go in."

I repeat, "I want to see my husband."

Jenny comes into the operating area with me. There is no heartbeat on the monitor. I start to sob from somewhere deep within and without me: "Armand, I love you. You are the love of my life throughout all time. Jenny and I need you. Please come back to us."

Jenny is standing next to me, and not a pin drops among the hospital workers listening outside. It feels as if everyone is holding their breath. Suddenly, the staff in the OR look up at the monitor, abruptly break the stark silence, and start shouting at us: "Get out! We have a heartbeat. Get out! We are starting up again!"

Armand had heard me and had come back to us. I sit in the chair outside the operating area, not knowing what had happened, and then they do what they did to me when my father died in the hospital, and what they always seem to do. The nurse comes out of the surgery room, says nothing, and hands me Armand's watch. He had run out of time. He would never see the new watch that Jenny and I had bought for him to open on Christmas morning. When we return home, I find an envelope that Armand had left on his desk: "For Vivian's Eyes Only . . . Happy Thanksgiving, as always." Inside is a note to me, written on one of his memo pads:

> Dear Vivian:
>
> My dearest and lovable Viv. Your words to me last night made me feel truly loved and loving in every way. You know, Jesus loves you. Jesus loves us all. Thank you for everything you are and mean to me.
>
> Love,
> Armand
>
> We have had a wonderful life together.

His farewell letter. Somehow, he knew.

We hold Armand's wake at a renowned funeral home in Manhattan. Jenny makes and displays beautiful collages of our lives together. On the final night of the wake, when the priest comes to say special prayers, Jenny suddenly looks like a faun that has been cornered by a mountain lion, starts shaking, and runs to the bathroom, vomiting uncontrollably. I am there with Jenny, trying to console her, and I want to somehow protect her in every and any way that I can from the fact that Armand's death has struck such a devastating blow to our small family, but how? This is a catastrophe, and our lives will be permanently altered. At the funeral mass, Jenny delivers an amazing eulogy that touches people's hearts for many years to come and that inspires others who read her moving tribute on the internet.

We are utterly alone. The weight of my responsibilities has multiplied. Nevertheless, the next two years fly by. Jenny sleeps in bed with me for the first six months following her father's death, as she is traumatized and plagued by petrifying nightmares. I enroll her in a new, more normal, and much less expensive school, and she makes new friends. I spend every day with Jenny going through her coursework, and she does well. We are very busy with her professional voice-over work, her training in the opera company, and her classes in singing and dance. We have many wonderful times, and we cleave together as a team. Jenny is one of the finalists for a major role in a Broadway production.

Finally, I run out of money, and I sell every piece of furniture that is not bolted to the floor and nearly every item of jewelry that I own, but I must return to work.

As I commence the interview process, I notice that Jenny's behavior is starting to change for the worse. I still have not learned my lesson, and I am about to make another major error. I should sell the apartment, move, and continue to stay with Jenny. However, she is now thirteen years old—no longer a small child—and I mistakenly think it is important to hold on to the residence so that she will not have to endure the loss of her childhood home. Therefore, I am going back into the law game, and Jenny will suffer more than I can ever imagine. Adolescence is a very fragile and turbulent stage in development, with all its physical, social, psychological, and emotional changes and the accompanying anxieties about oneself.

Mom's Back to Work: What Will Happen Now?

I secure new employment and take Jenny out of her Manhattan school, placing her in a boarding school on Long Island. This allows me to stay at the office until midnight on many evenings, with a reasonable belief that Jenny is safe and that her activities are supervised.

At precisely 3:00 p.m. on the beautiful afternoon of Good Friday, April 2009, when Jenny is home for spring break, I pick up my office phone, which is ringing with a display screen that says "EMS." I think that it must be a wrong number, but I receive a message that knocks me over.

"Ma'am? Are you Jenny's mother? I am an EMS worker. It is OK. Don't worry. Everything is OK. Jenny was hit by a taxi. Our EMS vehicle was there on the street at the time, and we took her to Citadel Hospital. She is all right. Don't worry. She is OK. But can you come to the hospital right now? Because she is a minor. Can you come? Immediately?"

I quickly leave my Midtown office, and I run into a colleague in the elevator who tells me that it will be OK. However, I already know that it will not be OK.

When I arrive at the ER, there is turmoil. EMS wants statements, the police are present, there are witnesses to speak to, and Jenny is lying on a bed in a neck brace, looking very fragile, stunned, and frightened. I rush in to comfort her. The doctors tell me that they are going to release her because none of her bones are broken, but this does not at all reassure me about Jenny's actual condition. I know that it is Easter weekend and that they want to discharge as many patients as possible because they are short staffed, so I protest, "How can you release someone who was just struck at very high speed and thrown into the air by a taxi? You need to keep her for observation. She has suffered a dreadful impact. No one gets hit with such velocity and force without something being wrong." I know now that this was only the beginning of a long pattern of quick and premature discharges by all the health care facilities we henceforth dealt with.

But the doctor and the nurses wave me away and inform me that they will monitor Jenny for only another fifteen minutes, and then I need to take her home. That evening and the next morning are a blur. We meet with a detective who comes by to speak to me and Jenny about the accident, and I set Jenny up on the downstairs sleeper-sofa. Early the next evening, Jenny looks at me with analytic fear from her mattress in the living room and questions me in a frail and tentative voice:

"Mommy, do you see snow on the ceiling?"

I feel a dangerous presentment. Looking up and searching the ceiling, I wonder what Jenny can be talking about because I do not see anything unusual. I answer that I do not see anything. Now I look at Jenny very intently.

"Mommy, but I do. I keep seeing it," she says. Five seconds later, she asks,

"Mommy, do you see flashing lights? I see lots of fuzzy gray-and-white specks buzzing around like snow on a TV when the channel is not working. Do you see that, Mommy?"

Finally, she tells me, "Mommy, I have a cracking pain in the back of my head."

Jenny then suddenly passes out cold, but she is in a form of unconsciousness so unlike sleep that it is alien and jarring. Her body is here, but even though she appears to be breathing, Jenny seems gone. I scream at her, shaking her, throwing water on her, but I cannot wake her up. Jenny resembles a fish just brought home from the market lying on the kitchen counter. I lift her arm, and it drops. I raise her legs, and they slump. I move her, and she stays where she lies. After I call EMS, it takes fifteen minutes for them to appear.

When they transport Jenny back to the ER of Citadel Hospital, she is placed in the same room that she was in yesterday. The scheduled ER physician enters about a half hour after we arrive, but no matter what any of us do, we cannot wake Jenny up. I flick my hands in her eyes, which look glassy and vacant, and her eyes do not blink. There is no muscle movement anywhere on her face or in her body. I pray that my Jenny will speak. I keep telling her, "Mommy is here, Jenny," "Mommy loves you," "Please wake up, Jenny." I ask God to please let Jenny wake up.

At last, one tear streams down Jenny's immobile face, and she starts to mumble, barely audible, and I think that she is going to say "Mommy," but instead she says,

"Daddy, Daddy, I see you. Daddy, why did you have to go?"

Jenny then goes completely silent again. It is clear that she is right at the edge of deciding whether she is going to stay on this earth or leave it. We have been here for hours. *Where is the neurologist?*

I turn to the nurse:

"She is in a coma!"

The nurse replies with slow and deliberate enunciation:

"Well, she is in an *al*-tered state."

"An *altered state*? You mean she is in a coma!"

"Yes, an *al*-tered state."

"Please, where is the neurologist? Please get the neurologist! We have been waiting way too long, and we need the neurologist right now!" The nurse looks at me with a detached, calm regard, says that she will try paging again, and gradually turns to pick up a phone.

In a state of desperation, I pace down the hall, feeling that I am in a terrible and unbelievable battle against death itself, and I start to pray:

"Dear Jesus. I know that I seldom pray to you, but you are the only one who can bring Jenny back. Please, Jesus, save her life. I beg of you."

I return to Jenny's bedside, and shortly afterward the neurologist appears. I guardedly allow myself to feel hope. It is now 10:00 p.m. I tell her everything that we have been doing and that Jenny is not waking up. We try shouting, and water sprinkling, and gentle shaking, but Jenny is still unresponsive. Then the neurologist pulls out a technique that I will be using ten or more times over the next three months: the "knuckle rub to the sternum." She crooks her forefinger while placing the rest of her right hand in a fist. She then leans over Jenny and thrusts the knuckle of her forefinger into Jenny's collarbone in the area adjacent to her neck. The neurologist keeps applying this pressure over and over, with a few rests between pokes, and I keep praying. Finally, after approximately ten minutes of this procedure, Jenny's eyelids start to flutter as she slowly awakens. My gratitude is unspeakable. It seems like a miracle. I ask the neurologist, what we can do to make sure that Jenny does not go into another coma. She just looks and me and does not provide an answer.

It is now after midnight, and the doctor on duty comes in and tells me I must take Jenny home. *Why do they keep doing this?* I reason with the doctor that Jenny is likely going to relapse. At 8 o'clock the following morning, Jenny begins to lose consciousness again, and I immediately start to call out to her repeatedly. I apply the knuckle rub to the sternum myself, and finally the doctor appears and agrees to admit Jenny to a floor upstairs and order neurological tests. I sleep in the room with Jenny all weekend, and Monday morning, Jenny starts to go under again. I call for help. The neurologist covering this floor comes into Jenny's room and tells me he is going to inject her with Ativan, because Ativan is used for seizures. I am horrified: "What are you doing? This is not a seizure. She has been going into comas. If you inject her with Ativan, you will put her into a deeper coma."

I push ahead of him to reach for Jenny. I ask him to take the syringe away, and he leaves the room, looking perplexed. I continue to speak to Jenny in a loud voice:

"Stay awake, Jenny! Stay awake! Stay awake!" I lift her into my arms and place her high up on the bed and then apply the knuckle rub to the sternum quite forcefully. I throw water on her while repeating, "Stay awake! Stay awake, Jenny!" Finally, she regains consciousness.

The kindly couple whose teenage child is in the bed next to Jenny's does not want to become involved, but God bless them, they tell me, "You better demand to see the head of neurology, and right away. That doctor did not seem to know what he was doing. You have a life-and-death situation this very second, and you cannot wait. You better call for the head of neurology of this whole hospital."

This is exactly what I do. The hospital's head of neurology and I meet in the "bubble room"—the typical glass-walled holding area—along with a lady from human relations. He asks me, "Why would someone give a coma patient Ativan? You want to bring a person out of a coma as quickly as possible. The more time out of the coma, the better. The longer in a coma, the worse it is."

"That is what I would like to know."

It appears that "Dr. Ativan" has been taken off Jenny's case. Later that afternoon, the partner head of our law firm practice group calls me, and I tell him about Jenny's comas. I mistakenly assume he has telephoned to see how she is doing, but he cuts to the chase: he wants me to follow up on a certain deal he would like for me to work on. I wish that I had gone to medical school, where I was headed until my mother developed Alzheimer's, instead of to law school. Most attorneys have a billable-hours clock where their hearts ought to be.

I give Jenny lots of hugs, read to her, help her through all the tests, keep trying to cheer her up, and watch her like a hawk. I tell her, "I love you, Jenny—across the universe!"

"I love you, Mommy—across the universe—to infinity! I win!" she replies, smiling her sweet and sheepish smile. She looks like a winsome faerie with electrodes in her hair.

I am afraid to go to sleep, and I have been glued to the chair in her room for the past three days. The doctor comes in to tell us we will be leaving tomorrow. I must arrange for twenty-four-hour nursing care for Jenny at home for at least two weeks, and I need to call her boarding school to debrief them on how to recognize Jenny's precoma warning symptoms and how to apply the knuckle rub to the sternum. It is clear to me, although no one has a medical term for it, that these returning bouts of coma have the semblance of reoccurring human tsunamis that keep washing over Jenny.

God has been so very good, but I am still an idiot. I should look to sell our house so that I can afford to stay home with Jenny, but instead, I just go back to work, planning to reenter her in school, as the doctors have mistakenly told me that Jenny is "fine" because the CT scans and the MRI are "clear."

Post-traumatic Stress Disorder (PTSD)

Although undiagnosed at the time, Jenny is afflicted with a powerful concussion, traumatic brain injury, and PTSD. Two months later, her personality changes dramatically, and Jenny is completely immersed in something she has never even thought of trying ever before in her life: drugs.

3

AN AERIAL VIEW OF THE DRUG SCENE

NO HELP HERE

The Scary Site

It is late spring 2010. Jenny is fourteen years old, and we are living on the Upper West Side of Manhattan, just off Central Park. Right underneath the highly polished surface of the Upper West Side are the gangs, the countless bodegas that secretly sell alcohol to preteens and teens, and a raging drug marketing system on every corner. Jenny is now hopelessly addicted. She still desperately misses her deceased father and can neither mentally nor emotionally process his passing. In addition to the searing pain of this loss, she is unable to recover from her PTSD and her repeated comas after being hit by the taxi, as well as all the other traumas she has been subjected to throughout her short life, which, I believe, is why she is self-medicating.

Our remaining family unit is only me and Jenny, and (not knowing who else to blame) she holds me responsible for everything, asking me why I can't be skinny, rich, and married to a super wealthy man like the mothers in her former "one-percenter" school, and then maybe she wouldn't have been treated so badly there. Jenny wants nothing to do with me, her "loser" mother, in our intensely materialist locale, and she feels rejected by everyone else, so last year, she went out looking for family and companionship in the notorious street gang "The Bloods," whose turf begins only a few blocks north.

It was a hot summer night in August 2009. When Jenny did not arrive to meet me and my friend for dinner, I called the police, feeling that something dangerous had happened. At the exact same instant the police showed up, Jenny collapsed into the front hall of our building, begging me, "Mommy, please help me. . . . You were right . . . you were right. . . . Please help me, Mommy." She had suffered a "thirty-one-second gang beat down" and "curb stomping" that broke her nose and gave her yet another head injury. Her face and hair were saturated in her own blood, and her forehead was covered with massive lumps. The beater, a girl named "Sauce" (whom Jenny had rescued from a prior brutal attack by a gang member and whom she thought cared about her) had turned on Jenny, holding up a trophy towel soaked in Jenny's hemoglobin. Sauce thanked Jenny for giving her "the thirty-one seconds" needed for gang entry, warning Jenny that if she ever returned "uptown," she would be killed on the spot. One of the NYPD officers who took Jenny to the hospital told her, "They [the officers] do not go 'up there,' and they are not going to go 'up there' to rescue anybody from anything." Despite some "authorities" telling me that Jenny requires "more freedom," the truth is that she desperately needs to get off the streets, where she is constantly in peril.

Now it is nine months later, and although I do not fully realize it, Jenny has fallen victim to an insidious cocaine habit, and she is living outside the margins. I feel both powerless and clueless, holding onto the memory of the Jenny that was prior to Armand's death and unwilling to admit the truth that is staring me in the face: that childlike Jenny is long gone, and we are at the mercy of the ravages of drug addiction and all that it entails.

I no longer have a husband with whom to share all of life's joys and considerable demands, and my daughter's plummet from normalcy parallels my crash into single motherhood. I am still working fourteen to eighteen hours per day as an attorney in a highly competitive law firm, where I excel in client contact but fail miserably at back-corridor connivance. There are daily calls with the teachers at Jenny's new Midtown school and with outpatient program directors, psychiatrists, and social workers about how best to "manage" Jenny.

Jenny has abandoned her career as a child voice-over artist and performer, hopelessly and mournfully telling me that she feels as if "that life is dead and gone forever, and that [she] can never get it back again." What harrowing sentiment from a fourteen-year-old girl!

Two months ago, I received an urgent Friday evening communication at my upper Midtown office from an outpatient rehab friend of Jenny's telling me to race down to Union Square, as Jenny was meeting a classmate there to do drugs—which is what Union Square was known for. In a panic, I rushed to the square, searching for Jenny and querying almost every homeless person and drug addict in the park. I found a police car at the edge of the Fourteenth Street section, but no officers were inside the vehicle or anywhere nearby to ask for assistance. Not knowing what to do, I then received a phone call from Jenny's fellow runaway, Carol, who told me that "everything was OK," that she had taken Jenny with her to her home in Staten Island overnight to help her and talk to her about things, that Jenny did not want to speak to me right now, as "she just needed a little space," but that she would make sure Jenny was all right. I calmed down and felt I had been granted a reprieve from angst and worry, as this girl sounded so mature and sincere, and maybe I believed her because I wanted to believe her, and perhaps also because I was still ludicrously dense about how convincing drug users can be.

The next day, Carol's father informed me that he had allowed both girls to go to a Friday-night party in Brooklyn at 11:00 p.m., but they were coming back to Staten Island on that Saturday afternoon.

I took the ferry (which I had never ridden before) to Staten Island to retrieve Jenny when she arrived at Carol's residence.

However, when I asked Carol's father why he allowed the girls to leave for Brooklyn so late at night, he grabbed me by the arm, applying relentless pressure while telling me that whatever his daughter did or did not do was of no consequence to him. I barely left the apartment in one piece.

I then called the Staten Island police, who suggested riding the ferry back and forth to try to catch Jenny, and their officers agreed to help me find her and detain her once she was recovered. After three round trips over the chilly waters, we intercepted them on Saturday at approximately 8:00 p.m. She and Carol were so high that it was almost comical, because, hey, desperation is the engine of comedy. Their jaws dropped when I found them, and they looked up at me and the ferry officers goofily, with bleary eyes, bobbing back and forth against each other, hardly able to stand, let alone speak coherently. I was just thankful to God that no one had taken advantage of them, waiflike and so young as they were, in their obviously totally incapacitated states, wearing skimpy dresses and with naked feet in worn-out flip flops on a very cold day. At that point, I was in a state of shock and exhaustion, but with my adrenaline pumping and my head buzzing—trying to match the energy of a drug-fueled teen—I was desperate to save her.

Jenny was furious that I was taking her home and became violent toward me during the car ride back to Manhattan, flailing and kicking at me and breaking and flinging in my face the pretty bracelet I had recently given to her. All this was accompanied by a barrage of cursing.

Once at our house, I telephoned her current therapist, who overheard Jenny threaten to jab herself in the stomach with a long kitchen knife (which she was wildly swinging about) if I tried to force her to go to the hospital. I could not believe that everything had escalated to an even more dangerous situation than the one I had just rescued her from. I froze, terrified that she would stab me if I tried to take the knife from her or stab herself if I called the police. It was like being trapped in a horror movie, unable to switch channels. There is no getting out, because I don't yet know how to extricate her on my own, and I will not leave her alone.

The therapist did what I was hesitant to do because I felt I would be betraying Jenny, as I had never yet committed her against her will. The police arrived and took Jenny to the emergency room of Citadel Hospital. Jenny had denied she was on drugs, so I took a video of her behavior with my phone to present her with a future reality check. Jenny later laughed at her own false indignation when she saw herself, with her head lolling, her speech thick and slurring, and her eyes rolling back in her head while she kept insisting, with great outrage, that she had not used any drugs and that my saying that she had was "ridiculuuuuus" and that I was "ridiculuuuuus!" When you are living in the funhouse of distorted reality, everything starts to become a farce. Normal rules no longer apply.

The psychiatric hospital social worker and doctor convened with me after Jenny was an inpatient for three days and asked me what I wanted from them. I sat in their "negotiating" room, sobbing and telling them, with innocent sincerity, that I wanted them to save my daughter. They exchanged pointed glances of hard and dry amusement and then abruptly released Jenny the next morning, noting in her medical chart that I had rejected their advice to send Jenny to the $60,000 (for one and a half month) Colorado wilderness program that they had recommended in our brief meeting. The social worker told me that she could offer us no other alternatives, even after I explained that as a single, working mother, I could not afford $6,000, let alone $60,000.

The day after Jenny comes home from "the Citadel," I walk into her room and find her staring at her computer screen, crying, with her arms pouring blood. Jenny has cut herself and shows me the scars of prior lacerations to her legs, telling me that she has been doing this for several months. She starts weeping. "I am a horrible person, and there is no one who I am more hurtful to than you! I hate myself. I am an awful person. I hate myself!"

I cannot believe what I am seeing. This is not real—it cannot be. But if it is real, please, God, let it not be that serious. However, I know full well that this is deadly dangerous and that I have no idea whatsoever how to stop it. I tell Jenny that she is a very good person and do all I can to comfort her. Yet I perceive that her urge to cut herself is a powerful compulsion with a will of its own that Jenny cannot control. And I am alarmed because I can see that my words will be no defense against it. Her arms are butchered, and I treat them as best I can. On some level, I feel I am losing my own mind. But I am the parent, so that cannot be permitted to happen. Jenny's slicing herself with razors will continue over most of the next decade.

Throughout the year, I have put locks on all the windows of our house. I clean Jenny's room, try to keep her well, and endeavor to make sure that she stays in school for the day and attends after-school programs. I go out to look for her when she does not come home on time. I buy her puppies and kittens and parakeets to stave off her severe depressions and to nudge her toward responsibility. However, she quickly loses interest, so I dutifully find each pet a very loving home. I could open a pet store.

Faithfully, I buy drug test kits and administer one to Jenny on a daily basis, but she knows how to beat the tests. I give her numerous psychiatric meds every day, locking them in a tall, strong metal filing cabinet, but Jenny tells me, and it is obvious, that the pills do not help. I hide the keys to the filing cabinet and those to the illegal inside lock on the front door so that Jenny will not run away at night. Then I hide my wallet and my purse, separately, trying to remember where I have hidden everything, because I must secret each item in a different location to avoid a jackpot discovery. If I had kept them in my bed, she would have unceremoniously wrenched them from me, as she is very strong. I take my showers after midnight, when Jenny truly seems asleep, so she doesn't go through the house to find all my hiding places while I am in the bathroom. However, Jenny does find everything, when I finally passed out at

2:00 a.m., and she does get out of the house. I vaguely recall her coming up to me, at around 1:30 a.m., putting her face close to mine, and asking me very sweetly, "Are you asleep, Mom?" I answered this seemingly innocent query with a somnambulant, side-leaning "Yeeesssss." (Years later, in a rehab program, Jenny will admit that, in several ways, she had stolen over $50,000 from me without my knowing it, such was my state of total exhaustion.) Jenny is seriously out of control again, needing to be in a long-term facility with twenty-four-hour observation and supervision. We mothers of "in-crisis" teens know the necessary steps to get them there.

How to Get Your Child Seen in a Hospital Psych ER

The required first step to having your son or daughter transferred to a longer-term inpatient psychiatric hospital is to have him or her seen in the psychiatric emergency room of a hospital. This is almost always while in the throes of an urgent medical crisis, and under police escort (as your child will not go willingly), and from there to a long-term residential therapeutic school/rehab/psychiatric facility. The hazards will increase every day, so you must take decisive action upon the next incident.

If the police have not received an emergency call from a reputable third party, you must induce law enforcement to intervene. Report that your teen has been missing for a substantial length of time, has a serious psychiatric condition, and may be in a life-threatening situation. Tell the police that your adolescent is very ill and that she self-medicates when she does not take her psychotropic prescriptions, as this will most likely ensure that your child will go to a hospital, and not to the Rikers Island Juvenile Detention facility, when she is found with drugs in her system or on her person. So many "therapeutic professionals" will berate you that you have "done your child a great disservice by keeping her out of jail," but the public will learn in 2015 that the juveniles at Rikers have been ruthlessly targeted with sexual violations and all kinds of abuse for years.

In addition, you must present a totally convincing case for police rescue, with the performance of a well-honed thespian, or the officers will not feel compelled to become involved. You must have already printed out eight-by-ten photos of your child with a biography and telephone numbers to hand to the police precincts and to plaster around the city. You must post, "I love you so much, [insert your child's name], please come home," on your child's Facebook wall and plead with her friends to do the same. You must work closely with the detectives (who are usually wonderful) to try to find your child by using the GPS tracker you have installed on her cell phone. If your child has cleverly turned her phone off to deactivate the tracker, swiftly proceed to your phone carrier's website and copy the cell numbers of her last calls and texts. You must have already cracked her cell phone password and surreptitiously duplicated all her cell phone contacts so that you can match names to numbers. You then must hire an expensive private investigator (if you can still afford one, as the time will come when you will no longer be able to) and ask for the PI to do an illegal "ping" to determine the geographical location of the phone of the person your child last spoke to. Then you must pray with every cell in your body that this person is *the* person who knows where your child is and that the detectives can persuade them to tell the police officers where to grab your child before it is too late.

All the foregoing is every mother's "Get Your At-Risk and Addicted Child to the ER" manual.

Jenny Goes Missing

I ask the detectives, "I can put a microchip in my cat; can't I put one in my child?" I seriously wonder if I can find someone who will do that for me.

If I could afford it, I would like to pay an international facilitator to have Jenny kidnapped and taken to a high tower in Sicily, guarded by men with machine guns out of *The Godfather*, until she is twenty-five or thirty years of age. I would arrange for her to engage in farming during the day, attend chapel every morning and every evening, study the classics, copy ancient manuscripts, and wear a chastity belt. Where are the good old days?

At this point, I am a total wreck, sleepless for almost twenty-four hours, and in a complete state of cortisone overload. My eyes carry more baggage than the entire Samsonite collection. I have said several rosaries and prayed for God to make me a better parent. If only they will find Jenny! I say to myself, "I must have been very bad in my last reincarnation to deserve this."

It is now 8:00 p.m., Friday, May 14, 2010, and Jenny has been gone, without any contact, since sometime in the first morning hours of this same day. A two-man police officer team comes to the house after the detectives take their leave. As providence would have it, I am overjoyed that at this exact time, Jenny turns on her phone, and the GPS tracker places it (hopefully she is still with her phone) as located just under the Brooklyn side of the Brooklyn Bridge. These cops are not in a good mood. I ask them to please come with me to Brooklyn and follow the tracker so that we can locate and retrieve Jenny. They both regard me with prejudiced hostility and then look at each other. The toughest one, Officer "Adverse," speaks to me with a brutish roughness:

"Get yourself to Brooklyn." His facial expression tells me that he is subvocalizing, *You snooty, Central Park West, privileged pain in the ass*. Instead, he says, "You can get yourself to Brooklyn."

I explain to them that I have no car, that I am not familiar with Brooklyn, and that I need their help to rescue my daughter, who is very emotionally fragile. I am hoping that the less overtly antagonistic one, Officer "Grumpy," will relent, but they are refusing to take me. There is a knock at the door, and the police sergeant (who is older, tall, and gentlemanly) enters the front hall along with his sympathetic female partner. He sees my heartache, is empathic and concerned for me, and demands that these officers go with me to search for Jenny. He locks eyes with his partner, and they both seem to approve of the fact that I want to go out, myself, in pursuit of my daughter and not merely leave this in the hands of the authorities. I am so very grateful to the sergeant because, although I have lived in New York City for thirty years, I have no idea where Brooklyn is. Why would I? Most of my life exists within a forty- to sixty-block Manhattan rectangle of work and Jenny's schools, like a gerbil's habitat. There never has been time to go anywhere outside of this geometric space. No vacations, no side trips. Nothing else.

We arrive at the Brooklyn police headquarters, which the GPS tells me is only three blocks away from where Jenny is located. Both officers go inside the precinct building. I exit the police car to give the desk sergeant a photo of Jenny so that it can be copied and distributed to Brooklyn law enforcement, which will help us in our reconnaissance efforts. Officer Adverse then descends the outside steps, abruptly puts up his hands in the "halt" position, physically moves to block my entrance, and tells me I cannot give Jenny's picture to this precinct. He is citing some bullshit about jurisdictional conflicts between Manhattan and outer-borough offices. I know this division needs and wants a likeness of Jenny because their desk sergeant has just told me so over the phone. Nonetheless, Officer Adverse tries to prevent me from setting foot inside—while flashing his holster at me. I issue a declaration of my impending plan of action:

"I am giving them the snapshot of my daughter so that they can find her, and you are not stopping me."

He is a big guy, and I guess he might handcuff me and arrest me, but I do not care, and I walk past him anyway. I am officially out of my mind due to this scary situation that may sound unreal to anyone who has not experienced it, alone to handle.

When both officers rejoin, we follow the GPS tracker, which leads us only a few streets away, to some alphabet avenues where the midtwenties grad students cook pots of various drugs to feed to the age-thirteen-plus Manhattan girls so that they can have their way with them at "underwear parties" held at strips of approximately twenty illegal wobbly clubs. No, the authorities are not shutting these places down. We are standing in the crossroads of ramshackle bars reminiscent of Old West saloons on the outside and eighties discos on the inside. A young adult male roadhouse impresario points to his right and tells the cops,

"The age twenty-five and up are in the clubs on this side. The age fifteen to twenty-five are in the clubs down to my left."

The police do not bat an eye, even though the legal drinking age is twenty-one.

I first go searching in the older-aged dives and then in the younger ones. The faces of the teenage girls I encounter look up at me in a depressed and confused blur, but no Jenny. I want to reach out to them, but I know this is impossible right now. They all look sweet, frail, sad, and lost. After about forty minutes of inspection, I receive a call from her. Jenny was tipped off that I was looking for her with the police and cabbed it back to our building. I ask for the concierge to (please) keep Jenny with him, but he refuses. Thankfully, Officer Grumpy springs into action, takes the phone out of my hand, and tells the concierge who he is and to "sit on Jenny, if necessary," and keep her there until we arrive. I am so grateful for this officer's change of heart. Jenny gets back on the phone with me and asks me to promise her that I will not have the police take her to the hospital if she stays where she is. I feel very bad about doing this, and my chest clenches with shame, but I lie, promising that I won't make her go to the hospital and that I will take her back home.

When we reach our address, the sergeant and his partner pull up simultaneously, and I request that they transport Jenny to the emergency room of Gideon Hospital. They tell me that if they do so, they will be required to handcuff her. And incredibly, I allow Jenny to be manacled, because this time I mean business, and I am not letting Jenny come home. This is it. I have been mercilessly berating myself over the past twenty-four hours because I, once again, foolishly believed her promises to stay home and stay sober, and my naïve trust has endangered her very life. When will I learn? Jenny acts childlike, lovable, and fragile, and my heart is breaking because she is in my charge and I love her so very much.

She looks at me with doe eyes, my determination starts to melt, and I want to keep her with me. However, I don't know what else to do. How many times can we both play Russian roulette? I feel defeated and robbed of my relationship with her but must put a stop to her running away, with the constant risk of overdose and rape. Also, I must get her out of the clutches of "Inner Sanctum," the teen outpatient program Jenny has been attending. She needs inpatient treatment again, and this time, for many, many months.

Out of Inner Sanctum and into Cresting View!?

As I wait to speak to the ER psych doctor on all-night duty at Gideon Hospital, I recall that Inner Sanctum, the shiny, newly minted, worse-than-useless teen outpatient drug program that Jenny attends, gave lithium to Jenny even though they knew she is still struggling with heavy alcohol use and that mixing lithium with alcohol could result in potentially fatal convulsions. This, of course, is exactly what happened, and Jenny underwent a smack-down, blue-lipped, cardboard-stiff seizure in Union Square and was rushed to the hospital by ambulance. Now Inner Sanctum has tried to cover its ass by demanding that Jenny belongs in a "tough-love," out-of-the-way facility called "Cresting View" in Southern New Jersey. Cresting View is very expensive, and they have hired a super aggressive, slick sales marketer. I cannot help but speculate about the potential kickbacks in this never-ending web of referrals to the preferred and extravagantly priced therapeutic schools, rehabs, wilderness programs, and outpatient centers. Indeed, I will later learn that just this sort of quid pro quo and payback practice has been taking place and was exposed by *New York Times* reporter Megan Jula in 2016. Various expensive treatment centers across the country make explicit offers of thousands of dollars to drug rehab staff members for referring heroin or pain-pill addiction patients with good insurance to their programs.[1]

During my personal inspection visit to this "school" two weeks ago, I witnessed the confession of a returning boy who had relapsed onto heroin and who was sneered at (during a public meeting) in very nontherapeutic language by a man with a dirty beard who was dressed in a soiled T-shirt and spoke like and resembled Charles Manson. My tour guide later showed me the very narrow, white, windowless padded room where they locked the kids who "got upset," and which presently housed a girl. The young female resident selected to accompany me on my tour with ongoing testimonials noted my discomfort and dutifully stated, "She needed it." This young attester herself appeared skeletal, and her eyes had dark circles, which concerned me greatly. I pondered, *Do they starve her?* These girls slept in rusty trailers on a terraced hillside, even in the depths of winter, reportedly sometimes seven to a trailer. I got a very uneasy feeling. There was no way I was going to send Jenny to Cresting View, and in subsequent years, this place would be hit with numerous accusations of child abuse and ultimately shut down. Nonetheless, this is the location that everyone, including one of the most highly respected treatment centers in the country, said that I and other parents must send our addicted children if we wanted to "do the right thing." The right thing for whom?

Navigating through the System

Finally, I speak to the thoughtful psychiatric physician at Gideon Hospital, and then he talks to Jenny. She tells him the truth about everything: her gang involvement, high-risk behaviors, cutting, drug use, overwhelming depression in the wake of her father's death, and feeling acutely suicidal after being hit by the taxi one year ago.

Right now, she is furious with me because she feels that I have deceived her by turning her over to the police, and also her addiction hates me. As she waits inside the psych bubble, cursing me out, I frantically call every "dual-diagnoses" (treating both addiction and mental illness) hospital in the area to see if there is an "available bed" so that I can say to the emergency room psychiatrist, "There is a bed at Halcyon Headland Psychiatric Hospital, and if you telephone them now and call EMS, then we can get her transferred there at 8:00 a.m." I implore the Halcyon Headland employee on duty at 3:00 a.m. (because these things always go down after midnight) to arrange with his friend, the 7:00 a.m. admissions person, to admit Jenny in the morning and grant us the priceless pallet. I express profound gratitude for his agreement to do so, and I mean it. Then we need to race up there with rocket blasters on Jenny's hospital gown, or we might lose the one open juvenile addiction/psych spot, as there is a burgeoning demand. If we miss our appointment, Jenny may be transferred to a hellhole of a mental ward somewhere, and I will not be able to stop it, as she has already been determined a "danger to herself" and in need of psychiatric admission anywhere. The ER psychiatrist looks at me funny because this must all be my fault—because I am the mother, right?—and because I am shaking and terrified for my child, in an almost complete state of emotional dysregulation. I have already lived through Jenny's two near-fatal overdoses. (There will be four more, in the next five years, and much worse than that, when I thought that nothing else could be worse.) I am very close to being a full blithering idiot. However, in stark contrast to my out-of-control appearance, my child, with enormous amounts of alcohol and drugs in her system, is *calm*. She lies to the police that I am bipolar, and the cops tend to agree with *her*. After all, they have just driven with me (in a state of near hysteria) to Brooklyn and back.

I am having a nice talk with a young African American girl sitting opposite Jenny in the psych ER holding room of Gideon Hospital. We like each other (every child other than my own always seems to appreciate me). This sixteen-year-old does not approve of Jenny's rudeness toward me. She tells Jenny,

"You should not speak to your mother that way. Your mother cares about you and is doing everything to help you. Quite frankly, I should not even bother to tell you this, because we do not tell people like you this, but your mother is right. In my neighborhood, we just look at girls like you and say, 'Oh, good, another stupid private-school girl on drugs.' You need to listen to your mother."

Finally, a badly needed clear thinker! I am very grateful to this young lady, who has tried to shock Jenny into stopping her self-destructive behavior, but unfortunately, this young woman's selfless honesty has not made a dent.

Jenny is then strapped into a stretcher and loaded into an ambulance on her way to the designated psychiatric treatment center in the countryside. The EMS partner requests information, and I again relate Jenny's history.

The night before last, a handsome young man who seemed very troubled appeared to me in a dream that truly felt more like a visitation. He looked at me, seeming both burdened and sympathetic. I asked him if Jenny was going to be OK. He came up to my face and stared intently into my eyes, never letting go of my gaze, to be sure that I really understood what he was about to say:

"*Did you ever think that she has just been through too much?*"

I woke up crying. What he told me was the truth in a nutshell. Is there recovery for a person who has been through too much? I believe there is a cure for everything. There has to be. A friend of mine who had become a rabbinical student once told me that when Moses went up the mountain of Mt. Sinai, he not only was given the Ten Commandments but was also shown the "Three Books of Medicine," which contained every malady that ever was or ever would be, along with its remedy. However, God was so angry at humanity's unfaithfulness that he deemed us unworthy of the books and withheld them. Therefore, it is up to us to find the cures. (The point being that they exist.)

However, for right now, Jenny is a prisoner in the back of an EMS van, and she glares at me and says,

"I hate you. I *hate* you *so much*! I wish that you had died and my father had lived. Why did he have to die and not you!? . . . Go die in a hole."

One week earlier, Jenny stole my work BlackBerry, and they had to retool my law firm's entire security system. I am a fifty-year-old lawyer who does not have a razor-thin corporate figure, and I need my job, which I am about to lose. I know super affluent women who can afford to be home and not work, as well as the bodyguards who pick up their children from the Upper West and East Side private schools. They and their families are fortunate to be protected by layers of money like a myelin sheath around a nerve transmitter. However, my nerves are frayed, and as is the case for so many millions of single mothers, I must perform a head-of-household economic function. Regrettably, I do not have the super-PAC funds it takes to throw against the problem of teen addiction and trauma in a Spencerian/Dickensian world. There is no way I can afford for Jenny live at Beautiful Shore (an upscale psychiatric facility) for $500,000 per year out of pocket, although I am acquainted with people who do, and even as it is Jenny's most fervent wish. She remarks that Beautiful Shore is nothing more than a beautiful hotel and a celebrity Band-Aid, but she wants to be protected from her ungovernable anxieties and from this cruel world in lovely surroundings forever. I have already spent some $76,000 sending Jenny there for slightly over two months, and they only contained her. They did not cure her or even help her, and she underwent an alarming episode on her second day out.

I must be gainfully employed to support Jenny for years to come and ensure her higher education. Illness took everything I had saved, and Jenny's addiction will take our home. In addition, as my husband was a psychologist, it looks like the shoemaker's child truly has no shoes. This does not help anyone's assessment of me, especially because I am all by myself and appear unprotected. Armand used to say,

"You don't want to look like the 'wounded caribou.' You think that other people will have compassion for you, but unfortunately, knowing what I do of human nature, they will come after you all the more if you admit to any problems—even those who are supposed to help you."

I have to acknowledge that I do look just like a wounded caribou. I try my best not to, but I just do. I can't help crying and sobbing, and there is no getting around it. I recall that he also told me, "Hospitals are places to get out of, not to go into. I know. I have worked in hospitals."

Nonetheless, we are now on our way to yet another dual-diagnosis hospital, and I pray, I pray that this time someone will do right by my child. I have been told that Halcyon Headland will help Jenny. However, that "little voice" tells me I am just bargaining with the seasons, and I wonder for how many more weeks, months, and years, Jenny and I can last in this never-ending mental "stealth/re-bad" shell game. The truth is that I have that sick feeling in the pit of my stomach, and I already know that this is going to be much worse than I ever could have dreamed it would be. The signs are all here. I shove this foreknowing way down, determined to discount it.

On the car-service return ride to Manhattan, after Jenny's eight-hour admission to Halcyon Headland, I meet a fashion retail executive mom, Joanne, whose daughter knows Jenny (all "Les Miserables" seem to be familiar with each other). Joanne has been dealt a similar fate. She is a single mother, and she also does not have the money to send her child to a $40,000-per-month facility for at least two years. She recently found her daughter in a gutter, nearly comatose from alcohol poisoning. Joanne points out to me that New York City touts itself as so safe for visitors and the super rich. She then says it is no coincidence that violent crime has gone way down while teen addiction has gone way up. I go into mind freeze. What is she talking about? Joanne states,

"It is we single, middle-class, and poor mothers who are paying to keep the violent crime rate down because the criminals are being sated by marketing drugs to our kids. Why mug a rich person when you can sell crack to children? It is a very good business." I think she may be right, and I feel unwell and furious. In addition, she tells me, just before jumping out of the vehicle that we have shared into New York City,

"Stay away from the social worker!" I have no idea what she means. "Stay away from the social worker! Do not talk to the social worker! They will call you tomorrow, and do not pick up the phone. They are not there to help you. They are there to get Jenny discharged as quickly as possible from the hospital. That is their job."

I am still gullible, and I cannot fathom what Joanne is talking about. My daughter's pediatrician has told me, "They really know what they are doing up there, and they will sort everything out for Jenny at Halcyon Headland. They will work with you to keep her there if your insurance runs out." I have had faith in Jenny's pediatrician since she rescued Jenny from that major asthma attack when she was two years old. Therefore, I believe that the social worker who will be assigned to Jenny's case will be one of a Halcyon Headland group of high-minded and caring intellects who seeks to heal every patient and who will come to an understanding of what it is that plagues Jenny, truly restore her soul, and get her well. I have visions of Bette Davis and Claude Rains in the 1942 movie *Now, Voyager*, wherein Davis's character suffers a nervous breakdown and goes for transformational inpatient psychiatric treatment at a sagacious manor on a hill in Massachusetts. However, the day after Jenny is admitted, I receive the call from the social worker that Joanne predicted. He tells me that he is not speaking to me to discuss Jenny's case but is only contacting me to ask where I am going to send Jenny when she is discharged, as she has to leave Halcyon Headland in a few days. In a complete state of shock, I ask him,

"What are you talking about? Jenny just arrived, and you are calling me the very next day to ask about discharge planning when she only just got there?"

He almost laughs at me over the phone. "Well, this is the way it is. So we just need to know." Once again, where, indeed, will Jenny go?

Avarice, Abandonment and Angels

Unbeknownst to me, it must be written somewhere in a book that by April 2016, Jenny will have been psychiatrically hospitalized more than twenty-five times, attended four therapeutic boarding schools, four outpatient addiction programs, and five inpatient rehabs. I will have hired two special education attorneys, one educational consultant, three guardianship attorneys, ten separate therapists (including psychiatrists), and a private detective on four occasions. I will have employed a private driver to take me everywhere in emergency situations of all sorts, because one person needs to drive while the other is attending to the crisis, especially in the dead of night. The total monetary cost will be in the millions of dollars. The total human cost (physical, mental, and emotional) will be incalculable.

I will learn that 99 percent of the juvenile rehabs, therapeutic residential schools, and psychiatric hospitals are commercial enterprises and that it is all about their economic augmentation. Our children's mental illness and addiction ensure the flourishing of these lucrative ("nonprofit"/profit) centers. Then, after all of them have taken everything that Jenny and I have to give, the court will terminate my guardianship of Jenny at age eighteen, setting her loose, out on her own and unprotected. As a result, Jenny will undergo devastating events.

I will, nevertheless, over the course of the next eight years, learn about the power of prayer, that there are forces of good and evil, that there are angels and demons, that there is this earth and another realm, and that the veil between life and death is very thin.

In Jenny's Own Words . . .

Very recently, Jenny herself told me she had not expected to make it beyond adolescence. She said, looking at me with stunned reflection, "Mom, it was a good thing that you constantly went out to save me and that you sent me away to all these rehabs and places and got me off the streets, or I would not be alive today."

I then asked her, "When actually did all this start, Jenny? These suicidal thoughts?"

"I never even thought of doing drugs, and it was something that I never wanted to do and that I knew to always stay away from. But right after I was hit by the taxi, all I could think of was suicide. All I could think of was killing myself. All I wanted to do was die—every day, all day long, and all night long, all I wanted to do was end my life. And with all that I was taking—cocaine, Ecstasy, Vicodin, Xanax, Valium, Klonopin, Ambien, Ativan, ketamine, OxyContin, heroin—and mixing it all with alcohol and going to very dangerous places, I was sure I would be dead at fourteen. If you had not rescued me, I would not be here. I did not expect to be here."

The first guardianship attorney told me, "You kept her alive!" when I said that I felt I had not cured Jenny.

Yes, the Money

For people without the money, it is impossible to do many of the urgently necessary and right things to save your loved one who is suffering from mental illness and/or addiction. I lost every penny I had, plus my car, which I sold, my furniture, jewelry . . . any material possession that someone was willing to buy. But I would do most of it all over again.

Ultimately, the court took away my legal power to safeguard Jenny because she came under the influence of unscrupulous people who urged her to request it and obtained my removal. Thankfully, these predators were out of the picture after one year's time, but she had suffered greatly, and my custody of her was never reinstated.

Jenny, therefore, required even more help from me, as she was often in trouble and because I could not force her into a facility for treatment. I was left having to find her when she was missing and in great danger, to answer her calls for help, all to try to avoid having Jenny destroy herself. And I was in a state of constant worry, day in, day out, always waiting for the next shoe to drop.

Perhaps some may think this means I "enabled" Jenny. However, that is too facile and superficial a label to stamp on someone. Had I not rescued her numerous times, she would have annihilated herself and be dead by now. She would not have learned by her own mistakes, because developmentally *she was still a child*, suffering from untreated PTSD, and lacked the capacity, the maturity, the judgment, the self-control, and the brain health necessary to do so. Nor did she have the support and healing help of truly effective one-on-one psychotherapy. Most glaringly, 99 percent of the medical and psychiatric inpatient hospitals, outpatient mental health clinics, inpatient and outpatient rehabs, schools, social workers, psychologists, and psychiatrists refused to offer Jenny and her peers any access to spirituality as a possible source of strength, love, hope—and cure.

4

THE SCARY-GO-ROUND, PART I

The Slippery Slope

It is now early summer 2010, and the past year has felt more like five. Jenny is still fourteen years old and still reeling with the brain injury caused by the taxi crashing into her the year before. I have returned to work to earn money to survive.

My palms are sweating as I wait on the blue-cushioned sofa outside the evaluator's office at Halcyon Headland. Jenny has been speaking to the psychiatrist, so he can assess the best discharge referral for her, as she will be dismissed in three days. I am still deluded and therefore hopeful that Halcyon Headland will arrange for a considerate and affordable transfer to an enlightened and helpful place of remediation and recovery.

Jenny exits the doctor's office with vigorous gusto and regards me with penetrating eyes that glisten with laughing daggers. It is a visual I have lived with for a long time. Clearly, Jenny has not achieved any new insights, let alone a change of heart, in her five-day stay thus far. But neither have I, as no one has given me a clue as to what is really going on. That is what I will have to find out on my own, through years of compelling experiences and painstaking research.

Now, as the door closes behind me as I enter the doctor's office, I attempt to position myself with a semblance of dignified posture in the narrow black-plastic chair placed next to the examiner's desk. But surprised by the hardness of the seat, I fail miserably. I wonder if this is an intentional strategy, as every parent who struggles to gather his or her thoughts while teetering in this crude and uncomfortable contraption has already been placed in a physical and psychological state of discomfort, disadvantage, disrespect, and devaluation. To boot, I am dismally aware that I have run out of both time and money. The physician, a tough but friendly realist from Taiwan, looks me full in the face and says, "Yaaaahhhh, Jenny hates you; she hates you so much. She is uncontrollable, and she is doing massive amounts of drugs. She wants nothing to do with you. Maybe in ten years from now, she might have a relationship with you, maybe never." I feel hit with the worst kind of unexpected blow to the gut and like I sort of want to die. He continues: "The only thing that might help Jenny is sending her to a wilderness program for several months."

The wilderness programs in the summer of 2010 were regarded as the holy grail for troubled teens when in fact they were most often places of abuse and financial rip off; however, no one knows this at the time, and the doctor means well.

"You are an attorney, yes? So you should have no trouble paying $40,000 per month, yes?" He smiles at me.

I explain that after spending some $100,000 over the past six months on various places to cure Jenny, the only asset I have left is my home, and I will not be able to sell it overnight. I also clarify that Jenny overdosed on a bottle of ibuprofen to get herself out of the famous "accountability development" school I sent her to last January. Recommended to me by an expensive educational evaluator and by attorneys with sons, this well-known facility allegedly routinely ordered students who committed minor infractions to run 5:00 a.m. "suicide laps" around the gym until they dropped. And the administration had required Jenny to be part of the daily "chop-the-ice work crew," even though she is severely asthmatic, and freezing weather is a dangerous trigger for an asthma attack. I highly suspect that if someone were to confront Jenny at the top of a cliff in a wilderness program, she might just say, "I don't need this!" and jump off. Familiar with Jenny and her reactions, I am sure that "tough love" will only worsen Jenny's PTSD and underlying traumas.

"Well, then," Doctor "Wilderness" replies, "I do not know what to tell you."

As I am about to catch the hospital transport service to return to the city, I again run into Joanne, who has been visiting with her daughter, Susan. "Listen," Joanne tells me, "while we wait for Susan's IEP, we are going to be here at Halcyon Headland for a few months because we have a connection with one of the people who runs this place. However, there is a residential drug rehab for adolescents in a western section of New York State on the border with Pennsylvania called Mountain Pass Academy, and they are wonderful, and they have a school and over 150 acres of land! Yes, they actually have a school right there! That would be perfect for you."

I am "on it" right away, as Mountain Pass seems to be the only game in town because their program fees ($1,500 per month for room, board, school, and rehab) narrowly fit within my budget. Adding to the pressure, I now realize that there is something I need to get called an IEP. I don't know what it is yet, but I know that I need one, and right away. I eventually discover that an IEP is an Individual Education Plan, devised by the Board of Education of New York City for children who have motor or mental challenges or who are emotionally and socially fragile. The board of ed determines that a child requires an IEP after administering a series of interviews and a battery of IQ and psychological tests. In addition, they also review letters from doctors and therapists regarding their consultations with the student and their recommendations for education and treatment. If the board of ed finds that an IEP placement is required, then they will pay for the youth to be sent to a special-needs or residential therapeutic school up through the age of twenty-one. Conclusion: until I can obtain an IEP for Jenny, a process that takes many months and usually requires $8,000 in attorney's fees, I am the agent placing Jenny in Mountain Pass—at my expense.

What Joanne does not tell me in the taxi but only relates to me two years later, is this: "I would never have done what you did. I would *never* have sent Susan to Mountain Pass Academy, because I did not like the demographics." And Jenny recently said, "Mom, I know you did not realize it at the time, but you really sent me to 'juvie.'"

Some thirty days after Jenny enters Mountain Pass, I learn that she is one of only two white girls out of approximately 160 adolescents of both sexes and that the "minority" population constitutes more than 95 percent of Mountain Pass's student body. This is way outside the state norm of 50 percent, and ironically, one of Jenny's problems is that she has always felt like the odd girl out. I nevertheless feel confident that she will make friends. However, I do become concerned when I discover that almost all the residents have been sentenced by court order to attend Mountain Pass as an alternative to time in prison and that many of them have already been inmates in Rikers. It is a running joke among the teens that most of the students have been "*man*dated" to Mountain Pass, but Jenny has been "*mom*dated" there. Mountain Pass is full of members of the gangs of New York City—the Bloods, the Crips, the Latin Kings, and the Trinitarios—and some of these groups have been enemies for decades. Students are not allowed to wear certain colored T-shirts because they are gang colors, and other items, such as rosary beads, are prohibited for the same reason.

This information is worrisome, but Mountain Pass is the only residential school/rehab facility that I can afford to pay for out of pocket at this point, and I am desperate for Jenny to be off the streets. In addition, despite their tough histories, I find something to like in every young person I meet there, and I feel a natural affection toward them. I can see that these are children who desperately want and need to receive love, understanding, kindness, encouragement, and hope and that underneath everything, there is sweetness. Also, I believe that, for the near future, Jenny will be safer on the interior of Mountain Pass than running wild on the exterior, especially as I am still working sixteen to eighteen hours per day. In the meantime, I am trying to sell my home so that I can afford to self-pay for Jenny to attend an all-girls dual-diagnoses boarding school while simultaneously trying nonstop to advance the process of obtaining an IEP for a school that provides both a breadth and depth of therapy for Jenny. Whichever option comes through first is the one I will take.

I am not allowed to see Jenny and barely allowed to speak with her for the first month she is at Mountain Pass. After this initial period, group family meetings every two weeks are the only opportunities for parent/child contact (unless, after many months of good behavior, a student has earned a home pass). All of us moms take the three-and-a-half hour drive to the "Western Hills" location in a Mountain Pass van that collects visitors at a gathering point in New York City. Jenny is relentlessly hostile almost every time we meet. I send her cards and presents weekly and bring lots of Chinese food on visiting day to share with the mothers and their children, but she remains antagonistic. She keeps telling me that she wants to leave, and I think that she just wants to get out and do drugs again, so I am terrified of what would happen to her on the outside. Unbeknownst to me, I should be just as afraid of what is happening on the inside.

Mountain Pass has received celebrity endorsements from rock stars, one of whom has even donated a recording studio. Politicians tout the great work they are achieving at Mountain Pass. The grounds are vast and beautiful, especially in autumn, and the building seems sparse but clean. Nonetheless, I should look behind the curtain. I should notice that the children are strangely silent at the family gatherings and that the number of drug counselors seems to be way too slim to manage the 160-plus souls in their care in an effective and therapeutic way. Nor does the staff-to-student ratio appear to be sufficient to truly ensure adequate supervision and safety. As this is a population of teens who have been severely traumatized and abused from a very early age, the need for a sizeable team of highly trained and attuned mental health and addiction practitioners is even greater than in most facilities. More than other groups of juveniles, these children require comprehensive, compassionate, and devoted treatment on so many levels. We parents do not see anything other than the inside of the family congregational "bubble room" for about two hours twice per month. Other than that, I do not view or know anything more. The fact that everything else is hidden from inspection should give me pause. I do not acknowledge my skepticism. I am swathed in my own wishful thinking because I am so afraid for Jenny to come home. The truth is that Mountain Pass is little more than a para-correctional facility with a school, some rehab talk, and extremely negligent oversight verging on callous indifference. For the next six years, Jenny will tell me that she can never forgive me for having sent her there and that her experiences at Mountain Pass constitute a book unto itself.

However, today, Jenny thanks me for placing her in Mountain Pass, saying that because she never had to grow up in a destitute area and be exposed to the unimaginable hardships of hunger, violence, extreme deprivation, lack of quality education, and emotional pain that beset these children from birth, she never understood what she came to learn here. Jenny reflects that anyone in those circumstances would turn to drugs, and perhaps worse, just to have something in this world and that all her traumas did not compare with the traumas of the teens she met at this facility—some of their stories being almost unrepeatable. She has remained in touch with many of the young women she knew and has decided that her goal is to become a therapist who will help youths who struggled as she did, reach out to people who are misunderstood, and work in underprivileged areas. Jenny believes that those who dwell in the bereft sections of our inner cities are citizens whom society has just forgotten, dumped, and given nothing. She says that they see very little opportunity and feel they have nobody, and they need to know that they have someone on their side. Jenny tells me that it was the heedless staff at Mountain Pass and not the young people ordered there who made the institution so terrible and unsafe. She now thanks me for exposing her to a side of life that she never would have known or been able to comprehend and empathize with had I not enrolled her in Mountain Pass.

During the family "therapy sessions," various collections of parents and children form a wide circle in the large bubble room with high floor-to-ceiling windows on two sides, 1960s green-colored paint on the other two walls, a few inspirational posters, several IKEA-style sofas interspersed with plastic chairs, and collapsible, cafeteria-style tables for eating lunch. Ninety percent of the parents are single mothers. All of them are very guarded in what they say and are careful to praise the staff at Mountain Pass, because the bottom line is that their children need certificates of completion to present to the judge. Attending the group meetings is like sitting on a powder keg while receiving therapy by strangulation.

One weekend, a male resident "loses it" and accuses the group leader, Patricia (a petite, middle-age woman with Harry Potter glasses and a bowl-shaped haircut), and the staff of knowing perfectly well that a lot of residents are using drugs inside of Mountain Pass but doing nothing about it. He shouts that everything that Patricia is spouting at the family meetings is just plain lies and hypocrisy. Two other mandated young men agree, but their mothers tell them to be quiet, and they quickly retreat from their support for the renegade.

There is a "crisis." Patricia demands backup and says that she "feels threatened" and "not in control." At first I am thinking this woman is a coward, because no one is threatening her. All she has to do is answer the charge, but she will not. Then, on second thought, I realize that she perceives the strangulated aggression in the residents and fears its explosion. On the other hand, God bless these young men, despite the danger of losing their "get-out-of-jail" card, for striving for honesty in a "therapy session" and no longer stomaching the mendacity. A male senior staff member is summoned to manage the meeting and explains to the parents that Mountain Pass is drug-free; however, occasionally visitors will smuggle in illegal substances, but they always catch them.

"Yeah, sure. Another lie!" booms the initial accuser. At the next convocation two weeks later, we discover that the "outer" fled the premises that same day. We are told that he was "mentally disturbed."

Occasionally, a few overtly religious mothers break down crying in the presence of their sons and daughters. You can see that these children are moved by their mother's tears, and it appears that these youths may stand a better chance of rehabilitation. No one is sure why these group meetings are being conducted or what is happening in them. Perhaps they are being held to receive Medicaid money for therapy per person, in bulk, and to have a written record that Mountain Pass really does engage in rehab work? The meetings do allow us to see our children, but why can't we visit with our children privately at other times as well? That is never explained by the staff.

The practical name of the game (for most of the families at the meetings) is *pretense*: to go through the motions, "make nice," mark the months, and escape jail time. Nonetheless, the emotional pain in the room is real. One sees the anguish of the mothers who desperately want a better life for their children but seem to be fighting a losing battle against poverty, guns, and fatherlessness. One also feels the torment, rage, and despair of disillusioned, suffering, and drug-addicted youths. All of them have endured horrific experiences, but no one is talking about that and how the traumas affected them. No one is speaking about why these young people were doing drugs or about how to heal family relationships. Is it because there is no possible improvement, no solution to be hoped for? Where are the caring and empathy? Where is an honest discussion of the real heart issues and the sources of the pain and the anger? Where is insight? Where is hope? Where is faith? Where is there a mention of God? Where is Father Flanagan from Boy's Town?

During one group family meeting, I confront Jenny because I have read her diary, which reveals that she has lied to me for months and that her best friend (whom Jenny swore to me was sober) got her hooked on Ecstasy. I am openly attacked by Patricia, who informs me that I had no right to read Jenny's diary and that I have "impermissibly and illegally violated Jenny's right to privacy." It almost sounds as if Patricia is going to somehow bring formal charges against me. A visiting preppy mother and her daughter join in the "politically correct" chorus. Jenny turns to the daughter and calls me a "stupid, dumb bitch." There is instant shocked silence, and Patricia is not correcting Jenny for insulting me this way in front of everyone. You can hear all the air in the room being sucked into a vacuum seal.

Suddenly, a very attractive and sharply dressed black mother stands up and explodes at Jenny:

"Your mother has every right to read your diary because you are a minor, and you left your diary in her house, and she wants to know that you are safe! She buys you a puppy and brings you Chinese food and presents and comes up here to see you all the time! I am here today with my mother and my grandmother. My father was a drug dealer, and he got shot and killed right in front of me! And now my son is a drug dealer, and your mother comes up here and does all this stuff for you, and you call your mother 'a stupid, dumb bitch?' I would stand up if I was your mother and say, 'I am taking back the Chinese food, and the puppy, and the presents, and I am leaving, and I would walk out of here, right now, on you!'"

I do not leave, but I am so incredibly grateful for this mother's support, because Patricia encouraged, rather than corrected, Jenny's overt disrespect toward me, and this will only hobble Jenny. The fact that Patricia allowed her to be openly contemptuous of me will just reinforce Jenny's drug-addict attitude, which is rife with hostility, defiance, and arrogance. In addition, I think Jenny will have to pay a price for the subconscious guilt that she must bear for the way that she most often treats her own mother. I believe that guilt will make Jenny hate herself even more, and cause more self-punishment and self-destruction, and lead to more drug addiction. The group leader should know this—and I believe she does know it but behaves in a very disingenuous, ineffectual and manipulative way that makes me think "the renegade" was right about her. Sadly, however, I must admit that most of the family therapists I have met, and whom I will meet in the years to come, seem to follow the same pattern of unreliable and unworthy conduct.

When it is time for our return ride to the city, Jenny meets me at the van, crying. Her eyes, which are almost a pale saffron in this light, are oceans of sorrow. Her soul is exposed, and she wants to come with me. I love Jenny so much that my heart is bursting. I put my arms around her, and I want to take her out of Mountain Pass. However, especially after her display of disdain for me, I am still extremely afraid of what she will do if she is released. Therefore, I tell her that she must stay at Mountain Pass—otherwise, Inner Sanctum will hand her over to the Administration for Children's Services (ACS)—and that, in addition, there are coyotes and bears around Mountain Pass (which is true) that will attack her if she runs away. Jenny is not sure about the ACS story, but she is afraid of coyotes and bears, and that holds her in place.

When, many years later, we are discussing the news that Mountain Pass is closing its doors before the end of the summer, Jenny asks me why I never responded to what she was writing in her letters concerning the incidents there.

"What are you talking about?" I ask her.

"I wrote you letters every week," she replies.

I am stupefied and cannot believe what I am hearing.

"I wrote you several times, every week, telling you everything that was going on and why I wanted to come home."

Jenny and I then both finally discover, for the very first time, that none of her letters were mailed to me by the staff. Therefore, she felt betrayed, trapped, terribly depressed, and furious because she thought I did not care about what she was going through in that place. There are no words.

Back to October 2010: I am still ingenuous and think things are OK at Mountain Pass. Jenny is achieving As in their school and is number one in her class, so I believe that this is progress. In addition, at a special family visitors' day, when we are finally allowed to see the girls' rooms, all the young women whom I meet seem to like me and Jenny. One young lady says to Jenny, "You should be nice to your mother. She is pretty." I am not quite sure what this means in terms of how Jenny has been talking about me to her peers and to Patricia and how Patricia may be fueling Jenny's resentments. But we have a good time, and I take pictures with the residents and their families. I am introduced to some of Jenny's new close friends, who will help me rescue her from desperate situations in years to come. These comrades, I later learn, are the young women who guarded Jenny from the girls who were gang members. However, Jenny's allies cannot protect her all the time.

I do not yet know the truth, which is that Mountain Pass is, in many ways, a war zone. There are frequent fights, widespread instances of substance abuse, and sexual relations between residents and allegedly between residents and staff. Jenny is threatened almost nightly by the toughest females, who tell her they will sneak into her room when her defenders are not awake and break her neck while she is sleeping. In addition, the staff just look the other way on the occasions when lone girls are dragged into the bubble room, stripped naked, and held down by female gang members. Jenny later informs me that the purpose is to demean the victim and to show dominance. Another young woman is forcibly raped by a male in the downstairs bathroom. This is where she went for protection, therapeutic guidance, and help toward self-knowledge, understanding, and confidence in order to extricate herself from the magma of drug addiction?

After Jenny is there for six months, her drug counselor calls, yelling at me over the phone, telling me that Jenny is a "bad person" who has engaged in consensual sex with a male student. Why are they calling me when she is in their charge, and they should be supervising the residents? After I ask a lot of questions, I discover that the boy at issue is allegedly twenty years of age to Jenny's fifteen. In addition, I learn that the school psychiatrist has been giving Seroquel to Jenny and that Seroquel will make a person very drowsy and dizzy and might be almost as effective as a date-rape drug. I tell the counselor that this is a case of statutory rape, not "consensual sex," and she is wrong in blaming Jenny for being raped.

The counselor realizes that the cat is out of the bag. She calls me back one hour later, this time with a total change of tune, and apologetically admits that they determined that there had been a lack of proper supervision at the facility. A friend of mine points out that they may be in "cover-our-ass" mode now because I am an attorney. Patricia then telephones me to inform me that now Mountain Pass will convene with Jenny and the police (only because the truth has been revealed, so they must adhere to the proper protocol or suffer possible legal consequences themselves). I ask to be present, but Patricia refuses. Therefore, I contact the local police department, and the officer in charge states that I must be in attendance, as Jenny is a minor, and I am her mother. I cannot believe that I am the one who has to teach them what is right.

At the meeting, Patricia keeps asserting that the "sex was consensual," openly urging Jenny to state the same. I keep interjecting that, in view of the difference in their ages and because of the medication that Jenny was prescribed, there is no way the incident was "consensual." The police then speak to me privately, telling me that they think Jenny has been traumatized by her father's death and that she does not need any more trauma. In this regard, they advise me that I should not seek to press charges against the offender. In addition, they point out that the young man has already run away from the property and is a member of a gang with headquarters located not far from where we live in New York City, which could place us in danger if we pursue this any further. Finally, at the never-ending prompting of Patricia, Jenny insists that she refuses to testify.

Was this an instance of "parental intrusion and overinvolvement"? Parents need to be perceptive to what and how "treatment" is done, and be alert to point out obvious unprofessionalism, negligence, misconduct, and malpractice in our institutions.

At my present point in time, I have learned that the internal culture that has been allowed to develop in institutions can often be geared toward the good for the institution, or the easiest for the worker, or (much less often) the good for the patient. A philosophical debate could ensue, but the point is that these dynamic forces exist and determine practice. We, as the often clueless, helpless, and beleaguered buyers of their services, must be vigilant.

The literature on rape bears out that many rape victims do maintain that the sex was voluntary, attempting to protect their sense of control and pride and to ward off feelings of shame for having been overcome and used. However, in addition, Jenny most probably felt trapped: fearing being deemed a "snitch" by the other residents and anticipating Patricia's revenge for her having dared to disagree. Mountain Pass has everyone in a vise and keeps them there with blackmail, brainwashing, and bullying. This place is not much better than the streets. But I am scared. What can I do?

I want to take Jenny out right away, but where can I send her, immediately? Jenny was statutorily raped on the inside, but there is the danger of violent rape, drug overdose, physical brutality, and possible abduction on the outside. Following this incident, I work with desperate urgency to find an alternative facility for Jenny, doing all I can to obtain offers on my house in a collapsed real estate market and earnestly pushing for the IEP to come through from the New York City Board of Education so that Jenny can be transferred to a therapeutic boarding school.

As I am not initiating a lawsuit, the head of Mountain Pass promises me that she will pair Jenny with a twenty-four-hour "one-on-one" escort, pending Jenny's admission to another residential institution. I believe that this constant supervision will keep her protected until the transition occurs. However, without my knowledge, Mountain Pass never keeps its word, and there is no escort. Also, I am completely unaware that right after the rape,

Jenny started cutting herself again, at one point savagely butchering her arm in an attempt to kill herself. And she began heavily snorting drugs, becoming powerfully readdicted inside the rehab that was supposed to get her clean.

The day after I obtain the IEP and send Jenny to a special education school, Jenny will almost end her life by overdosing on narcotics.

"Open-Campus" Jeckyll Center

Jenny is admitted to a well-known coeducational, therapeutic residential facility located just outside of Albany, New York, called the Jeckyll Treatment Center. The Jeckyll Center boasts an impressive website, with various write-ups and photos, specifying their education and therapy, individually designed programs, grief treatment sessions, and creative arts studies. The student demographics are in line with the state norm, none of the residents is court mandated, and some of them even attend without an IEP, with their parents paying some $300,000 per year out of pocket. It seems like therapeutic Disney World, but that will turn out to be a fragile illusion.

Located in venerable Broadview, with its spanky modern architecture and lakeside view, it is quite enticing. I buy a comforter imprinted with roses, matching sheets and pillowcases, and everything else on the residential checklist for Jenny's ensconcement in one of the girls' houses. This is a fresh start, and I so want Jenny to be happy and safe and to receive the education and the right kind of guidance and therapy she so desperately needs.

In early February 2011, I drive Jenny from Mountain Pass to the Jeckyll Center and help her settle in. However, when I go to say good-bye, tell Jenny that I love her, and try to hug her, she recoils and turns away. She appears ill, shriveled, and tiny, and she will not face me.

"Come on, Mom, you always do this. Just go! Good-bye! I already said good-bye. How many times do I have to say good-bye to you?"

I know that this is not a good sign and that Jenny's failure to look me in the eye is always an indication of very serious self-harm to come. The next day, I receive a telephone call from Jenny's school therapist telling me that Jenny is being taken by ambulance to the emergency room but that she is "OK." I anxiously recall that EMS told me that Jenny was "OK" two years ago, just before she went into a coma.

"Jenny took something," the therapist says. "She went to class and started acting funny. She started falling down the stairs. Someone had to catch her. We were finally able to wake her up."

I race up to the emergency department wing of the hospital in Broadview. Jenny has overdosed on eighteen Klonopin, assorted other pills, and a Percocet that were sold to her by one of the school's student drug dealers as soon as she arrived. Thank God Jenny took the Percocet, because it made her throw up profusely. When I run into the room where they are treating her, she looks at me in stunned horror and speaks to me like the little girl she used to be:

"Mommy, help me. Please, help me. Mommy, help me. I could not stop myself. Mommy, please help me. I could not stop myself."

Again! The enormity of this truth regarding the power of the forces arraigned against Jenny (and myself) is beyond overwhelming. I feel like we are battling the White Walkers from *Game of Thrones* without any dragon glass. I need some Valyrian steel, and I need it fast. I hold Jenny and try to comfort her.

I sent Jenny to the Jeckyll Center to be safe, and once again, Jenny is not safe. This is a special education school vetted and funded by the taxpayers of the state of New York to treat socially/emotionally fragile adolescents, but the school accepts no accountability for what has happened to Jenny on their grounds. Evidently the facility has an "enjoy it off on the hillside" loose drug-use policy, and the student who allegedly gave the drugs to Jenny is reportedly well liked by the owners and permitted to remain at the school. In addition, there is a free smoking policy, with the dormitory moms and students inhaling upward of one pack of cigarettes each per day. The Board of Education of New York City tells me that the Jeckyll Center needs to take responsibility for the lax conditions on its campus, but the board does nothing about it. To top it all off, the local police inform me that the AWOL (absent without leave) problem at the Jeckyll Center is a "joke." I worked so hard to find and have Jenny admitted to what I thought was the best possible school for her, and I feel fooled and defeated once more. It is as if an unseen entity keeps punching me in the face and is laughing its head off.

I bring Jenny to our home in New York City, and we enjoy an idyllic two weeks together, during which time she is very grateful and respectful and never leaves my side. I treasure this time with Jenny, who is so sweet and loving, as she has not been for years. We go to the zoo and to the Metropolitan Museum of Art, and she quits smoking. In addition, I have found a wonderful psychologist for Jenny, and we visit with her almost every day. Jenny, who has been writing poetry since an early age, presents me with a beautiful poem from her heart:

I'M SORRY TO YOU FOR EVERYTHING I'VE DONE

I'm sorry to you for everything I've done
I'm sorry for faking the battle that you had thought I won.
I'm sorry to you for everything,
especially crushing your dreams.
I'm sorry for making you look stupid,
while I acted terribly obscene
I'm sorry to you for everything,
every time I made you cry.
I'm sorry to you for everything,
especially when I would lie.
I'm sorry I made you love me,
even though you thought it was not in return.
I'm sorry I made you die inside,
as you watched me crash and burn.
But most of all I'm sorry,

I always put you last—it's true.
But the past is the past and
I really do love you.

Jenny's poem moves me, and others, to tears, and I feel that she has made a breakthrough.

It is all wonderful until Joanne appears and tells me that I am a terrible mother for forcing Jenny to give up cigarettes right away and that "it is more difficult to stop smoking cold turkey than to quit heroin." But I counter that Jenny is so much better and that smoking is very bad for her asthma and her vocal chords and is even considered by some experts to be a gateway drug. However, Jenny overhears Joanne and starts smoking four cigarettes per day, claiming that she will taper back, which never happens. As Jenny resumes smoking, her attitude becomes more evasive, and by the time she is ready to return to the Jeckyll Center, I can sense that something foreboding, but hidden from view, is ready to spring forth again, although Jenny claims that everything is fine.

I realize that I have to accept the one low offer that has come through for my residence, as it is becoming more and more impossible for me to work and to care for Jenny and as I sense that she will probably not be able to stay at the Jeckyll Center. Because Jenny suffers from acute intrapsychic pain, very high anxiety, and proneness to impulsivity, she may not be equipped to resist the easy access to drugs on their "open campus," and I will likely have to self-pay for the right place for Jenny, if there is a right place. It is emotionally and personally devastating to have to sell my beloved home of twenty years, and I know that it is a monolithic economic mistake, but there is no other solution to save Jenny.

The therapists and educators at the Jeckyll Center are good, well-meaning people and helpful, but the fact that the school allows drug use, cigarette smoking, and running away undoes any benefit that their therapy can provide. Jenny is drug tested once per week and is assigned a drug counselor, who tells me she is sober, but each week I tell him that I doubt it. I know the signs of drug use, and I know it is easy to beat an every-seven-day drug test. This goes on for three months, until I receive a call from Jenny's "house mom" in the middle of the night:

"Jenny has fled the premises."

I immediately telephone the local police, who are not yet "on the case," as the Jeckyll Center has not contacted law enforcement to report that Jenny is missing. Therefore, I hire a private driver at 2:00 a.m. to traverse the 140 miles from New York City to go out looking for Jenny on my own. I call my girlfriend Judy from the car and ask for her to please pray for Jenny, which she promises to do. As we enter the town of Broadview, I see a lone girl on the street who I think is Jenny. I jump out of the cab, grab her, and tell her, "Get in the car right now!"

The girl looks at me with concern and asks, "Are you all right?" This girl is very kind, but this girl is not Jenny, and no, I am not all right. I have been through this too many times.

It turns out that at that very same moment, only a few blocks away, Jenny has obtained drugs from a local gang member who believes that he will get something personal in return for the drugs, but then Jenny bolts, thinking that she can outrun him. Like a guardian angel, a friend of Jenny's has miraculously followed her, sees what is happening, and quickly speeds to a bar that is—again, miraculously—still open. The bartender calls the police and protects Jenny and her friend from the pack of males who were in hot pursuit. The police officers bring her back to her dormitory, where I am waiting. I read her the riot act, and the girls' residence head (who cannot believe that I have come up from New York City at 4:00 a.m.) tells Jenny, "Wow! Your mother is a gangster." But it does not end here.

The next day, Jenny's roommate calls to inform me that "I have to do something right away" (again) because "she cannot remain silent anymore": Jenny needs to leave the Jeckyll Center because she has been taking at least ten pills every day and mixing them with a bottle of vodka and a blunt of marijuana for the past three months. I confront Jenny, who admits that her roommate told the truth. Although Jenny has straight As, she will not be able to complete her semester, so now she will be two years behind academically. I do not want to take her out of school right before the end of the year, but I am petrified of another possible overdose or that she will be kidnapped the next time around. The newspapers have reported that local rings have captured young girls who have then disappeared, only to be found years later, held prisoner in basements in the various boroughs of New York City. Times have changed, and this is not the Broadview of yore. Jenny is clearly spinning out of control, and the risks are too great.

I send Jenny back to Halcyon Headland, and from there to Heliotrope, one of the foremost and most expensive drug treatment programs in the country, perhaps in the world. I will use the money from the sale of my apartment to be able to pay for Jenny's stay at this establishment, which I have been told is Jenny's best chance at recovery, long-term sobriety, and a normal life.

Jenny will be there for just short of three months. I will observe that while Heliotrope seems to have some success with treating adults, for many adolescents, their program is a failure.

Heliotrope's Help and a Move to Suburbia

When I tell people that Jenny is being sent to the Heliotrope Addiction Facility, located in southern Illinois, they respond with "ooohss" and "ahhhhs." "Well, that is the place," they say with hushed and awed respect. They act as if I have just moved into a McMansion in Greenwich, Connecticut, and drive a Bentley. Jenny almost backs out of going, but then she learns that her friend Kensie (Kensington), a gorgeous girl and a heavy Ecstasy user, whose boyfriend is a drug dealer, is already at Heliotrope. Kensie's old-money grandparents have forked over the $90,000 for a three-month stay. Her brother, Arthur, was also at Heliotrope with Kensie, but Arthur ran away. The interventionists hired by his parents chased Arthur down with a helicopter, and Arthur is now "far out West." The exact location is a secret. Kensie's mom, Liz, just tells me "way far." Liz is initially happy that Arthur is near Rocky Mountain High, at a place recommended by Heliotrope; however, Liz is later informed about Arthur's best friend, who ran away from the horse ranch/rehab. Liz learns that the heroin problem out West is even worse, and the heroin itself is much more lethal than it is in New York. Arthur's friend is dead.

On our way to Heliotrope, I have flashbacks to Halloween 2009, when Jenny went to visit Kensie in her well-to-do New Jersey town upon Liz's promise that she would watch Jenny and Kensie constantly: "I'll never let them out of my sight." However, she allowed both girls to stay with her ex-husband, and the girls went out to do massive amounts of cocaine, hooking up with a notorious heroin user and dealer named Sally.

Then I think back to Thanksgiving of that same year, when I had to block Jenny from going back to New Jersey. In a complete rage, because I would not allow her to exit the house, Jenny caused $10,000 worth of property damage by smashing in walls, bending door frames with her leg thrusts, and almost breaking my arm with the handle of a scooper pan. The problem was that I had used myself as a human shield to bar Jenny from departing. Finally, in the living room, afraid of the perils of letting her leave, I grabbed her by the hair, and she then grasped my hair as well. Now she was locked to me—glued—because I was not letting go and neither was she. And there we were in a swirling fury, a mother-daughter tornado twisting across the floor, yanking at each other's scalps, each trying to defeat the other. We smashed into furniture, punching, swatting, kicking, screaming, maniacally laughing—doing all that we could to weaken the other. We were both incensed and filled with determination—Jenny trying to bolt and me resolved to stop her. Round and round and round we went, finally hurtling to the ground in a raucous rumble. I felt like a completely disreputable mother, in a worse-than-barroom brawl with my own fourteen-year-old daughter. How, I wondered, were we ever going to survive any of this?

The cops arrived. The lead officer was a realist. He looked at Jenny and said, "You are doing drugs and breaking up this house, and your mother is trying to save you. She is doing all she can to save you. I want her to take out a restraining order against you, but she won't. You are going down, and all you are doing is taking your mother down with you, and there is no reason for your mother to go down too. I will take you up to juvie lock-up in the Bronx right now, with the green peeling paint and the chicken wire, and you'll be saying, '*Mooommmy, Mooommmy, please get me out of here*!' But Mommy won't be able to get you out of there, not for six months or a year. All your mother has to do is to give me the word and I am taking you up there right now." I think about it. Would this wake Jenny up? He continues: "If you keep doing what you are doing, the next time I see you, I am going to be zipping you up in a body bag, and I won't care. I'll step right over you and go home to eat my Thanksgiving dinner."

Suddenly my reflections are interrupted as Jenny and I arrive at Heliotrope. The Heliotrope driver ferrying us from the airport had regaled us with stories about all the wealthy international passengers and celebrities—whom he is not allowed to name—that he has transported to Heliotrope. He tells us how wonderful it is when he takes these same young people back to the airport and "they are no longer wearing hoodies. . . . Such a change."

Jenny and I enter the admissions room, where the initial order of business is the presentation of my certified check for $30,000 for the first month. Then we fill out all the paperwork, and I am told that I will not be able to speak to Jenny for about two weeks while she settles in but that there will be a family weekend, which I will need to attend, around that time. I ask for the telephone numbers of the nurse and the overseer of the house where Jenny will be staying.

I learn that individual therapy only takes place once per week for only a half hour, and not with a psychodynamic psychotherapist, but with a drug counselor. The focus is on "group rehab," not on the safe individual therapeutic exploration, understanding, and working through or even cognitive-behavioral treatment of the personal problems of the individual users that underlie their addiction.

In all my seeking of help for Jenny, it is always "either/or," and no facility seems to combine both drug education/rehab work with individual talk therapy in a rigorous, interlocking, and comprehensive way. Could it be to prevent a perceived conflict between two different messages: getting to know oneself versus buying into the program? Then again, one-on-one therapy is more expensive and will not allow the facility to realize the greatest profit margin, which depends on treatment in volume. Would insurance cover individual therapy? But then therapists would have to be hired and paid for.

I know that Jenny must get to the source of why she self-medicates to quench her overriding craving for drugs. In order to bring this about, I believe Jenny should be able to speak about her experiences, her traumas, and her troubles with a skilled, highly trained, caring, empathic therapist who can contain and regulate Jenny's anxiety while truly wanting to hear her whole story—a therapist who can help her discover and understand how she got to this point and then aid Jenny in recognizing her own strengths and what salutary options there are for moving ahead to better choices and meaningful relationships with others, a productive and rewarding life, and healthy living. As an adjunct, why not use eye movement desensitization and reprocessing (EMDR)—a relatively brief treatment that has been successfully used to treat post-traumatic stress? Furthermore, to assist juveniles in reprogramming their thinking away from self-defeating patterns, dialectical behavioral therapy (DBT) might be effective, training them to utilize mindfulness techniques on a minute-by-minute basis. This could help them identify harmful impulses and come up with constructive ways of coping with stress.

I am sure that Jenny needs individual sessions at least twice per week. In addition, I believe that at $30,000 per month, she should be entitled to receive this kind of quality treatment. However, I am informed that Heliotrope has "their program," and "that is how it works, for everyone, with no exceptions."

I will come to see that Heliotrope's "program" is all about the Heliotrope "formula," and that the formula is all about the groups, and that the groups are all about the money. Financial earnings are maximized by the presentations of lots of prefab materials by schooled, low-salaried, single lecturers to the exorbitantly charged and paying "clients," packed in throngs. Yes, Heliotrope, in a very businesslike manner, refers to the souls who have come to Heliotrope in search of human redemption as "clients." The counselors keep dutiful notes that track the stapling of each client to the daily format, with the same mechanical efficiency with which Con Edison marks individual usage on a utility grid:

"Went to breakfast, went to group, went to lunch, attended group lecture with AIDS Network, participated in (*group*) lecture with Tom, went to dinner, attended the 12-step AA [Alcoholics Anonymous] (*group*) in-house meeting in the evening, discussed the movie *Mean Girls* (*in group*)." Only surface behavior is addressed; there is scant acknowledgment, let alone exploration, of each individual's personal emotional and cognitive reactions to what, most often unconsciously, motivates his or her impulsive reactions and behaviors.

That said, there are some worthy aspects of the curriculum. Some of the groups have useful topics, such as "The Dangers of Mixing Energy Drinks with Alcohol," "Boundaries," "Defenses to Progress," and "Anger Management." In terms of the general drug-information part of the plan, their approach appears to be thorough and educational. But excellent and pertinent topics such as "boundaries" or "defenses" or "anger" require in-depth work, individually, over considerable time, in order to be adequately understood and assimilated.

Most importantly, their psychiatrist, Dr. T, is the first (and will be the only) mental health expert to agree with me that Jenny is suffering from traumatic brain injury (TBI) and PTSD and that her drug addiction is secondary to the trauma she endured when she was hit by the taxi and went in and out of six comas. He updates Jenny's diagnosis to include "personality changes due to traumatic brain injury." Jenny is prescribed Trileptal to address the symptoms of PTSD. The Trileptal requires the monitoring of Jenny's blood. Dr. T sees that the underbelly of Jenny's addiction is trauma. This diagnosis is of utmost importance and should have a pivotal role in Jenny's treatment, which should be geared toward addressing both the brain and the emotional traumas that cause the addiction. Unfortunately, that is not the modus operandi in these "conveyor belt" treatment venues. Why does the psychiatrist not have the power to prescribe the appropriate treatment as he sees fit?

I beg for Jenny to receive more one-on-one therapy on a consistent basis, but this request is rejected. However, around this time, Jenny has the good fortune to be assigned to a counselor, Erica, who is one of those rare individuals who truly seems to care and have a heart. Erica writes about the love that Jenny and I have for each other, and she is the only therapist whom I will meet at any facility who dares to use the *L* word and who talks about love in her counseling sessions. Erica seems very unlike anyone else at Heliotrope, and in having the ongoing support of Erica, Jenny starts to improve. It is a validation of the belief that she, and others like her, would do well with more intense individual therapy with a loving and compassionate therapist.

When I attend the family meeting, all of us parents are herded together into a medium-sized room, lectured on drug addiction, given our leaflets, and then joined by our children two hours later. The group leader throws cards on the floor and tells us that we are one or several of what these cards depict: "Rescuer," "Enabler," "Lost Child," "Hero," "Helicopter Parent," "Cop," "Detective," et cetera, et cetera. We are then bidden to pick up the cards that we think represent us, and our children are asked to do the same. We are told that these are the cards/representations of people who we should not be if we want our sons and daughters to be sober. I do not like any of this because I know it will only give Jenny more ammunition to use against me. In addition, the lecturer's premise seems false to me. You are damn right: if your children are in an emergency, you must "rescue" them, and to find out where they are going and what they are doing, you have to be a "cop" and a "detective." These children are too young. They need intervention. You cannot just leave them to their own devices and to a fate based on a coin toss. The group leaders/lecturers/therapists do not offer the parents any better alternatives, nor do they offer guidance on how to change any maladaptive roles identified and replace them with something that works.

Jenny's "client" notes read as follows:

> During the course of treatment, patient was provided with services that consisted of group therapy six days per week, community meetings (*groups*), one weekly session with a primary addiction counselor, . . . recreational therapy (*groups*), and educational process groups on the disease of addiction, recovery life skills, self-diagnosis, and self-motivation. Patient was introduced to the concept of positive peer culture and retroflexive reformation (*What in the world is that?*) as vehicles for positive self-change (*in groups*). Extensive work on the first four steps of the 12-step recovery process (*in groups*), as well as issues of relapse prevention and developing sober life skills (*in groups*).

Is all this useful information? Yes. Is the fact that Jenny is sober while inside of Heliotrope—as opposed to her drug use inside of Mountain Pass Academy and the Jeckyll Center—of great assistance? Yes, absolutely, as this drug-free time is allowing Jenny's brain to begin to heal. I was hoping that Jenny would adopt and believe in the group philosophy and would perpetuate it, but it was not sufficient. Jenny told me that almost exclusive reliance on group programs does not provide enough motivation to keep one going and that it did not work because it was the equivalent of trying to solve a personal problem with a mathematical formula.

Many of the young women I met who were with Jenny at Heliotrope relapsed almost immediately upon discharge. One girl from Long Island disappeared for three months, and when she was finally found, her face was so beaten in that she was almost unrecognizable. Kensie started using drugs just as often as before. Another Heliotrope girl from New Jersey became Jenny's OxyContin supplier.

In this regard, Jenny expressed to me that Heliotrope was not really preparing people for the outside world after placing them in the Heliotrope "fairy-tale bubble" and then dropping them fast with a program that did not address each addict specifically.

In addition, Heliotrope failed to provide the adolescents in their program with a detailed aftercare plan. This was like ejecting these youths out of a plane without a parachute. Heliotrope did not set them up with actual drug outpatient centers, psychiatrists, AA meetings, sponsors, and therapists that they would immediately need when they returned to their respective locales.

Heliotrope followed the twelve-step AA model, which seems to be successful for a good number of adults and is most often meant for mature individuals who have usually achieved more solid identities prior to drug addiction. They were doctors, lawyers, bankers, advertising executives, and so on, and they can return to their former career personas. For those for whom the AA model is effective, the AA meetings then become the center of their lives after work, and AA people become their new friends and family. However, this is almost impossible for teenagers to achieve, as their identities are still forming, and they will find their peers not in nightly AA meetings but in high school, which is rife with drugs and lots of angst. Given the current statistics regarding teen drug use, it is time to install daily young people's NA (Narcotics Anonymous) and AA meetings in high schools across the country, as well as a stable of compassionate, in-house one-on-one therapists, trained in the treatment of childhood and family trauma, who will privately treat both students and parents—also, pastoral counselors and DBT programs.

The Heliotrope format appears to stress the neurology of drug dependency and what happens to the brain when drugs hook into the receptors. But the Heliotrope literature underlines that addiction is a disease with genetic constituents and that it is a primary disorder, not caused by another mental illness. Certainly, the neurology of addiction is a vital component, and one needs to have a thorough understanding of how it works. However, that is not the only aspect of addiction that needs to be addressed, as Jenny, like so many victims of PTSD, uses drugs to forget and to self-medicate when she feels overwhelmed by the inner emotional pain, unbearable anxiety, rage, shame, guilt, fear, and most often, dissociation. What Heliotrope teaches is helpful, but it is like using a wooden fence to try to hold back a tank when the monster of personal unresolved traumatic material and intrapsychic agony attacks the individual, alone, back out on their own.

I ask the expert who delivers the lecture on drugs and neurology at Heliotrope how we cure teenagers of addiction when only 25 percent of the prefrontal lobe (the decision-making, impulse-control center of the brain) is formed in juveniles and is not completed until the age of twenty-five. His only answer is that "it is very, very difficult." Heliotrope needs to develop a genuinely effective paradigm for treating adolescents. (As does the rest of the country.)

During Jenny's three months at Heliotrope, she gains more than thirty pounds chowing down on waffles, because one method of preventing the girls from running away seems to be switching unlimited access—from drugs to carbs. On the Fourth of July weekend, I have an argument with "Ms. Crunch," the administrator who runs the "ongoing program" and who is Erica's boss. Ms. Crunch is a termagant with no obvious professional credentials, such as social worker or psychologist, but with tremendous power (a business degree? perhaps closely connected or related to someone at the highest organizational level?). Jenny has gotten into an argument with a peer whom she perceived as being disrespectful toward her, so Ms. Crunch has ordered Jenny to stay indoors alone for the entire day and evening of the Fourth of July while everyone else at Heliotrope is celebrating the national holiday.

Jenny becomes severely depressed, starts cutting her legs, and wants to leave. I protest that this punishment is too severe. Erica intervenes on our behalf, and Jenny is then permitted to participate in the Fourth of July festivities, is much happier, and now wants to stay at Heliotrope. However, my opposition to Ms. Crunch's draconian measures will come back to burn us three months later.

One day, Jenny and Erica call me on the phone together: Jenny states that she absolutely has to leave New York City. She tells me, "There is a drug dealer on every corner in Manhattan," and she begs for me to move to "the country" where my mother's sister lives as soon as possible, prior to her being released from Heliotrope. This is something I had already considered. So having sold my little duplex in New York City at a loss, I purchase a modest apartment in the same building where my aunt resides, in a small, suburban town, and I prepare for Jenny to attend the highly rated local high school. I look forward to a wonderful beginning for Jenny, newly sober. Finally, the Heliotrope psychiatrist writes me a letter, which states in part,

> Jenny is suffering a syndrome that is the result of the severe head injury she suffered in the accident. . . . I think for the near future you will have to perform as her executive power and will need to exercise much more oversight than one would normally expect of a young woman of sixteen. She will require therapy, medication management, drug and alcohol treatment, and specialized training and schooling, which may last for two years or longer. It will likely be impossible for you to work during that time, given her high level of impulsivity. I am recommending that you take whatever leave is necessary to supervise her rehabilitation until such time as she is able to take more responsibility for herself.

This is a most important and accurate assessment of what is ailing Jenny and one that future counselors and rehab directors need to pay attention to rather than try to separate Jenny from me.

So this is what I do: already prostrate with guilt, I decide to give up my career and devote myself and anything that I have left to taking care of Jenny. I am determined to do everything humanly possible to see her healthy, happy, and well.

Life Begins in the Suburbs

We move to the visually beautiful, upscale town of Round Bridge, and Jenny is dropped into a historic suburban environment, like Alice falling down the rabbit hole. The landscape is poetic, but the village seems very strange and lifeless to this child of Manhattan, raised in the cultural richness, eclectic population, and bustle of the "city that never sleeps." In Round Bridge, there is a complete absence of diversity, and (in general parlance) "nice" means "loser," "hello" means "good-bye," "a promise to help" means "don't count on it," no one ever raises their voice, and the silence is deadly. There is something unsettling about Round Bridge (which sits in its own terrarium along the Hudson River, almost two hours outside of New York City), and soon after we arrive, we learn that there has been a recent rash of parent suicides. These tragic events, like much else in Round Bridge, are addressed by neither the residents nor the media and so just seem to be absorbed into the atmosphere, adding to the heaviness of the viscous air mass that envelopes this 325-year-old settlement. Jenny had asked that we move to Round Bridge as a safe haven, but neither of us had any idea what truly lay beneath its perfect, picture-postcard, placid surface. Does a perfectly safe haven exist anywhere?

Although Heliotrope fell short in several important regards, it had at least provided a cogent, solid diagnosis and recommendations by the psychiatrist and an informative and safe in-house detox/rehab program. In addition, Jenny formed a positive bond with her good counselor, Erica, who encouraged a loving mother-daughter relationship between Jenny and me and inspired Jenny to truly want to be drug-free. Jenny is very proud that she has been sober for ninety days inside of Heliotrope, and for ten days on the outside, and I am grateful to Erica for that.

There is, however, a hard-and-fast rehab rule, which we were not informed about, that states that no one leaving an inpatient recovery facility should engage in any major life changes for at least the first three to six months immediately following their discharge date. Moving to a totally different area would be high up on the list of things not to do. And Heliotrope had released Jenny home with no treatment plans, nor did it discharge her to an identified outpatient individual therapist, with an appointment in place, which is an absolute must. Jenny felt jettisoned into a foreign land, or like a saltwater fish dropped into sweet water.

Given these two major strikes against us, maintaining sobriety will not be possible for Jenny in Round Bridge, where I learned many of the teens use drugs, but the town turns a blind eye to it. The administrators at the nationally highly ranked public high school will not admit that they have a very serious drug problem, as it would negatively affect the real estate values in Round Bridge. Moving was a rushed decision, and I should, somehow, have enlisted the help and advice of someone who could have honestly described this environment at all levels—but I doubt that such a person would have dared to come forward.

The basic tradeoff that should have been first noted is this: in New York City, there were lots of drugs, but there were so many other things to do besides drugs, and young people's AA and NA meetings were more frequent and only a subway stop away. In Round Bridge, there are lots of drugs, but without the abundance of alternative activities that abound in the city, and there is no readily accessible network of peers in recovery.

I scramble to arrange for Jenny's class schedule, make a chart of all the Monday-through-Sunday AA and NA meetings in the county, and attempt to find therapists for Jenny. One highly recommended social worker from the high school quits after only one session with Jenny, stating that she is not an addiction expert. Only one year later, I discern what everyone is well aware of: that just five minutes away, in the next village, there is a major psychiatric hospital named Mother of Guidance that specializes in the treatment of teen addiction. However, I am not apprised of this by anyone. And evidently Heliotrope does not agree that researching and arranging for effective outpatient planning is a part of their $30,000-per-month "client" package. But that is a vital part of an appropriate discharge.

It all goes downhill very fast.

Jenny stops attending classes after three days. She sleeps until 2:00 p.m., leaves the house in the afternoon, and does not return until many hours after midnight, night after night. Her eyes are bloodshot, she has asthma attacks all the time, and she becomes increasingly hostile and verbally belligerent.

The weekend of the first week of school, Jenny demands to go to New Jersey:

"Mom, please give me $250 for a car service round trip to New Jersey. I have to go see Antoinette, who was with me at Heliotrope. Antoinette is so positive, and it will be so good for my sobriety. I really need to see her. Please, Mom, please! I am so unhappy."

I know that Jenny's "unhappiness" invariably leads to relapse. And although I do not trust the Antoinette scenario, I have no choice but to accede to Jenny's request, hoping against hope that she and Antoinette will bond over a desire to stay sober after their stint at Heliotrope.

Over the phone, Antoinette's mother tells me that she watches Jenny and Antoinette all the time, and they go to AA meetings together, and "They are doing so well." But Jenny later admits to me that Antoinette's mother is a "recovered" addict herself, and she strewed painkillers in candy dishes, the way other people sprinkle jelly beans, throughout their custom-built palatial abode. Antoinette is providing Jenny with large amounts of OxyContin.

Two weeks pass, with Jenny having essentially dropped out of school. Even though I ferry her to AA meetings almost every evening and bring her back home, Jenny's late-night disappearances are ongoing. Then Jenny starts walking out of most of the meetings, as they are almost exclusively populated by fiftysomethings with whom Jenny has nothing in common. Jenny shares with me that going to AA/NA meetings "and hearing alcoholics and addicts talk about all the dangerous antics they used to engage in" just triggers Jenny to want to see if she can get away with the same risky behaviors. Many nights, I go out looking for her, driving around the neighborhood and calling the telephone numbers (that I pilfered from her cell phone) of new acquaintances who turn out to be mostly Vicodin dealers from the neighboring town of Bottle Bay. I leave messages that if Jenny is not home in one hour, I am calling the police, and this always gets a reaction. Jenny's breathing is becoming increasingly shallow, her behavior is wild, and her speech is garbled. Every weekend, she goes to New Jersey, and I absolutely cannot hold her back. Jenny is in the middle of a full-blown relapse.

As a result of the stress, I am hit with incredible pain in the left occipital lobe of my brain, and I lose muscle control of my left eye, which I cannot stop from crossing. I start to drive with the afflicted eye closed. At one point, I collapse in the living room. EMS is called, and I am rushed by ambulance to the hospital with very rapid heart palpitations and an abnormal EKG. I am admitted overnight, and the conclusion, not surprisingly, is that I've had a "panic attack."

Jenny's chief defense is to avoid any open and meaningful conversation concerning what she is really doing, her personal feelings of deep sorrow and intense fury, and her addiction. If I attempt an honest discussion, her ultimate weapon is to blackmail me by threatening to create such a clamorous disturbance that she will cause a dreaded "noise alert." This would result in my being forced to sell our apartment—which I will ultimately need to do, as a disturbance will occur.

Her "home contract" with Heliotrope, drafted and signed by Jenny and Erica, states that if Jenny relapses, she should immediately return to Heliotrope for detox and rehab. She refuses to go. Finally, the interventionists are willing to pick her up and physically take her to Heliotrope. Jenny overhears my phone conversation with them and confronts me mano a mano:

"I swear to God! I swear, before they can touch me, I will break everything in this house, and scream and yell my head off, and get you kicked out of here! All of this—everything in this place—will be smashed and gone! Just lay a hand on me—go ahead and touch me. I swear to God! I dare you. I hope you do!"

Complex PTSD, Addiction, and Entities

It is hard, at times like this, when one is goaded, not to take the bait. Jenny is too enraged to be engaged verbally, and she is physically too strong to subdue. Somehow, one never expects that one's child will be hit with a major illness, and in order to maintain as rational an approach as possible, I must keep reminding myself that Jenny is very sick. I know that none of this is her fault, any more than Jenny would be to blame if she was suffering from cancer. Through my research, I believe that Jenny is stricken with a form of PTSD known as "complex and chronic post-traumatic stress disorder" and that her drug use is a secondary and dramatic symptom that expresses the severity of the traumas that Jenny has suffered. Sigmund Freud wrote, in *Beyond the Pleasure Principle*, that because there is no obvious physical injury when abuse is internal, it is far deadlier and more difficult for the patient of trauma to recover than it is for the patient to recuperate when there is visible bodily harm.

I must keep my eyes focused on the invisible adversary, the addiction, as Jenny is its hapless victim, and it is torturing her mercilessly. "What," Jenny cries out to me when she is in the throes of craving drugs, "*What do I do with my pain?*" I must somehow succeed in reaching the rational Jenny, whose psyche is being overrun by this "thing" that is not Jenny. If I answer with anger to her expressions of animosity and contempt, the result will be disastrous, and this alien intruder will win. That said, my breaking-down body is telling me about the cost of being Jenny's human shield. I pray that, with God's help, I will not give in and never give up.

While rummaging through Jenny's folders of rehab self-help printouts, hoping to find the "magic words" that will motivate and strengthen her to stay sober, I rediscover a "letter" that I picked up at an Al-Anon meeting at Heliotrope.

Dear Friend:

I've come to visit once again. I love to see you suffer mentally, physically, spiritually, and socially. I want to have you restless, so you can never relax. I want you jumpy and nervous and anxious. I want to make you agitated and irritable so everything and everybody makes you uncomfortable. I want you to be confused and depressed so that you can't think clearly or positively. I want to make you hate everything and everybody—especially yourself. I want you to feel guilty and remorseful for the things you have done in the past that you'll never be able to let go of. I want to make you angry and hateful toward the world for the way it is and the way you are. I want you to feel sorry for yourself and blame everything but your addiction for the way things are. I want you to be deceitful and untrustworthy and to manipulate and con as many people as possible. I want to make you fearful and paranoid for no reason at all. I want you to wake up during all hours of the night screaming for me. You know you can't sleep without me; I'm even in your dreams.

I want to be the first thing you wake up to every morning and the last thing you touch before you black out. I would rather kill you, but I'll be happy enough if I can put you back in the hospital, another institution, or jail. But you know I'll be waiting for you when you come out. I love to watch you slowly going insane. I love to see all the physical damage that I'm causing you. I can't help but sneer and chuckle when you shiver and shake, when you freeze and sweat at the same time, and when you wake up with your sheets and blankets soaking wet.

It's amazing how much destruction I can do to your INTERNAL ORGANS while at the same time work on your BRAIN, destroying it bit by bit. I deeply appreciate how much you sacrifice for me.

The countless good jobs you've sacrificed for me. All the fine friends that you deeply cared for—you gave up for me. And what's more, for the ones you turned against yourself because of your inexcusable actions—I'm more than grateful.

And especially your loved ones, your family, the most important people in the world to you—you even threw them away for me. I cannot express in words the gratitude I have for the loyalty that you have for me. You sacrificed all these beautiful things in life just to devote yourself completely to me. But do not despair my friend, for on me you can always depend. For after you have lost all these things, you can still depend on me to take even more. You can depend on me to keep you in a living hell, to keep your mind, body and soul—FOR I WILL NOT BE SATISFIED UNTIL YOU ARE DEAD, MY FRIEND.

Faithfully yours,
Your Addiction and Drug of Your Choice

Addiction is often spoken of as an "entity." It not only depletes brain cells; it also steals a person's soul. It destroys who one was meant to be—a healthy subject in the world exercising one's own will in fulfillment of one's God-given potential—and holds its prey hostage while feeding on its spirit over and over again.

Two and a half weeks have passed since her outburst in opposition to my returning her to Heliotrope, and Jenny keeps claiming that she is sober. But her respiratory condition and her overall health are rapidly deteriorating. This crisis is escalating, helter-skelter. I call the police and urgently try to have them escort Jenny to a medical/psychiatric hospital, but she is noncompliant, and the young, tough male cops who come to our home tell me that Jenny is "fine" and that I (the worn-down "fuddy-duddy") am "the one who has the problem."

As the situation becomes more desperate, I have a dream in which I see a demon of addiction. This phantasm appears as a very malevolent, tall, extremely thin, pasty, light-skinned woman, whom I can only view from the side, with long, dark hair, a red mouth, and pale-blue eyes that glitter with a ravenous malice. She is standing, seething, in the bathroom located between Jenny's bedroom and mine. It is clear to me that her aim is to torture me and Jenny as much as possible and finally kill us both if she can. In my dream, I am determined that I will oppose this enemy with every ounce of strength I have.

I do not tell Jenny about my dream of an evil being, but several weeks later, Jenny has a nightmare about the same demonic spirit, and she describes the identical apparition that showed itself to me, feature for feature. *Go figure!* In Jenny's nightmare, the woman is trying to kill me. *What is going on? Why are we receiving the exact same mental image during our sleep?*

Recently, Jenny related to me that she researched the phantom in her dream and that the woman we both saw was Lilith. I reminded her of a subsequent Lilith nightmare (recounted in chapter 6), but she had no recollection of it. I mention this same experience Jenny and I both had because it is a curious phenomenon that lends itself to interpretation and certainly to further explorations of its meaning and of potential other forces or "entities" involved.

The next evening, when Jenny gets home after midnight and is gasping for air, I telephone EMS and the police again. This time I am fortunate that headquarters dispatches two female police officers who agree with me that Jenny requires medical and psychiatric attention—immediately. EMS arrives and confirms that Jenny is having a very serious asthma attack, with her oxygen level at only 72 percent. They inform Jenny that she is breathing like an eighty-eight-year-old woman with emphysema and must go to the hospital by ambulance.

They then transport Jenny to Restful Valley Hospital, in the early morning of September 18, 2011. From there she is transferred to a psychiatric facility known as Byron Hall. Jenny will be at Byron Hall for one month, and she will barely escape with her life.

On to Byron Hall

> "*Flores. Flores Para los Muertos. Flores.*" "Flowers. Flowers for the dead." The Mexican woman attempts to sell flowers, to drape over the graves of the departed, to Blanche DuBois before she is later raped and dragged off to an insane asylum. "No, not yet!" screams Blanche. "Not, yet!"
>
> —Tennessee Williams, *A Streetcar Named Desire*

I am familiar with this hospital. Byron Hall is a long-established New Jersey psychiatric facility on the New York border, and in its far distant past, it was subject to a blistering exposé that brought about an outcry for reforms. The more things change, the more they stay the same.

Sections of Byron Hall are very old, and it gives me the creeps. While Jenny completes the private portion of her admission procedure, I wander into a side room of the main building. On one wall, hung six feet high and upward, I see one black framed photo after another of thirty or more of the early psychiatrists of Byron Hall. I can discern their sense of mastery and arrogance as they look down upon me. They are suspended there, men from seventy-five to one hundred years ago, fading but, it seems, still making their lingering presence felt.

Jenny's admission takes about four hours. The kind young woman who comes to review Jenny's paperwork with me shakes her head with great sympathy and says, "She went to all these places, and no one helped her." I write across page 1 of Jenny's admissions sheet in big, bold letters, "NO THORAZINE PERMITTED AS A PRN DUE TO HISTORY OF SEIZURE AND COMA," and I underline my writing for added emphasis.

I go to visit Jenny every day and inform the psychiatrist in charge, a physician named Dr. Q, that I am arranging for Jenny to reenter Heliotrope, as she and I both want to honor her contract to return if Jenny relapsed. Dr. Q is a late-thirtysomething male who looks pale and moist, and his eyes are a transparent blue of the same icy tint that shimmers through his skin. This effect is exacerbated by his balding cranium, accented only by his silver-sided, rimless glasses that, combined with his peering manner, create the overall impression that he is viewing everyone under a microscope. One feels he is constantly considering enacting some unexpected surgical-psychiatric procedure that does not require patient consent. His demeanor and manner of speaking are semi-military and matter of fact. He shares with me, on September 22, 2011, that he is glad that Jenny is reentering Heliotrope, as Dr. Q finds that (1) "Jenny is very, very suicidal, and her addiction is very powerful"; (2) "Jenny's addiction has a life of its own" (again, that entity thing); (3) "Jenny is very, very addicted"; and (4) "Jenny requires lots and lots of treatment for years to come and inpatient rehab and inpatient hospitalization." Jenny has been diagnosed with bipolar disorder and is prescribed Lexapro (15 mg), Abilify (7 mg), Wellbutrin XL (150 mg), Trileptal (300 mg), and Strattera (40 mg), all to be taken daily. This seems like enough medication to fell an elephant, let alone my petite daughter. And all these medications carry possible side effects: Abilify allegedly can cause numerous harmful compulsive behaviors, giving rise to claims against the pharmaceutical manufacturer.

When I spend time with Jenny, she is remorseful, loving, and respectful toward me, and she is looking forward to seeing Erica at Heliotrope once more and to becoming sober again. I have received an email from Erica, and I share her caring message with Jenny.

Subj: Jenny
Date: 9/18/11
From: Erica at Heliotrope
To: Me, Jenny's mom

Dear Vivian:

I just got off the phone with you and I am very concerned about Jenny and what you have been telling me has been going on. I feel like she needs to come back here to get detoxed and to get grounded in recovery. Right now, she is unable to see herself the way she is using and behaving. I know from working with Jenny she is not the kind of person I was hearing about just now. *WE love her here*. I think she needs to come back to get back on track. She needs to get back to sobriety. She will not accomplish the things she needs and wants to do if she stays on this path. I know that the Jenny I know (the sober Jenny) wants to be a good person and is a good person (you see this when she is not using). This is not her now at all.

If there is any way that I can help, please let me know. I would gladly speak with her if she wants to talk. I am afraid for her, and what will happen if she keeps going on like this.

All the best. I am thinking of you both.
Erica

Jenny is so excited and encouraged by this correspondence from Erica and, most especially, by Erica's writing that they love Jenny at Heliotrope. I call the head of admissions at Heliotrope and secure the approval for Jenny's readmission in two days' time.

Perhaps it was my prior opposition to Ms. Crunch's proposed punishment of denying Jenny any participation in the Fourth of July celebrations at Heliotrope that now exacts a deadly consequence. Or perhaps it was Byron Hall's very strong and damning report that alarmed Heliotrope, but the day before Jenny is scheduled to be transferred from Byron Hall, I receive a call from the Heliotrope Adolescent Division instructing me to cancel all plans for Jenny's arrival, as Heliotrope will no longer admit her. The pretext is that Jenny has PTSD, so she does not belong at Heliotrope. However, Jenny was at Heliotrope for three months with a PTSD diagnosis and was never asked to leave because of it, and most of the adolescents at Heliotrope were suffering from undiagnosed PTSD, which is why they were doing drugs. In addition, Jenny's "home contract" with Heliotrope emphatically stated that she should return to Heliotrope if she relapsed. And while there are a few PTSD treatment centers for members of the military, there are almost none for civilians, and only for those who are over the age of eighteen. The first order of business, in any area of medicine, is to "clamp the bleeding," which, in Jenny's case (as Erica stated in her email), is the out-of-control addiction and the need for detox.

After Jenny realizes that I have exhausted my appeals, going all the way up to the CEO of Heliotrope, she is completely devastated by this major rejection, and her behavior starts to change radically. I have a terrible feeling and inform Dr. Q and the social worker (Gretchen, an athletic-looking, attractive, and unhelpful lady with wavy, streaked blonde hair and a flawless manicure) on September 24, 2011, that I believe that Jenny is doing drugs inside of Byron Hall. Jenny will not look me in the eyes, appears irritable, and asks me to leave as soon as I arrive for my visits. The affectionate and regardful Jenny is gone. She tells me,

"Get me out of here! You are undoing all the good that I accomplished at Heliotrope by keeping me here!"

At the time, I have no idea what she is talking about, but I will later discover, after Jenny is discharged from Byron Hall, that she was able to snort Thorazine, twice per day, for twenty-five days, inside of the hospital. Jenny will become heavily mentally, emotionally, psychologically, and physically readdicted inside the very same medical facility that was expected to keep her safe and free of substance abuse and where she was supposed to receive detox, sobriety, quality therapy, and healing.

Jenny easily obtains the Thorazine from other patients, as the nurses are not adhering to medical protocol. The staff do not perform cheek and hand checks to make sure these juveniles have verifiably swallowed their medications and have not stashed them. One of the nurses, according to Jenny, just hands the pills to the adolescents and lets them walk down the hall.

Thorazine, a powerful antipsychotic medication originally used as an oral alternative to lobotomies, has not been prescribed for Jenny and is the one medication that I wrote on Jenny's admissions form that she should not be allowed to receive due to her history of coma and seizure. Jenny will become increasingly and dangerously ill inside of Byron Hall, and by the time I rescue her, she will be collapsing in my arms.

Dr. Q tells me that it is "impossible" that Jenny could be using nonprescribed pharmaceuticals inside of their hospital. They are the professionals, so why am I the only one who sees it? I wonder why they don't check the inside of her nose, just to disconfirm what I am telling them. If they had done so, they would have found numerous fresh lesions. Jenny's hospital notes read:

> 10/6 "Patient seen at rounds, sleepy and sad. Slept yesterday due to a headache; has low frustration tolerance and needs redirection."
>
> 10/7 "Patient displayed a flat affect."
>
> 10/8 "Patient admits had a dream about using OxyContin last night" (*a classic sign of substance abuse*) "and admits to having cravings. Denies problems with meds. Notes decreased energy. Mood reported as bad."

All along, I keep telling Dr. Q that Jenny is displaying the classic signs of active addiction and that I believe she is accessing unauthorized drugs inside Byron Hall, but my concerns are discounted as being "absurd and ridiculous." Dr. Q also makes a note in Jenny's chart that he totally disagrees with my reporting that Jenny is suffering from PTSD, despite the diagnosis of Dr. T from Heliotrope and Jenny's obvious PTSD history.

On September 29, 2011, I am called suddenly into a meeting with Dr. Q and Gretchen. In this meeting, I am spoken to very harshly. Despite Dr. Q's having told me only six days prior that Jenny was very sick and addicted, requiring lots of treatment for years to come and inpatient rehab and hospitalization, Dr. Q now declares, "Jenny is stable and doing fine" and must be discharged this same day to come home and enroll in an outpatient rehab program. If I do not immediately comply, I am told that I will have to pay $2,000 per diem, out of pocket, that will not be covered by insurance.

Then Jenny appears at the meeting and has a major meltdown in front of everyone, acting defiant, cursing, and exhibiting classic, blistering relapse behavior. Clearly, she is not ready to be discharged.

Dr. Q reacts to Jenny's disturbed conduct by claiming that he, Dr. Q, "has never seen her this way before," that "Jenny needs distance from her mother," and demands that I pay $65,000 to send Jenny to a Colorado wilderness program. So which is it, Dr. Q? Jenny is stable enough to go to an outpatient rehab program and come home? Or Jenny is so out of control that she needs the extreme discipline and harsh environs of a wilderness program? Both cannot be the case; I refuse to be intimidated, and I inform Dr. Q and Gretchen that I am not taking Jenny out of Byron Hall without an acceptable and proper discharge plan to an inpatient rehab, as her life is in very great danger of possible overdose on the outside. Dr. Q and Gretchen then resort to insisting that my insurance will not pay for inpatient rehab, so "Jenny has to leave right away."

With some investigating, I discover that incredibly (on Monday, September 19, 2011, the very first full day that Jenny was on the unit) Gretchen had sent a submission for Jenny to be admitted to a well-known inpatient rehab with a second establishment in the area. Gretchen's communication included a detailed accounting that contained alarming and negative statements about Jenny, so the application was rejected by both centers. I discuss the matter with a prominent psychologist, who informs me that the usual procedure is for the hospital simply to send the rehab a discharge summary with a recommendation after the patient has been in the hospital for a while. However, it is now too late for this customary approach, as Gretchen has "jumped the shark," and her initial assay (submitted without having observed Jenny for even one full day and without having allowed a reasonable amount of time for patient stabilization) has made her "radioactive" to ongoing mental health/rehab facilities. Furthermore, Gretchen now refuses to change one word that she has written in her premature "report" and states that this is the document that she is required to forward to any future place to which we may wish Jenny to be transferred.

After gleaning this information, I no longer believe Dr. Q's contention that my insurance company has refused to pay for inpatient rehab, and when I call to verify this representation by Dr. Q, the insurance company case manager tells me that the insurance company "would not pay" only because the hospital had told them "not to pay." I cannot believe my ears. *What?* I then contact the insurance company's physician supervisor, Dr. Y, who informs me that my insurance company would pay for inpatient rehab *but that the hospital had told them that "they were not recommending inpatient rehab, because Jenny would not benefit from it."* I am beyond shocked at the outright lies of Dr. Q and Gretchen. Their disingenuousness is chilling, as this is the medical arena, where the highest ethical standards of honesty must be required, and with a young girl's life at stake.

Dr. Y grants me an appeal, wherein I ask that my insurance company completely reject Byron Hall's false assertion that Jenny "would not benefit from inpatient rehab." The insurance company sides with me and issues a finding that Jenny should have a proper discharge to an inpatient rehab and not to an outpatient rehab. Now Byron Hall must pay for Jenny's stay in their hospital until Byron Hall can arrange for a suitable transfer.

As the weeks elapse, there are distressing incidences on the adolescent ward, which is a very narrow, small wing of the hospital. Jenny tells me that she is terrified at Byron Hall and "does not trust them." She recounts that a girl came onto the unit who had taken so many drugs that she was hallucinating and was very loud. She confides to me, under her breath, that on top of the massive amounts of drugs this girl had ingested, the person in charge on the floor had ordered that the girl be forcibly lifted in the air by the male orderlies in the hallway and shot full of "booty juice" (likely high doses of Thorazine or Ativan syringed into one of the cheeks of her bottom) to keep her quiet. Jenny whispers to me, wide eyed,

"She could have died from their doing that. They did not know how many drugs she had in her system, and they could have killed her. They just wanted her to be silent, and they did not care. If she had died, they just would have said that she overdosed on the drugs she had already taken."

Jenny divulges to me that because she is now so afraid of the doctors and the social workers, she "tries to stay away from them," adding, "The medical staff at Byron Hall are really and truly crazy."

One evening, as I am visiting Jenny, two boys get into a fight. One overpowers the other and breaks his nose. There is blood splattered everywhere. *Where are the hospital personnel?* Jenny's eyes fill with sorrow, and she asks me to leave. She begs me,

"Mom, please go. Please go! I don't want you to see what they are going to do next. I don't want you to have to go through that. I am used to it, but you are not."

Four beefy men appear. There is a rough scuffle, and one of the boys is yanked into a wrestling hold, forcibly raised some four feet off the ground, and vigorously jabbed in the buttocks with a large needle. Jenny starts crying and crying, as the whole situation is very stressful for her, sobbing to me that these kinds of things go on all the time. I am desperate to take her out of here, but I am so afraid of what she will do absent any confinement, free out on her own.

Clearly, there is almost a complete lack of supervision on the floor, and this unit is nothing more than a way station for displaced souls. At Byron Hall, psychiatry is not being practiced as it was meant to be, as a serious profession. To the contrary, the social worker is trying to eject the patients as soon as they enter if she thinks they require too much work or expertise.

The situation is becoming increasingly dire for Jenny, with Dr. Q and Gretchen claiming that they cannot find an inpatient rehab that will accept her. Furthermore, Dr. Q has reported that Jenny is psychiatrically stable, so she cannot be discharged to another psychiatric hospital. We are in no man's land. When I come to visit on October 16, 2011, Jenny tells me that "the team" just tried to pressure her into saying that she did not want to live with me. She informs me that the entire psychiatric crew appeared in her room and addressed Jenny, asking her,

"Wouldn't it be better for you if you did not live with your mother?"

Jenny is trembling when she shares with me that she was so terrified that they were making a concerted effort to try to get her to speak against me and that she was panic stricken that the mental health contingent was attempting to make a case to hand her over to ACS.

Jenny answered the gulag squad,

"Why are you saying this to me? I want to live with my mother. I love my mother more than anyone in the whole world."

If our living together, if our relationship, posed a true psychological problem, the way to address that would have been a private meeting with truly well-meaning and competent clinicians, who would "embrace" us both and explain what they feel is a problem, how, and why. They would be empathic and supportive to both of us and make recommendations for ameliorating the situation. Then there would be some follow-up. Their approach was beyond unprofessional.

I send a report of these machinations to the head of human resources at the hospital, and I again request that my daughter be transferred out of Byron Hall ASAP and into inpatient rehab where she belongs, in accordance with the directives of even the insurance company's physician.

Finally, I meet Dr. A, an East Indian doctor in charge of the adolescent unit on the weekend when Dr. Q and Gretchen are gone. I feel that this is our one chance to liberate ourselves from this incarceration, and I have to seize it. Dr. A sees what is going on, is both brilliant and humane (*how was she ever hired by Byron Hall?*), and truly wants to help me spring Jenny from this trap. We devise a plan together, and I call both Halcyon Headland and my insurance company. The insurance company agrees to pay for an admission to Halcyon Headland, as it is a dual-diagnoses hospital, and Dr. A and I succeed in having Jenny affirmed for transfer there, because unlike Dr. Q and Gretchen, Dr. A says what needs to be said and submits a new, nontoxic discharge summary that clears Jenny for admission. This arrangement is concluded none too soon, for Jenny's drug addiction inside of Byron Hall is now so acute that she rips the soap dispenser from the wall and is taken to the white padded room.

The next day, Monday morning, I arrive to retrieve Jenny for her transfer to Halcyon Headland. I go straight to the nurses' station and move to collect the discharge papers from the clerk as quickly as possible, without making any contact with Gretchen or Dr. Q. I feel like a secret agent rescuing a prisoner in a *Mission Impossible* episode.

Jenny's complexion appears green and disturbingly pale, and she has deep sepia-colored rings under her eyes. She resembles the actress Ingrid Bergman in the movie *Notorious*, when Bergman's character is locked up inside of the mansion of her SS husband and slowly poisoned. Jenny begins to faint outside the ward as we are leaving the floor. I ask her why she is so ill and she answers that she feels "lightheaded." I lift her up and try to carry her down the hall, but her knees are buckling, and she collapses in my arms. I feel alarmed, desperate to complete Jenny's escape and in need of immediate assistance, but there is no way that I am asking Byron Hall personnel for help, or we may never make it out of this chamber of horrors. A Good Samaritan reaches out to support Jenny as she starts to fall again and assists me in gathering her into our waiting car service. On the way to Halcyon Headland, Jenny finally admits that she had snorted Thorazine that morning and that she has been doing so twice per day ever since she discovered that Heliotrope had broken their promise to readmit her.

At Halcyon Headland, the medical staff discover that the inside of Jenny's nose is filled with lesions and scabs, and the nurse tells me that these abrasions were caused by her snorting drugs over the past twenty-five days inside of Byron Hall. The medics at Halcyon Headland start treating Jenny's nasal sores with Bacitracin.

I speak to Jenny over the phone on the morning after her admission to Halcyon Headland, and she tells me, sounding very frightened, that she was up the entire night hallucinating that she was seeing the girl from the movie *The Ring* and that this was terrifying for her. She is so petrified that this hallucination will return tonight. This is thanks to Byron Hall's care.

Now Jenny says, "I do not care anymore about getting off drugs, and I will always do drugs." After snorting Thorazine at Byron Hall for almost one month, Jenny has redefined herself as a drug addict. She tells me that she warned me not to send her there from Restful Valley Hospital, that all the good that was done at Heliotrope and her desire to be sober are gone. Of course, Heliotrope put the nail in our coffin by refusing to take Jenny back, breaching their own contract with us. Jenny is so angry and feels so betrayed and so misunderstood, but she is also not able to exercise some self-control, which is frustrating to me at some level. She tells me, echoing her earlier statement,

"I now crave drugs so badly that I can't stand it. I will always be a drug addict and will do anything I have to do to get drugs, and I do not care." I feel devastated by her feelings of hopelessness and defeat and exasperated by the entire situation.

Jenny tells me that she loves me but feels that no one else ever cared about her and that she feels worthless. The second day at Halcyon Headland, Jenny has a breakdown, bursting out of her dinner chair, hungering for drugs. She screams and cries hysterically, requiring that she be sent to the "quiet room." I have never seen Jenny in this state.

A private psychologist famous for founding the adolescent wing of an outstanding therapeutic institute opines that Byron Hall is guilty of a complete lack of oversight. The insurance company informs me that Byron Hall failed to follow medical protocol, but at the same time, the company refuses to do anything about it.

Liz (the mother of Kenzie, who attended Heliotrope with Jenny), who is also a nurse, insists that for Byron Hall to allow Jenny to snort Thorazine (when it was not prescribed and when I specifically forbade Jenny's use of that drug) would be the equivalent of their administering the wrong medication to a patient on a daily basis, twice a day, for twenty-five days, and poisoning her.

There is no blood or urine test for the presence of Thorazine in the system. Only the wounds inside of Jenny's nose, discovered by Halcyon Headland, as well as her hallucinations, visible infirmity, and swooning in the hall of Byron Hall, bore witness to what she had to say. Clearly, had I not taken Jenny out when I did, she might have died there, and the accurate cause would never have been discovered.

Yes, Byron Hall is an *American Horror Story*, and Heliotrope's promises to Jenny and to most of her friends all turned out to be nothing more than fake sunshine.

As of October 2011, every time I suggest to the "professionals" that PTSD is Jenny's true diagnosis (save for the finding of Dr. T at Heliotrope), I have been dismissed. Therefore, I often feel in the dark and disbelieving of my own thought processes—doubting my intuition. My primary aim is to keep Jenny protected, drug-free, and secured. Safety first—for without it, nothing else can exist. Still, like the little boy who persists in digging a hole in the sand, thinking the waves will not wash up, I keep hoping, naïvely, that the experts in the next facility that Jenny goes to will somehow be able to "fix" her and make this nightmare go away. I am well meaning but incredibly *dumb* and trusting. In our travels, I will discover the sad truth that none (but a very few high-caliber therapeutic practitioners) are pure of heart and possessed of the inner goodness, the sincere compassion, and the erudition and skill that are the requirements of one who would be a healer of souls.

5

THE SCARY-GO-ROUND, PART II

Foundering in Flowering Glen

Halcyon Headland, unlike many other places, ensures that their nursing staff follows medical protocol, so at least their patients are safe and secure while they are inside. The residential houses of Halcyon Headland are architecturally charming and clean, and their programs seem to be comprehensive and conducive to the achievement of insight. Unfortunately, like almost all the mental health facilities in the United States, it is an insurance-driven "get them in and out" psychiatric hospital. Therefore, incisive perception is unlikely to be attained within three to five days, which is the usual amount of time insurance will allow. Halcyon Headland is the raft in the middle of the ocean that you clamber upon while you try to book passage on the next ship of wrecks.

During this round at Halcyon Headland, Jenny's therapist is a social worker named "Ms. D," who seems well read and cutting edge. Ms. D tells me that Jenny has borderline personality disorder (not cited on her discharge summary) and recommends that I read the latest book on the subject. While Jenny is at Halcyon Headland, she hears about a young people's rehab, located in a rustic area of New York, called Revision and whispers to me that not a lot of people know about it, but it is supposed to be excellent, and her friend at Halcyon Headland is going there. Jenny's intuitions are usually on target, whereas I make the mistake of following the advice of "the experts." Jenny will attend Revision eight months from now, and it will be the single worthy facility I will encounter. Revision charges $2,000 per month (vs. the $30,000 per month cost of Heliotrope) for 24/7 residence and rehab, and Revision will keep Jenny safe and sober for almost one year.

However, for now, I listen to Ms. D, who tells me that I must not send Jenny to Revision. Ms. D looks at me darkly, aghast, and with a quick shake of her head whispers her secret factoid: "Revision is no good. You do not want Jenny to go to Revision." She tells me that I must instead send Jenny to Flowering Glen, headquartered in a manicured, upscale environ in the middle of New Jersey horse country and a one-and-a-half hour drive from Round Bridge.

Flowering Glen is a therapeutic boarding facility for girls and boys (kept in separate residential quarters) that also provides high school classes. Prior to our final decision, Ms. D and the admissions director at Flowering Glen emphasize to me that they "will reach Jenny's underlying traumas to heal the causes of Jenny's self-medication," that Jenny will receive lots of individual psychotherapy, and that she will be treated with "compassion, love, nurturing, therapy (including pet and equine therapy), and care." Flowering Glen is very expensive and is mainly attended by those whose money grows on trees. Nonetheless, I am desperate after Jenny's experience at Byron Hall, and I take a deep inhalation of aromatic assurance, with Ms. D promising, "They will get her well at Flowering Glen." I am lulled into a false sense of belief and hope, but Jenny is still not convinced. Ms. D puts her hands on Jenny's shoulders, gazing lovingly into her eyes.

"Jenny, you trust me, don't you? I care about you, and you know that, right? You know that you can trust me, and that I want the best for you, and that I would always tell you the truth." Jenny agrees to take the trip to Flowering Glen.

What I do not discover until one year later is that it was not the practice of Flowering Glen to admit subjects who presented a great chance of running away, or resuming substance abuse or anorexic or bulimic behavior, or engaging in perilous acts. Jenny has not just one but all these behaviors that are supposed to exclude her from entrance to Flowering Glen.

Flowering Glen is built and staffed to accommodate a certain number of juveniles, and at the time that Jenny is admitted, there are only half that number in the girls' division. The logical impression is that Flowering Glen desperately needs more clients, to the point that they breach their own protocol to get Jenny's body through the door. And in violation of their stated requirements, they have also accepted a young lady with a very active eating disorder, which will cause her to require hospitalization while she is at Flowering Glen. This betrayal is another indication of how far some inpatient therapeutic institutions will go to achieve their own financial gain while misleading and endangering their residents.

Jenny enters Flowering Glen on November 4, 2011, and on November 5, I receive a telephone call from Mildred (a licensed marriage and family counselor), who has been assigned to be both Jenny's private therapist and our family therapist at Flowering Glen. Mildred begins by screaming at me over the phone, asserting that she will not work with Jenny because Jenny has admitted that she wants to do drugs (*duh*) and demanding that she go to a wilderness program. Mildred screeches, "One relapse and Jenny is out." As if her admission here had been all my own doing! The esteemed adolescent psychologist Dr. G, whom I am consulting to better help Jenny, tells me that Flowering Glen should work with Jenny and that relapse is often part of getting well; he advises that Flowering Glen should manage any relapse that might occur in a therapeutic way. I mention this to Mildred, who is on a nonstop rampage against Jenny being at Flowering Glen. Again, she shouts at me, ending with "Just shut up! Just shut up!" Then I receive a call from Jenny, who is extremely miserable and wants to leave.

Next, I am summoned into a meeting with Mildred and her male supervisor, Nelson, as they sit opposite me, shoulder to shoulder, on one of the contemporary-style sofas in Mildred's office. I thought I had readied myself for Mildred's attacks, but I am not prepared for her black belt in passive aggression. She is a very pretty woman with shiny, straight, Brazilian-treatment chestnut hair, a rich girl's tan, and a perfect figure with shapely bare legs set in red stiletto pumps. As she looks at me, she begins to seethe with animosity, because she wants Jenny out of Flowering Glen, and she seems to coil and uncoil on the corner of her cushion. She is getting ready to strike, fixes her eyes upon me, and then proceeds to say (with a slow shake of her head) that "Jenny is very, very *jaded*." She continues: "It is unfair to these [prosperous, upper-class] girls to have Jenny here, because she has been to Mountain Pass Academy, so the other girls are afraid of her."

Clearly, Mildred dislikes and looks down on Jenny, causing me to recall a passage from Dr. Judith Herman's *Trauma and Recovery* describing the therapist's negative transference reaction to her patient: "The therapist may feel revulsion and disgust at the patient's behavior or she may become extremely judgmental . . . [and] may have moments of frank hatred and want to be rid of the patient. . . . The first task of treatment is for the therapist to confront his/her own sadistic feelings, not only in response to the patient, but in terms of his/her own potential, as well."[1]

I reply that Jenny is not "jaded" but frustrated, tired, and disappointed, although bright, and that the children at Mountain Pass Academy may have come from disadvantaged backgrounds, but they are no less than anyone else in this world. I cite that the director of admissions and Ms. D have assured me that Jenny needs compassion, love, nurturing, and care, as Jenny has been through so much trauma. Mildred responds by first turning to look at Nelson and then facing me, speaking in a very deliberate manner, with knitted brows and great concern:

"I have a real problem. You are now telling us how you think our program should be run."

I reply that these are not my words but those of Ms. D and their own director of admissions—their representations of how therapy is conducted here. Mildred then states that she is tired of hearing about how much trauma Jenny has been through (hmmmm!), and Nelson concludes the meeting by saying, "We will see if we can move forward."

I feel as if my brain has just been thrown into a washing machine on spin cycle. Jenny meets me in the adjacent corridor in tears, saying that Mildred has called her "jaded" and that all the girls are judging her because she has been at Mountain Pass. Jenny is wearing rosary beads around her neck, and she is not even religious. Looking desperate and unhappy, she asks me,

"Why won't you just let me come home and do drugs? I am so tired of being sent away."

I feel terrible, and I can understand how it must affect Jenny to be taken to all these places and to end up embroiled in their own dysfunctional dynamics—feeling so lost, confused, and disconnected from her home, in an ever-shifting landscape. I want nothing more than to be able to bring Jenny home, but I am terrified of a possible overdose. One pill too many, just one mistake, one miscalculation, and it could all be over, as Jenny's tolerance to drugs and alcohol (which she freely mixes) is now greater than that of a three-hundred-pound man. Since her father's death and the car accident, Jenny has been away from me for almost two and a half years.

But going from one failed admission to the next and working up expectations and hopes for help and improvement, only to meet with hurt and failure, further exacerbates her condition and wears out trust, hope, and tolerance. This is a nightmare I cannot wake up from. *How can this be happening to us?* Yes, from time to time, I scream inside my head, so as not to be heard; I need to scream.

I convince Jenny to stay at Flowering Glen because I do not know where else to place her at this very instant, and I am trying to give her as much drug-free time as possible. Allowing Jenny's brain to convalesce is my number-one priority. Also, I am in a panic, as it appears we have been almost everywhere else there is to go in terms of an adolescent residential/therapeutic boarding school that is not across the country or that will even accept Jenny at this juncture, as she is now halfway to seventeen years of age.

I beg for Nelson and for the director of admissions to provide Jenny with a therapist other than Mildred, but Nelson refuses, claiming, "We never change therapists at Flowering Glen." Then Mildred does not have any one-on-one therapy with Jenny for weeks! Jenny is very upset over not receiving private sessions, as the other residents are. This is distressing, as we were promised that lots of individual therapy would be the hallmark of Flowering Glen.

Finally, when Jenny's once-weekly meetings do commence, Mildred seems to embark on a mission to turn Jenny against me and tells her I am a bad mother and responsible for her drug use. I am shocked: even assuming that these were Mildred's honest and valid opinions of me, I am sure there is a more appropriate and effective and less damaging approach than the slanderous attacking method she used. And that I am Jenny's only immediate family should have been given careful consideration before plunging into such an unethical strategy.

Jenny calls me that same evening, shouting at me, full of rage:

"I am so angry with you because you never mothered me. You were never a mother to me! You are a terrible mother! You never should have been a mother! No wonder, because you are such an overwhelming and changeable person." Jenny is now repeating Mildred's exact verbiage toward me from a previous joint telephone call, as if it is holy writ. "We do not have a relationship. How could we? We never had a relationship! You and my father were babies. You were not parents. You should never have been allowed to be parents! You should never have been allowed to have children! I can't wait till I am eighteen, when I can get away from you, and you will never see me again! You do not even know me!"

Jenny has never spoken to me quite this way before. Thanks to therapist Mildred, my relationship with Jenny, which I am paying a fortune to try to repair, is worse than ever. A friend of Jenny's later tells me that she and her mother (also a single parent) were assigned to family sessions with Mildred, who immediately tried to sabotage their relationship, so they quit therapy with Mildred after the first session. This same young woman reports that she has permanent liver damage due to Flowering Glen's psychiatrist prescribing very high doses of lithium and Geodon simultaneously without monitoring her blood in the manner prescribed. Two months later, that same psychiatrist will claim that Jenny has fourteen separate psychiatric diagnoses, and I subsequently will have to fight to have several of them condensed and some of them excluded from Jenny's record.

When I later ask Mildred how Jenny is doing at Flowering Glen, she tells me it is not the practice at Flowering Glen to discuss the residents with their parents over the phone "for reasons of confidentiality." However, Jenny is a minor, and I am her parent, who is responsible for her well-being, and no other facility Jenny has attended (egregious though they may have been) has ever used this justification for not informing me about Jenny's welfare.

I speak to Joanne, who has installed Susan in an upstate Individual Education Plan (IEP) residential school, where Susan has been grabbed, bruised, and thrown by a male guard. This incident occurred after the school abruptly discontinued Susan's SSRIs (selective serotonin reuptake inhibitors)—medications including, but not limited to, Lexapro, Prozac, Paxil, and Zoloft. These are taken for depressive and anxiety disorders and are supposed to be suspended only with tapered modulation, as to do otherwise can result in manic episodes and acute suicidality.

As a side discussion on SSRIs, how this class of drugs works is not exactly known, but it is believed to increase the levels of serotonin (thought to regulate mood balance and counteract depression) by limiting its reabsorption into presynaptic cells. Anecdotally, I am acquainted with many adults, as well as some young adults ages eighteen and over, whose lives have been dramatically and positively improved by taking SSRIs (Lexapro and Prozac in particular). When Jenny was an adolescent, the SSRIs did not seem to help abate, and may even have exacerbated, her suicidal ideation, which is one of the reported side effects, and there are many others. Indeed, approximately ten years ago, the Food and Drug Administration (FDA) added a "black-box warning" to a number of antidepressants used by teenagers, saying that they might increase suicidal thinking. This was because an FDA review found that 4 percent of those taking SSRIs experienced suicidal ideation or behavior at twice the rate of those taking a placebo. Still, studies on the effectiveness of SSRIs in adults, teens, and children seem to be split.[2] Most of these articles cite modest (although a few cite significant) improvement in those who suffer from severe depression, with minimal improvement in instances of mild to moderate depression, while pointing out the placebo effect in many cases as well as the bias of studies conducted with pharmaceutical company funds. However, WebMD asserts that "fluoxetine (Prozac) can improve depression symptoms and prevent relapse in children and teens. Studies have also shown other SSRIs work for children and teens, such as citalopram and sertraline."[3] Perhaps the most cogent summary is expressed by the National Institute of Mental Health, which finds (as have other studies) that "fluoxetine . . . can lead to significant improvement of childhood depression overall. However it may increase the risk for suicidal behavior in a small subset of adolescents. As with all medical decisions, doctors and families should weigh the risks and benefits." This piece also notes that in some cases, depressed children commence cognitive-behavioral therapy and/or psychotherapy prior to starting an SSRI. Other studies have shown that the combination of psychotherapy and/or cognitive-behavioral therapy along with an effective SSRI is more beneficial than medication alone.[4]

The bottom line, in my opinion, is that one should be thoroughly evaluated by a psychiatrist in conjunction with one's medical doctor before starting an SSRI and carefully overseen thereafter on a weekly basis. In children especially, one should attempt improvement via psychotherapy along with cognitive-behavioral or dialectical behavioral therapy and/or pastoral therapy prior to prescribing an SSRI. Although many patients respond positively, not everyone does, and an SSRI may have one or more negative side effects for some people. Studies disagree with one another's conclusions, and there are many intervening variables that often are not included in clinical research, such as whether the patient is also involved in one-on-one psychotherapy, his overall health, and whether he is suffering from diabetes, any other ongoing physical ailments or endocrine imbalances, or traumatic brain injury (TBI) or posttraumatic stress disorder. If an SSRI is commenced, then including one-on-one psychotherapy and cognitive-behavioral or dialectical behavioral therapy would be optimal. However, most people cannot afford private therapy on an ongoing basis, which is why community doctors resort to the pills. Overall, the biggest question is, *Why* has there been such a recent dramatic increase in the numbers of children younger than age thirteen who are suicidal or severely depressed? *What has happened?* Medication may paper over the symptoms in some cases, but for how long, and what is the underlying cause? We shall address this issue in part 2 of this book.

Joanne comments, "Unfortunately, it does seem that quite a few people in the medical/psychiatric field, in particular, like having power and being able to abuse it."

Years earlier, when Armand was trying to find a therapist for a family member with a specific issue, he sought advice from one of the foremost psychoanalysts in the field. This brilliant and devoted psychiatrist/analyst exhaled a weary sigh and told Armand that he was semiretired and that he could recommend but a single gentleman, whom he stated was the only person he knew whom he trusted. This was quite a commentary by an acclaimed worldwide "maven" regarding his actual opinion of most therapists.

Flowering Glen: On Mothers and Daughters

I learn that the other mothers at Flowering Glen are very disturbed by the calculated manner whereby Flowering Glen ruins their relationships with their daughters. One mother states openly in a meeting that the therapists never tell her anything about her daughter, who only ever says, "Hi, Mom . . . bye, Mom" on the phone, just as Jenny has started to do. Another single mother declares that she is consulting with the National Alliance on Mental Illness (NAMI), as the therapist has not even allowed her to speak with her daughter for more than a month and has placed this mother on a "no-talk policy" with her own child. She further reports that the counselor consistently blames her for everything and that she is so tired of having to spend all her time defending herself to therapists for the past six years as a single mother. In addition, the therapist has encouraged her daughter to habitually gang up on her. If there is a good clinically relevant reason for prohibiting mother-daughter communication, as is done with all patients during the initial period in some drug detox programs, it should be addressed at admission and the reasons explained with sensitivity in a manner that can be understood and accepted. Instead, their approach oozes belligerence.

At the same time, Flowering Glen practices what they call "holding," where a staff member (male or female) has one of the adolescent girls sit on or close to his or her lap while holding the juvenile like a baby. I was shocked upon first learning of this bizarre practice. And even though I communicate to Flowering Glen that they absolutely do not have my permission to employ "holding" with Jenny—due to her history of sexual abuse—they (both male and female "counselors") try to "hold" her anyway, and Jenny must repeatedly push them away on her own.

The practice of "holding" has come under scrutiny, severe criticism, and investigation due to the dangerous violation of personal boundaries, the inappropriate intensity of emotional arousal it produces, and the physical force exerted, which in the past has caused serious difficulties for patients. This is not a practice to be forced onto a child who has been sexually molested and is suffering from post-traumatic stress disorder (PTSD).

Flowering Glen should be healing mother/daughter relationships and encouraging healthy connectedness, but instead, they chisel away at these bonds and enforce parent/child separations. Through well-conducted family therapy, Flowering Glen should be facilitating mutual understanding, not implanting mental tapes of resentment and hate. Jenny has still not completely recovered from the falsehoods inserted into her mind that ripped open a rancor against me in her heart, courtesy of the cultivation of Flowering Glen.

Along the same lines, the workers in most therapeutic settings like to criticize parents as being "enablers." Some are, but the crux of the matter is the way in which the problems of "enabling" or "separating" are approached: they are crucial issues that should be dealt with in a thoughtful, professional, informed, helpful, personalized, and supportive and educative way with both the parent and the adolescent or harm can result. If someone is truly enabling one's child, then that person deserves and needs assistance to see and understand the dynamics involved and how to correct them. To slap a derogatory label on someone is not beneficial.

What I have done is to rescue my *child* once she was in grave danger or on the verge of irreversible disaster. Jenny has told me that I have not been an enabler because I have not overlooked, ignored, minimized, or facilitated her drug use. Furthermore, Jenny told me that I had to rescue her over and over again, as she did not know what she was doing, and she was *only a child* in her teens.

Thanksgiving at Flowering Glen

This Thanksgiving, the anniversary of Armand's death, is particularly difficult for Jenny. She gets into a verbal dispute with a resident who has made a pair of plastic earrings in an arts and crafts class, and in the heat of the argument, she throws the girl's earrings into a waste paper basket. Mildred telephones me to announce that Flowering Glen is going to call the police, because taking the earrings and flinging them into the bin constitutes "theft," and Jenny will be given a police record. Really!? I speak to one of the male administrators, Mr. J, who informs me (by way of example) that there is another institution for girls over the age of eighteen in a nearby town, and since they are short staffed at that facility, the young women there receive police records "on a regular basis." Mr. J lets me know that you can eventually have the police records expunged, "if you work at it, over time." Mr. J then proceeds to tell me that Jenny urgently needs "masculine boundaries" and that Flowering Glen uses the police department to establish such masculine boundaries for its residents.

I always think that I cannot be shocked any more than I have been, but wrong again. I reply that the police are not trained psychotherapists—far from it—and that it is not correct to use the threat of armed violence and prison sentencing in lieu of proper psychological therapeutic boundaries for children. With a very costly monthly charge to parents, Flowering Glen should not be employing the police department to conduct "masculine boundaries" therapy. I have kept Jenny out of jail for years, and I am not paying a small fortune every month for this place to stick Jenny with a rap sheet over a pair of plastic earrings cast into a wastepaper basket over a teenage contretemps. Flowering Glen finally backs down on this one. This incident would have been an excellent opportunity to work with the two girls and teach them to explore and resolve the issue. Instead, it was another therapeutic opportunity missed.

In Love at Flowering Glen

Evidently, there is a lot of lesbian sexual activity that takes place at Flowering Glen, and Jenny thinks she is in love with a girl who is a tall, slender, and almost platinum blonde haired, blue-eyed beauty from Scandinavia, named Astrid. I know that Jenny is just exceptionally vulnerable and looking for affection. (She even gave Astrid the blanket she had been crocheting for me for Christmas.) I also believe that if the day ever arrives when Astrid turns against Jenny, there will be a disastrous mess. She is trying to meet all her emotional needs through the person of a young, unstable adolescent fellow patient, and I express my advice, discouraging a relationship potentially disruptive to Jenny's own progress. It is my concern that when this bomb explodes, Jenny will be left with nothing, but naturally my objection only makes Jenny more hostile toward me, and she is going to have to learn by her own mistakes.

On the other hand, although Flowering Glen's residential facility is mostly dreadful, their classroom setup is fantastic. The instructors are excellent at imparting their subject matter, and they are kind and compassionate people. Jenny's teachers are warm and respectful toward Jenny and me, and Jenny is achieving straight As, including in chemistry, and receives a grade of 100 percent on her geometry exam. Nonetheless, her academic progress is about to be undercut because of her entanglement with Astrid and the untoward practices in the residential program at Flowering Glen.

One of the great disservices of Flowering Glen is the every-Sunday-afternoon residential "group family meeting," which is more like an episode of "Flowering Glen Survivor." Instead of conducting a session where legitimate concerns can be verbalized without inappropriate language and where children and parents together can be taught healthier interpersonal communication and family rapport and balance, the family meeting is a time when the girls vent their complaints and animosities regarding other adolescents in the residence and their parents lob gripe grenades against these targeted students. This results in the character assassination of the undefended, bullying, and mobbing. My perception is that the therapists just sit back and let the bloodbath run its destructive course.

On the one Sunday when the staff have been informed that I will be unable to attend, Astrid's parents (who fly to the United States every two months to visit Astrid) come forward and declare (in front of all twelve girls, with their siblings, parents, and therapists there assembled), that they and Astrid's therapist, Arnold, do not want Astrid to have anything to do with Jenny. They elaborate by stating that Jenny is a very bad influence on their daughter and that they are so proud of Astrid for agreeing to denounce Jenny, in front of everyone, at this family meeting. Astrid's parents announce that she "is committed not to speak to Jenny anymore, in order for Astrid to do what is right." Although I don't disagree that the girls should not be involved in a romantic relationship, I doubt that this public condemnation of Jenny, with the complicity of Astrid's analyst—especially when there is no one there to support her—has taught Jenny anything. The therapists who are running the family meeting, including Nelson, do nothing to modulate the recriminations and to put things into rational perspective. What do they expect from stirring up such powerful aggression and injurious sentiments, with no safe provision for damage control?

The day after this *Lord of the Flies* episode, Mildred and, Arnold join a Flowering Glen "community meeting" for a repeat performance and make Astrid tell Jenny, all over again, with all the children and staff who were not present the day before collected as witnesses, that Astrid cannot be friends with Jenny anymore. In addition, unfortunately, Astrid's parents have sent her a letter in which they describe Jenny as "a lost cause, whose life is over," and other girls are shown this letter, so its foul details have spilled all over the residence. This is very hurtful, and Jenny tells Nelson that she feels demeaned by the way she has been treated, but Astrid's parents are not asked to apologize to Jenny and to me, nor is any corrective action taken on Jenny's behalf. Jenny wants to kill herself. The public gatherings may have been strengthening for Astrid, but Jenny only received the rejection and humiliation that compounded her perilous lack of self-esteem and value as a person.

After this incident, the teachers in the educational division deliver the news to me that Jenny's grades have plummeted and that she received a 47 percent on her chemistry exam. The head of the academic program informs me that in his opinion, at the time all this was happening to Jenny, she had just given up. Jenny starts having drug dreams, nightmares, and drug cravings, as in the past only drugs could ease her emotional grief. She tells me now, "I don't care if I live or die, because I don't want to feel any more pain, and I will be a drug addict forever." But of course this is what Astrid's parents wrote in their letter, that Jenny's "life is over." In addition, Astrid tells Jenny that her own therapist at Flowering Glen "hates her."

On February 9, 2012, Jenny calls me, crying and sobbing into the phone, "Mom, get me out of here. I am falling apart. I cannot take it anymore. Please, Mom. Get me out of here."

I tell Jenny that I love her with all my heart and that I will call Flowering Glen, come up to see her tomorrow, and get her transferred back to Beautiful Shore. I then email and leave voicemail messages for Nelson and Mildred, requesting them to please be sure that Jenny is still on constant observation (CO), which was the "deal" when Jenny first arrived at Flowering Glen, as there is a great danger that she could harm herself. I also ask that we work on transferring Jenny to Beautiful Shore so that she may reintegrate herself after the harmful Astrid episode.

From Flowering Glen to the ER

The next day, February 10, 2012, I receive a call from Mildred that Jenny is being sent by ambulance to the nearest hospital, Castletowne Hospital, as she has come forward to say that she does not feel confident that she will not harm herself. I rush to Flowering Glen in time to meet the ambulance, and I accompany Jenny to the emergency room. She is at first very quiet and still, but then she starts to sob, admitting to me that she has been saving up her nightly Benadryl so that she can swallow a lot of pills all at once and overdose.

I am furious with Flowering Glen for the poor treatment they have given her. They were unable to provide a safe structure, and they lost control. I telephone my livery driver, Olaf, from New York City, and I call Beautiful Shore to arrange for Jenny to be preadmitted out of Castletowne Hospital, where the psych ER is little better than an organized riot.

When we arrive at Castletowne Hospital, one woman inside their psych bubble area is verbally expressive, so she is rushed, tackled to the ground by four very muscular men, and knocked unconscious on the floor—a use of excessive and unnecessary force, in my opinion. Now they have to try to get her to "come to." The psych ER doctor—a tall, lanky specimen who speaks in aristocratic lockjaw, wears a gold wax seal signet ring, and sports an Ivy League tie—does not want to let Jenny go to Beautiful Shore. Why not? I did not expect any opposition. Castletowne's psychiatric wing is nothing more than an open area with a broken TV and a corridor for shuffling back and forth all day. He is not budging, so it is time to take command, because too much is at stake for Jenny. I tell "Dr. Lockjaw" that he better let Jenny be transferred to Beautiful Shore so that she may reconnect with the doctors there and get the quality of care that she needs or I will report what I just saw his staff do to this woman. He flatly states that I cannot prove a thing. Olaf then whispers to me that I am in danger of being tased by the security detail standing nearby, whom Dr. Lockjaw can command with the flick of his wrist. However, since Olaf is located right behind me in the hallway and has also witnessed the patient "beat down," Dr. Lockjaw decides to authorize the transfer.

We undergo the one-hour drive to Beautiful Shore in the middle of the night in the worst snowstorm I have ever seen, with a visibility of no more than two feet in front of us. The large trailer trucks are whizzing past us and at one point push us to the edge of the highway. Finally, we arrive, safe to port. Olaf tells me he believes there were guardian angels on either side of us all the way. It certainly feels as if this may have been the only reason that we reached our destination safely.

Jenny is happy to return to Beautiful Shore, where she stayed for seventy-six days last year during this same season. The doctors remember Jenny and welcome her back. She feels comfortable here. After all, this is where Jenny has said she wants to live forever. Who wouldn't? It is idyllic. This little detour costs me $10,000 out of pocket, and I gladly pay it, considering everything Jenny has been through and with her life at stake.

At Beautiful Shore, Jenny opens up about the letter Astrid received from her parents denigrating Jenny and about how depressed she is because it's extremely debasing contents were shown to the other students: "Jenny is beyond help and ruined forever, and no one can save her," as well as other damning statements about her. Plus she reports that she overheard the staff saying that "Jenny is going to get kicked out of Flowering Glen." The psychiatrist, Dr. C, and the social worker, Mr. F, in charge of the adolescent wing at Beautiful Shore, empathically summarize that because of this, Jenny feels that no one at Flowering Glen likes her and that she is unwelcome. Jenny also reveals that the staff at Flowering Glen talk about other girls in an unkind way as well.

The Beautiful Shore psychiatric team calls Heliotrope to try to get Jenny transferred there; however, Heliotrope (at the behest of Ms. Crunch) refuses—just as they disallowed her readmission to them from Byron Hall. Dr. C and Mr. F then speak to Flowering Glen about how the Astrid incidences at Flowering Glen have harmed Jenny, and they request that they give Jenny a change of roommate. They also ask Flowering Glen to instruct their nursing staff to conduct medication cheek and hand checks, in accordance with proper medical protocol, to keep Jenny safe.

After ten days at Beautiful Shore, through their respectful and truly caring approach, Jenny is feeling better, and Dr. C and Mr. F, believing that Flowering Glen will follow the requests and advice of the Beautiful Shore psychiatric team, suggest that Jenny be discharged back to Flowering Glen. They hope this will enable her to complete the remaining two months of the spring academic semester (and thereby not fall behind a third year in school) while being contained in a structured environment. But it is not to be.

I bring Jenny back to Flowering Glen, and she is happy with her new roommate, who is a brilliant guitarist named Amy. Jenny and Amy share a love of music.

However, Mildred resumes her practice of insulting me in front of Jenny, now calling me "extreme" for asking Jenny to wear a seatbelt in the car. I think my request is reasonable, and in what seems like a role reversal, I make Mildred aware that if she continues to pervert Jenny's mind against me, then Jenny will not be able to turn to me when she is in trouble or overwhelmed by emotional pain. And as I am the only person Jenny has, she will be left with no one to reach out to for help.

It is March 8, 2012, and Flowering Glen now has a full residential house of twenty girls, with more students on a waiting list. Jenny places an urgent call to me, in tears, to tell me that Flowering Glen has taken her off CO and has made her sign a contract, even though she is a minor, stating that she will not hurt herself. Or what!? Jenny cannot promise this, especially if Flowering Glen is not following medical protocol while engaging in practices that make her feel very depressed. Now Flowering Glen uses the tactic of abdicating their responsibilities by forcing parents and juveniles into waiving their rights.

I place calls and send emails to ask that Jenny be placed back on CO per their original promise to me. I receive nothing but silence by way of reply. I will later discover that Nelson and Mildred have also been completely incommunicado regarding the fact that Jenny has been seeing the nurses at Flowering Glen for nosebleeds every day for the past two weeks and that her behavior has been markedly bizarre since shortly after her return from Beautiful Shore.

Doing Drugs in Flowering Glen?

On March 12, 2012, I receive an email from one of Jenny's teachers.

> Hi Vivian:
>
> For the past two weeks, Jenny has been scattered. She used to be an avid listener. Now, when I ask her a question, she has no idea what I am talking about. When she realizes it, she answers in

confusion: "Wait, what?" and "Kevin, I have no idea." This is very unlike her.

Her grades are below her normal As, with a 75 on her last test. Also, she came to classes on Tuesday and Wednesday without bringing a bag, homework, daily planner, or any books. I have talked to the other teachers and she has been unprepared for their classes as well.

Today, the reason that I am writing you is the fact that I cannot wake her up. From period one to two, she was described by other teachers as "rapid and hyper." Now, she has crashed in my room; she is refusing to get up and being noncompliant. She also slept through my calls on the first.

I have seen this behavior from Jenny for about two weeks. I was hoping that this was a little "slump" that would only last a couple of days. It has not stopped.

Thank you very much and have a good day.
Kevin H.
Social Studies and History

From this email, it is crystal clear to me that Jenny is on drugs, and I email her social studies teacher to please send Jenny to the Flowering Glen nurse immediately, as these are all symptoms of substance abuse, and she could be in great danger.

That same evening, Jenny calls me and admits that she has been snorting Benadryl and that she feels no hope for herself. She tells me that even though Flowering Glen was warned by Beautiful Shore, the nurses at Flowering Glen have not been conducting cheek and hand checks since the day she returned from Beautiful Shore. In the middle of Jenny's conversation with me, the staff force Jenny off the phone "due to time constraints."

I email Mildred and Nelson, letting them know that the nurses are still not following medical protocol, thereby allowing Jenny to snort her medication, and I ask them to please put Jenny back on CO immediately. What is so concerning is that the teacher had been observing Jenny's altered condition for the past two weeks when he finally contacted me. Had he already alerted the therapeutic division of Flowering Glen? If so, Jenny was obviously still ill, and he knew she needed help. The residential staff at Flowering Glen *must* have also seen Jenny's abnormal behavior. *Was this why they suddenly asked Jenny to sign a contract that she would not harm herself?* I point out to Nelson and Mildred that I have been alerting them since on or around February 24, 2012, that I suspected drug use by Jenny. How's that for "enabling"?

Then there is my request to visit Jenny on the weekend of March 17, 2012, due to her relapse and lack of follow-up with cheek and hand checks, which was approved by Teresa (one of the house "mothers") but immediately intercepted by Nelson, who emails me:

> Dear Vivian:
>
> I understand that you asked Teresa if you could visit Jenny on Saturday. Teresa is not in a position to grant such requests. My clinical recommendation is that you not visit with Jenny this weekend *in order for her to be held in relational tension*. If you choose to visit despite my recommendation, please respond to me within the time frame.

"*In relational tension*?" More Orwellian doublespeak.

The Heart and Soul of the Matter

As I edit this book, I am belatedly struck by a huge paradox: an obviously missing and vital link in the chain of rehab treatments, hospitalizations, procedures, and programs that Jenny went through. The reality is that not only do the children, the addicted, and the traumatized patients need help, but the parent or parents do as well.

The large, impersonal, sporadic "family" meetings held with all the other parents and the children are of no help and often have destructive qualities. Parents need to be embraced, privately, by a truly therapeutic arm of an institution as part of its program to treat the patient. The parents need to be shown kindness, understanding, empathy, and support, which builds trust, not authoritarian, condescending, bullying, antagonistic, or hostile attitudes by the staff. There must be regular, well-run, private therapeutic sessions with each family to address their own mental and emotional turmoil and trauma, to give them supportive insights and information on how to best deal with their child's illness, and to provide information on how the program is run and what to expect.

Had that been part of my experience with the institutions we frequented, perhaps I, and other parents, would not have been flailing and floundering, feeling scared, rejected, alone, and helpless in the face of the huge problem we were struggling to handle all by ourselves. But, of course, this did not take place because it is again a matter of money, which rules out integrity and compassion.

Also, it seems to me that medical, mental health, and rehab professionals should be rigorously trained, as part of the core of their education and licensing, to understand and truly internalize the ethical canon that their caring for another human being demands. Each of the mental health professions (psychiatric, psychologic, social work) holds its members to the principles of its own code of ethics or moral standards of professional behaviors. The modern Hippocratic Oath states, "There is art to medicine as well as science, and that warmth, sympathy, and understanding may outweigh the surgeon's knife or the chemist's drug." And further, "I will remember that I do not treat a fever chart, a cancerous growth, but a sick human being, whose illness may affect the person's family and economic stability. My responsibility includes these related problems, if I am to care adequately for the sick."[5]

It is clear to me that Flowering Glen's reason for handling the critical issues mentioned above as they do is that a more respectful and ethical attitude would cause more work for them and cost more money, or perhaps they simply don't know how to do adopt such an attitude. Money as the primary motive of health care/rehab institutions and the idolatry of the "system" really need to cease, as these motivations breed laxity, indifference, dishonesty, and phony treatment.

Basically, Jenny has been labeled a "difficult case," and the staff are reacting unprofessionally to quell their own frustration and aggression rather than thoughtfully to devise an approach that would benefit the patient and ultimately themselves and the system. And if one has the misfortune of being categorized as "difficult," who will treat and cure one? The organization must run smoothly, all gears and wheels turning relentlessly, silently, and in synchrony, very much like the assembly mechanisms of a combine, or jams and delays will occur, workers must be called, and repair often means cutting off the jammed piece (i.e., the difficult patient).

Bleeding Out and More Serious Problems at Flowering Glen?

On March 21, 2012, I receive a call that Jenny needs to go to the doctor right away because she is having a severe nosebleed. The doctor, Dr. Goode, informs me and Jenny that the membrane between the bridge of her nose and the brain is perforated from her drug use inside of Flowering Glen, it needs to be cauterized, and Jenny must be placed on CO at Flowering Glen. (Yes! They caught up!) Dr. Goode is sending Jenny to an ear, nose, and throat specialist, as the vessel is too high up for him to reach and cauterize. The nosebleeds are not stopping, and there is a danger that Jenny could "bleed out." A person can die of such a nosebleed in fifteen minutes or less. Mildred and Nelson had told me that I was "intense" and "overwhelming" for requesting that Jenny be kept on CO, but now their own doctor, to whom they send numerous referrals, is demanding CO for Jenny and does not care about his potential loss of business. At last, Dr. Goode, an objective observer, is overtly disgusted with Flowering Glen for what has happened to Jenny on their watch.

On Monday, March 19, 2012, I had informed Nelson and Mildred that Jenny had a major nosebleed when I visited with her the previous day, such that I had to clamp Jenny's nose for almost a half hour, replacing one bloody tissue after another, and that this was witnessed by the nurse, a counselor, and other residents. I related that Jenny told me that she had been having nosebleeds every day for more than two and a half weeks.

However, Nelson and Mildred denied any nosebleed incidents, except for Sunday, March 18, 2012. Nonetheless, to the contrary, Dr. Goode now informs me that Jenny has been having nosebleeds twice a day since approximately February 24, 2012—the exact same time I told Mildred and Nelson that I suspect Jenny of resuming drug use. Furthermore, Dr. Goode advises me that the nurses at Flowering Glen have been aware of these nosebleeds since that time, so for the past three weeks. Throughout the month of March, I have been urgently looking to find another residential facility that Jenny could be transferred to but have not been successful.

I report all these incidents to give the reader an idea of just exactly how treatment in these facilities is conducted and to forewarn parents and patients so that they can forearm themselves by staying alert.

On Friday, March 23, Jenny calls me, crying frantically into the phone that she wants to come to see me on a home pass, but Mildred again curtails our appeal, despite that Flowering Glen's own dereliction of duties has been so egregious. What game is Mildred playing? I email both her and Nelson about Jenny's complaint to me that the strain of being away from home for so long is wearing her down and she is suffering mentally, but Mildred is unmoved and Nelson will not dare to cross Mildred.

On Sunday, March 25, Jenny telephones, saying, "I just want to tell you that I love you, Mom." Alarm bells go off, because this is what Jenny always tells me right before she runs away. I call the staff to warn them, but they have been instructed not to talk to me. Jenny makes her escape from Flowering Glen with her roommate Amy, who was supposed to be on CO (but obviously is not), as she suffers from a debilitating eating disorder—yes, the one that Flowering Glen had declared they would not admit.

The mothers present at Flowering Glen at the time of the breakout agree that the staff were not watching the girls as they should have been. In addition, when the staff followed the girls to the getaway car, they did not even prevent them from entering the vehicle with an unknown man. Are the staff at Flowering Glen "enabling"? Maybe?

Jenny Is Gone?

Because they ignored my warning, Jenny is gone, but to where? I search the train stations around Flowering Glen, but there is no sign of her. The popular theory is that Jenny has gone to New York City, because that is where she grew up.

I need to make a quick decision. What can I do? I hire a very expensive private detective named "M." M has alerted the police, as he is ex-NYPD and a very tough guy who has seen too much. He dispatches a crew of seven investigators to search for Jenny every day in New York City. We work closely with the local police and the New York City police. The local police discover that the "unknown" young man in the vehicle was Amy's boyfriend, and they "ping" his cell phone, which traces him to Times Square. In the meanwhile, I am out with a private car service from 8:00 a.m. to 10:00 p.m., all day, every day, looking for Jenny and Amy in Times Square, Union Square, and Washington Square and on the Upper West Side. I am calling every person whom I am aware that Jenny ever knew.

I plaster posters of Jenny, with contact information, all around New York City, and I visit the Times Square police precinct, where the police call an old boyfriend of Jenny's, Guillermo, who lives in the Bronx. I speak to him over the phone, and at first he is snarky because it was a little upsetting to have the police contact him, but then he realizes that I am just a mother who loves her daughter, and he agrees to help me. Guillermo reaches out to Jenny and tells her to come home. He does this several times a day for two days, God bless him.

At night, Jenny and Amy are put up in different New York City apartments by a man named Tom whom they meet in Union

Square and who makes a practice of "welcoming" runaways. Tom deals marijuana in Union Square and is allegedly friends with the police. He tells Jenny,

"Wow, your mom is super fierce! The cops told me that there is tremendous heat out to find you."

In the early afternoon of March 28, 2012, Amy is caught jumping a subway turnstile. M prevents Amy from getting a police record and brings Amy to her mother. However, Jenny is not the sort to get nabbed and is still out there, but now she is all on her own, which is much more hazardous. Finally, at 11:30 p.m. that same day, she calls me from a phone booth and asks me to come pick her up on West Fourteenth Street at the bottom of Union Square, in front of the colossal Virgin Records store (which is now gone) on the promise that she never has to go back to Flowering Glen. I promise. What is the point? Not only have they been terrible, but they cannot protect Jenny from a possible overdose on the inside or prevent her from running away.

I call M and ask him to please go to Fourteenth Street right away, and I obtain a night car service out of Round Bridge to drive me to New York City. When I arrive at approximately 1:00 a.m., Jenny is talking with M in a huddle on the corner near the neon lights of the iconic Virgin Records store, both of them smoking, under a street lamp. The scene looks very Edward Hopper–esque. I give M a lift to his apartment and express my deep appreciation for all his help, but my voice seems to issue from another person, because my head is buzzing with exhaustion, and this has all been so terrifying that I am in a kind of netherworld.

On the ride back to Round Bridge, Jenny, who is fairly stoned, suddenly exclaims, "Mom, your rosary beads saved my life! I am never taking them off!" Jenny then explains that she was traveling the subways alone when she was approached by a menacing gang, but the gang members told her that because she was wearing the rosary beads I had given her, they were going to leave her alone. "You see, Mom?" Jenny bursts out. "It is a good thing you gave me those rosary beads!" She shares with me, thoughtfully, that she eventually listened to Guillermo, who told her how much I love her, and to call me, and to go home to her mother. *Finally*, reversing Flowering Glen' message!

There are no words to convey my relief, and I inwardly express my gratitude to God, because I have been praying nonstop, "Please, God. Please let me find Jenny. Please, God. Please let Jenny be OK." When your child is missing, and you have no family to help carry the burden, you are in a state of constant panic and adrenal overload. You do not rest, you barely sleep, and you cannot think of anything besides locating your child. The horrifying thing is that when your child has gone dark, you are never sure you will ever see her again. As the days stretch, you become more and more alarmed about whether she is now across the country, or even in a foreign land, and what could have happened to her. At times, your heart seems to stop beating. This is particularly true if your child is a beautiful, petite teenage girl who is mentally and emotionally fragile, addicted, asthmatic, without her medications, and a choice morsel for predators and abductors. Every decision is a major ruling with severe consequences, and without help to decide, often instantly, this task becomes overwhelming and risky.

In the morning, I contact the Board of Education of Round Bridge and suggest that Jenny be tutored at home for the remainder of the semester, and I obtain an outpatient rehab placement at Mother of Guidance in the next town. It is so wonderful just to have Jenny home, and I have placed inside locks on the front door and a padlock on Jenny's bedroom window, which leads to the fire escape. We are two flights up, more than twenty-five feet off the ground, so Jenny should be safe indoors—or so I think.

Jenny sends a letter to the board of education summarizing her experiences at Flowering Glen. The letter ends,

> In conclusion, I am making a plea to stay in Round Bridge and attend the "Achievement Program" at Mother of Guidance Hospital and have tutoring after Mother of Guidance so that I can be a junior in the fall. I understand that I must be drug tested and

remain sober and attend my AA [Alcoholics Anonymous] meetings and my therapy sessions with Dr. B. I am also looking into attending a DBT program in Morningsong County.

The only good part of Flowering Glen for me was the educational curriculum. The teachers were encouraging, and I felt motivated to learn until I became too depressed to continue.

Sincerely,
Jenny

"Interrelational Problems"

As of April 12, 2012, I am dealing with the Special Education Board of Round Bridge. In order for them to allow Jenny into an end-of-spring semester tutoring-for-exams program under the auspices of Round Bridge High School, they have notification, timing, and personnel requirements and request that I submit extensive documentation to be reviewed and distributed before they can hold a meeting on April 19, 2012. The board directs that I obtain Jenny's admission to the teenage drug outpatient "Achievement Program" at Mother of Guidance (which I have already done), arrange for Dr. G and a second psychiatrist to be present at the review session, and schedule the teachers from the Flowering Glen Lyceum to join in by telephone. All this costs me some $3,500.

The committee gives the tutoring/examination plan a green light, but as Jenny is still technically a freshman (although she is nearly seventeen years of age), it seems to me that these educational administrators no longer seriously consider Jenny's completing high school a reality. The school principal states point-blank that no other residential places will take Jenny now because of her age and indicates that she is not going to make it easy for Jenny to graduate. Then the board of ed drags their feet for an entire month, and by the time they have finally arranged for tutors to begin, Jenny is in the middle of accelerated drug use.

It is now May 16, 2012, and for four weeks, Jenny and I have been informing Ivy, the director of the Mother of Guidance outpatient addiction program, that Jenny has relapsed onto Vicodin, other assorted pills, and marijuana. Like a leitmotif of all the other places we have been to, Ivy refuses to believe us and says we are both seeking attention, because Jenny is passing their urine drug tests. So I take Jenny to a hospital to have her blood drawn, and the report shows that she has drugs in her system. Ivy then states that the issue is not that Jenny has relapsed on their watch and that their exams showed false negatives, but that "Jenny has interrelational problems with me." Dr. G, who is a highly credentialed psychologist, tells me that addicts *never* admit to doing drugs if they are not doing drugs. Dr. G asserts that addicts always say that they are *not* doing drugs, and he thinks they are so dumb at this program at Mother of Guidance. Furthermore, he points out that Jenny's confessing to me that she was using drugs showed a *lack* of interrelational problems—that Jenny trusted me, was honest with me, and wanted to be sober!

On May 18, 2012, feeling marginalized and disrespected by the delay of her education for more than a month and demoralized by Ivy's blatant skepticism of her drug relapse, Jenny becomes suicidal and is admitted to the Mother of Guidance emergency room and, from there, to the inpatient adolescent psychiatric ward. She says she misses her father so much and that her world just stopped and she felt shattered after he died.

Jenny tells me at a hospital visit,

"Mom, I have never told you this before, but . . . since the day those two nannies started sexually abusing me, I have not felt like the me I was before. Everything changed after that, and I feel that the girl I was is lost for all time, and I do not know how to get her back again."

Jenny is sobbing and looking terrified and destroyed. My heart goes out to her. I tell her that if I had ever known, I would have jumped on top of them right then and there and beaten them to a bloody pulp and that my doing so would have helped her, because she would have known that it was not her fault and would have felt vindicated.

"No, Mom." Jenny shakes her head. "That would not have done any good." I feel like a small boat alone in the middle of a stormy ocean, struggling to keep my precariously ensconced child passenger safe in spite of the huge waves striking us from all sides. I want to call out to God, to the winds, to the forces of the universe, *Somebody help us!* I have no family, no one person with whom to discuss my difficulties who will give me unbiased and honest advice. (I know, I'm repeating myself.)

Jenny continues: "Sometimes I am afraid I might hurt myself. I am afraid of that now."

Mother of Guidance

The Mother of Guidance psychiatric team listens to me when I tell them that since her father's death and her taxi accident in 2009, Jenny's behavior has been drastically different. I inform them that there were no drugs or psychiatric hospitalizations prior to these events—nor is there any medical record of same. I relate that I believe whatever underlying issues may have been at play, Jenny's condition has been severely exacerbated by these events and the attendant traumatic brain injury and posttraumatic stress disorder, which has only led to an out-of-control spiraling of trauma and addiction, especially as she is an adolescent.

The psychiatrist replies that Jenny's behaviors are possibly consistent with this, and Jenny then appears and tells us she is still very depressed and does not feel safe out on her own but would like to pursue treatment at a place that would really help her. This time, Jenny and I both decide to bend all efforts to have her admitted to the rehab she should have gone to when this all first started three years ago—Revision.

Revision! At Last

Revision is a one-of-a-kind rehab/therapeutic center, with its main "first-stage" rehab residential house located in a rural area of New York, headed by a recovered addict of some thirty years who is true of heart. If you look up the word *dedicated* in the dictionary, this gentleman's name would define its meaning. It is estimated that approximately 50 percent of the residents (young men and women between the ages of fourteen and twenty-three) are court mandated, but there are no gangs inside of Revision. The entire program is designed to last approximately three years, with eighteen months (the classic amount of time) in the out-of-city facility and another eighteen months or longer spent partly in the New York City headquarters and in apartments in the metropolitan area, which Revision locates for its "second-stage" recovering addicts. In addition, Revision helps residents obtain their GEDs and issues many scholarships to young people who wish to attend college.

Revision is outstanding, it is family, and in my estimation, it is how rehab should be done. Those individuals who complete the Revision program are very happy and successful. My friend Steve writes to me that "Revision could be a great place for Jenny. Safe but tough love. Let her realize how good you have been to her." And my friend Mario notices that there are superlative testimonials about Revision posted on the internet that state that "Revision saves lives."

The first week in June, Jenny goes up to their alpine house in the Revision van with her "kit and kaboodle," including her Alvarez guitar. In addition to the rehab program, I am told that there are therapy sessions. Jenny is not allowed to talk to me for one month, until "she has earned that right." Here the reason is explained. In the interim, I receive reports on Jenny from many of the staff members, who are very bright and caring. Jenny sends me the following letter on June 25, 2012:

Dear Mommy:

I love you so much. I would not be here at Revision if it wasn't for you. The groups and seminars are good here, and you can tell that the counselors really care here. This is *not* like any other place. It is so weird, but mostly everyone here follows the rules, and the people here care, even the guys. The guys here look at the girls like human beings and not just objects. I am so used to being treated like an object that it is weird to be cared about as a friend. Revision is not like any other program I've ever been to before. The counselors actually take time out of their day to talk to you.(!!!) The boys are like your brothers, and the girls are like your sisters. My big sister's name is Stella, and she's so sweet to me. She really cares. I know this is the right path.

I think Revision will help me a lot. I'm talking about things that I never talked about before. I don't know why I'm so open here. But I want you to be completely honest with me and tell me how you feel about my drug use. I hope you can forgive me.

I love you so much.

Love,
Jenny

When I am invited to visit on "family day" some six weeks later, I am beyond impressed. I would like to move in myself or become a therapist there, and I cannot help but think that the grounds, as lovely as they are in July, must be like a wonderland in the winter. The main house is a modern and pleasantly rustic A-frame structure, with high ceilings and windows that admit ample amounts of light along with sweeping views of the beautiful panorama. Affixed to this area are pleasant side dormitory wings with super clean and organized sleeping quarters kept shining and sparkling by the residents. The large dining area is bright, with inspiring framed motivational posters hanging everywhere. Amazingly, over the years, the residents themselves have built an incredible state-of-the-art, freestanding gymnasium/movie building as well as an enchanting Japanese meditation garden with classic wood-carved benches, and there is a lovely pond at the edge of the property with a charming bridge. Everything is very neat, immaculate, and tastefully minimal yet also pretty, warm, and picaresque. There is, in addition, a large and welcoming outside fire pit for roasting marshmallows and singing camp songs (where Jenny enjoys playing her guitar and singing almost every evening) and a wonderful mascot dog, a sweet German shepherd named Tilly.

The girls and the boys run the front office, cook the meals, do the carpentry, scrub the kitchen, and scour the bathrooms and everything else in the facility. Jenny has never looked so healthy and "bonny," nor has she been as affectionate and courteous toward me in a very long time. Jenny tells me that she loves being close to nature, as it is very pure and healing. She has made a lot of good acquaintances and introduces me to her two best girlfriends, Andrea and Gabrielle. These are endearing young ladies, and one of them is a recovering heroin addict. The shadows under Andrea's eyes tell of her struggles with this monkey that she has been unable to get off her back. Andrea is a very warmhearted person and a beautiful soul. Tragically, when Jenny decides to leave Revision prior to the end of August, Andrea departs shortly thereafter. The boys and girls have such camaraderie that no one is an island, and whatever actions one person takes will have tremendous repercussions for the other residents. Jenny will remain sober for another six months thanks to the sobriety ethic instilled by Revision.

On August 26, 2012, Jenny calls to tell me that she is leaving Revision because she "cannot take it anymore." I drive up to retrieve her, and I plead with her to stay longer, but she says that she has become very depressed, to the point where she fears a psychotic split coming on. Andrea confirms that Jenny has been so painfully afflicted that she stayed up all night with her. In addition, Jenny tells me that she has an eating disorder and throws up her food all the time (which several of the girls at Revision verify). She says that she has been having flashbacks about sexual abuse issues and that there was no help for that at Revision. There seems to be no help for that anywhere. Jenny will be admitted into

Mother of Guidance hospital, again, within three days of leaving Revision and coming back to live with me.

She's Gone Again

I awaken at 2:00 a.m. on August 30, 2012, and search the entire apartment in Round Bridge several times, but I cannot find Jenny. There is no way she could have gotten out, because I have placed inside locks on the door of our apartment and on Jenny's bedroom window to the fire escape, which are the only two possible exits. Then I notice the screen is up on one of the living room windows, which are some twenty-five feet off the ground below. *Nooooooo, this cannot be possible!* My mind starts to blear, and I feel as if I myself have taken a hallucinogen. Where is Jenny? Suddenly, there is a knock at the front door, and she appears, her eyes wide and crazed with fear and her body bruised.

"Jenny, what happened? Where have you been? What have you done?"

"Mom, I am so sorry. I jumped out the window. I don't know why I did it. I should not have done it. I jumped out the window." I cannot believe my ears, yet I know, only too well, that Jenny is so capable of pushing through the edge of the envelope.

"Jenny, you could have killed yourself!"

"I know. I hung from the ledge by my hands, then I let myself drop, and I rolled my body when I hit the ground. . . . I just need to go to bed. I will go to the doctor in the morning. Nothing is broken. I went to meet Blake at the park, and I could hardly walk, and I walked all the way back, so nothing is broken, but I have to lie down right away."

The next morning, I call my friend Mario, who relates to me that Jenny is very lucky, because a lady friend of his in Italy fell out of a window just ten feet off the ground and died. An inspection of the soil outside of our casement informs me that the dirt is still cushiony and damp, and the superintendent tells me it had rained several hours before Jenny jumped—probably what saved her life. Everything is becoming too freaky for words. Who or what made Jenny jump out of that window, and who or what saved her? The pediatrician determines that Jenny has bruised the cartilage all over her body but releases her, and I then drive Jenny to Mother of Guidance for admission to their inpatient psychiatric unit.

Jenny is sober and tells me she has been so hostile to me for the past several days for bringing her into the world, into a terrible situation. I think that now what Jenny needs is real, quality, compassionate psychodynamic psychotherapy in order to heal from her sexual abuse and PTSD, combined with safety, structure, healthy socialization, academic goals, and progress. This would give Jenny a sense of achievement and normalcy. Even at $200,000 to $500,000 per year, there does not seem to be any such place to be found. Of all the facilities, Revision, at $25,000 per year, seems to offer the best overall program with the most hope, in large part because their director, Mike, is sincere. For Mike, it is not about the money; it is about saving these young people and seeing them reclaim their lives. Where will Jenny go after she is discharged from Mother of Guidance? She is in desperate need of the right kind of treatment and is refusing to return to Revision.

Mother of Guidance attempts to discharge Jenny to the acclaimed sexual abuse program located in nearby Sunnydale, but they reject her because of her past history of substance abuse, even though Jenny has been sober for four months. Doesn't this program know that most sexual abuse victims use drugs to self-medicate? Who *does* attend this program—sexual abuse victims who have been stored in glass jars? It is so upsetting that Jenny has been denied participation by this highly acclaimed clinic. No compassion, again. Again, we are refused any help. The bottom line is that each of these problems must be addressed therapeutically by someone who knows what he or she is doing and is not just going by the prefab, one-size-fits-all programs for mass consumption imposed by most facilities that exclude individual intimate knowledge of and work with the patient.

What Is Left When Nothing Works?

My attorney friend Steve emails me that he thinks that religion and a belief in God would be of great assistance to Jenny. Nothing else has worked, so, as this is Jenny's wish as well, I request that Jenny be allowed to see the in-hospital priest. Jenny desperately needs hope and a restoration of her spirit. At this point, almost three years of psychiatric hospitalizations, rehabs, and therapeutic boarding schools have not helped Jenny deal with her sense of profound betrayal and with her loss of faith in herself and in charity in the world. Maybe a belief in a kind and loving God, and in the force of good, will be a great source of strength and solace for Jenny and bring about a renewal of faith.

The Mother of Guidance social worker, Brooke (a young brunette in her twenties with the sweetest smile who is nonetheless a power-hungry martinet with prejudices of her own and who likes to talk nonstop about how hard she works and how much she cares about everyone), is very hostile to the idea and sneers at me in front of Jenny: "Your mother always wants to bring God into it." I had mentioned God only once or twice, but why, I wondered, should this make it acceptable for me to become an object of derision by a social worker at a Catholic hospital in front of my own daughter? I tell Brooke that I want Jenny to see the in-house priest, as that is why he is here.

I go to speak with "Father K" (*K* for kindness) to inform him of Jenny's location in the hospital and that I have requested that he be permitted to visit with her. I express that I would be very grateful for his doing so. Father K is a meticulous, gentle, thoughtful, highly intelligent, elderly gentleman who has been relegated to a windowless six-by-six office. There is a sadness and a hopefulness about him at the same time. He is being treated as a sort of vestigial organ, but he still believes. Father K has wood carvings of Jesus and some saints on his desk and regards them wistfully as we end our conversation, and he stands up to say good-bye. Somehow, he had known Armand.

I meet with Jenny after she convenes with Father K, and her eyes are wide, bright, and filled with delicate hope and innocence. Jenny seems renewed in spirit, telling me, with great enthusiasm, "Father K knew Dad. He told me that he knew Dad very well and really admired and liked him!" There is a real connection here that can be built upon. The even greater irony is that the physician/psychiatrist who is the head of this psychiatric hospital was a student of Armand's. Jenny is more positively transformed than I have ever seen. However, when I follow up with both Jenny and Father K to ask if they have continued to meet, per my request, each of them separately informs me that Brooke has not allowed them to visit with each other. Brooke's pretext is that Jenny's seeing Father K was interfering with Jenny's "education" on the unit. This is a sick joke. Jenny tells me, and I have observed, that there is no "education" on any adolescent psychiatric wing. Jenny relates to me that there are just scanty visits at noon every day from supposed "teachers" who speak about whatever subject matter, at a generic grade level, in smatterings that are usually slept through or immediately forgotten, as the average hospital stay is three to five days. What is the point?

Both Jenny and Father K feel intimidated and defeated by Brooke's ruthless assertion of her authority to cancel their visits. After observing Jenny's very positive feelings and hopeful affect following her meeting with Father K, Brooke should have been doing all that she could to encourage them to continue to work together rather than brutally separating them and depressing their spirits, especially as Father K could have been an ongoing resource for Jenny after she was discharged, had a solid relationship been permitted to develop. Instead, Brooke foisted her own lack of belief upon them.

After Jenny's discharge on September 12, 2012, I keep begging the Round Bridge Board of Education to place Jenny back in classes in the high school, but they leave us dangling, even though Jenny is still drug-free and seventeen years of age. Out of frustration, Jenny starts to misbehave, going on rampages, telling me that she hates me and that she has always hated me, and infecting my computer with viruses by using Facebook for hours at a time, all night long. The detectives have told me that I can block all the telephone numbers I want to on Jenny's cell phone, but she and all these kids will find anything and everything and anyone and everyone on Facebook, and there is nothing a parent can do to stop it.

I advise the board of ed that Jenny is urgently requesting to return to school and that she is feeling more and more forestalled and stressed. Jenny becomes so upset that she walks over to their offices one day on her own and tells them that she wants to reenter school right away, and finally, in a state of despair, Jenny flees the town of Round Bridge.

Jenny does not come home in the evening of October 2, 2012, so I call the Round Bridge detectives and my private investigator, M. M works closely with the detectives, and I provide all parties with a list of the telephone numbers of contacts Jenny has most recently spoken to or texted. I match these numbers, which I have lifted from Jenny's online phone records, to the names of persons to the best of my ability.

I telephone Maria R., who was Jenny's close friend and protector inside of Mountain Pass, and I leave a message on Maria's phone to please try to reach Jenny and to tell her to come home. Finally, Jenny telephones me at 10:30 p.m. on October 3, 2012. She tells me she is with Maria in front of a bodega in the Bronx. Maria gets on the phone to say that she will keep Jenny safe with her until the detectives arrive. I am so grateful to Maria, and I telephone M and Detectives Stone and Guildhall, and they rush down to New York City to meet Jenny at the address I have given them. They pick Jenny up at 11:30 p.m., buy her some food, and talk to her. These guys are great. I am so relieved when they apprise me that they finally have her in custody and especially when they bring her home at 2:30 a.m. The Round Bridge detectives are the best, and I write a letter of commendation to the chief of police. These are chivalrous, truly caring professionals who go above and beyond the call of duty.

The PI bill is another $2,500. Evidently, Jenny told M that she had panicked, as she was afraid that the Round Bridge Committee on Special Education (CSE) was plotting to send her to another residential placement at an upcoming meeting. Jenny's suspicions were based on the fact that they were nonresponsive to her begging them, for four weeks, to let her go to school in Round Bridge.

The next day, Jenny tells me that during her runaway, she went to the Bronx apartment of a man in his twenties whom she hooked up with on Facebook and who is listed as having attended the Jeckyll Center. After Jenny arrived at his apartment, two other men in their twenties appeared from back bedrooms and told Jenny that they were going to cut her up with machetes, which they evidently were holding in their hands. I don't know where Jenny gets the "cajones," but she looks at me with fire in her eyes, telling me that her response was,

"Go ahead! I hope you do! My friend is right outside, and if I do not come out right away, she is calling the police. Good, I hope you go to jail for me! I would love for you two to go to jail for the rest of your life for me!"

While her would-be attackers were stunned by Jenny's verbal offensive, she quickly bolted from the apartment and sprinted as fast as she could to meet up with Maria, who lived several blocks away. *How much more dangerous can this get?*

The decision as to whether Jenny will attend school in Round Bridge becomes moot when Jenny (thankfully) decides to return to Revision, where she remains through December 6, 2012. Up until that date, the admitting evaluator, Harry, and the other counselors inform me that Jenny is doing so well, "so much better than the first time." However, the lovely gentleman, named Robert, who was the former head of the country program retires, and Revision installs a new supervisor, Edgar (Robert's assistant), who tells me that Harry's reports are not accurate and that Jenny has been doing poorly. Edgar did not like it when Jenny, as a severe asthmatic and because Revision had no air conditioning (save in the supervisor's small office), had to go to the ER during the over-ninety- to one-hundred-degree heat wave of the past summer, and when, just recently, Jenny was sent to the ER with severe abdominal pain. Edgar claims that Jenny was only "seeking attention" in both instances. Then Edgar decides to discipline Jenny—more severely than the actual offender—for not reporting the off-campus behavior of another girl who has confided in Jenny. (Jenny wishes this person had not disclosed her secret for this very reason.) Jenny will not be allowed to attend any of the holiday celebrations held at Revision, and I will not be permitted to visit her on Christmas Day, which I remind Edgar is a difficult time for Jenny, near the anniversary of Armand's death. I beg Edgar to at least let me see Jenny on Christmas, but to no avail. Jenny cannot take more pain at Christmastime, so she leaves.

I know that only disaster will follow Jenny's departure from Revision.

6

DANCING WITH THE DEVIL

It is the evening of January 25, 2013, and since leaving Revision in December 2012, Jenny has been attending the public school academic and fashion program in a town halfway across the county. She has been doing a superlative job. However, recently she is having another bout of antagonism toward me. Already tired from sleepless nights, I became upset and unsettled to the point that today I got into two sixty-five-mile-per-hour side swipes with other cars on the expressway. It was a miracle that there were no injuries and no car damages. Jenny had been screaming in the car, demanding that I drive her back and forth across the county to Birch Ridge twice: first in the early afternoon to visit with her girlfriend Ashley and then later this evening to go back again and bring Ashley to our apartment. I gave into her demands because, since she is not being contained 24/7 inside a facility and there is no way for me to neutralize and protect her from the ravaging internal forces that thrust her about, I know she is safe with her girlfriend under my roof. Barring her from leaving the house would unquestionably lead to her destroying the apartment, attacking me, and injuring herself. She has done it, and I know she would not hesitate to do it again. The alternative is for her to be left to run out looking for random and dangerous companionship when she can no longer bear to be alone with her demons. And the demon of loneliness drags out and incites all the other destructive emotions.

My mind suddenly returns to a nightmare of 2:00 a.m., the early hours of this same day. In my dream, I first gazed at William Blake's famous watercolor painting inspired by the book of Revelations, *The Great Red Dragon and the Woman Clothed in Sun*. In it, a woman stands on a crescent moon, and she is every mother who wants to protect her child from the malevolent forces that seem to rule this ruthless, pitiless planet earth. Still in the dream, I then looked up at my window. The almost-full moon was beaming like a flashlight. My bulletin board was hanging there, with a copy of my photo and résumé from my last career posting. The edges of the paper started to lift, repeatedly and markedly, but there was no breeze. In the dream, my brain did an inventory and a scientific analysis: it is winter, the window is closed, the heat is off, and I do not have a radiator, so what is causing the paper to continue to lift in such a pronounced way? I started to wonder if someone was playing with me, nonverbally making their presence known. I was very tired, but I decided not to ignore it, and I said, in my head, "If you are really here, then show me." In my nightmare, I wanted to know the truth, and I was not afraid of a confrontation. Suddenly, pictures, a hammer, and other objects from that side of the room rose and started moving toward me through the air. I began to pray the Hail Mary out loud. The items did not fall back, but they froze in midair and did not advance. I woke with a powerful jolt. I have had dreams like this before, and I know what this dream means. Although I have no actual proof, Jenny has relapsed, and whatever is coming will involve great anguish and struggle.

I now recall Jenny telling me that she had been attacked by demons at our home in New York, right after Armand died. She said that they seemed to appear to her while she was awake and in nightmares, and they bore down upon her mercilessly. Jenny only disclosed her experiences to me several years after they occurred, in a flat voice filled with defeat:

"Mom, you told me to say the 'Our Father' if anything bad ever happened to me, and I said it over and over again, but it did not help me. It did not stop them."

As a result, Jenny feels helpless against the demons, deceived by me, and abandoned by God. After all, Jenny prayed for God to save the life of her father on that early Thanksgiving morning, and her father died anyway.

It is now 9:00 p.m., we are all awake, and tonight there is a very bright and rather mysterious "wolf" moon set in the tableau of a navy/black sky and draped with portentous wisps of gossamer clouds. Abruptly, Ashley (who is a stunning young lady in Jenny's fashion program and who reportedly suffers from schizophrenia) crashes into Jenny's bedroom and starts yelling and frenetically waving her arms. Ashley shouts that she is "not covering" for herself or Jenny anymore and reveals that both girls "have been doing tons of ketamine," sold to them by a drug dealer across the street, at the Round Bridge recreation center. (*Why don't they just open a narcotics candy stand at the community sports arena, since the authorities are doing nothing to curtail the constant and open sale of drugs there?*)

At this point, I have never heard of ketamine before, but the very word will strike terror in me for the next three years. Ketamine, originally employed as a horse tranquilizer, is an abominable drug, used mostly by young people under the age of twenty-five, and it can give a twenty-one-year-old the bladder of an eighty-year-old in one year's time. (Jenny later tells me that she has a twenty-two-year-old girlfriend who must wear a diaper as a result of her ketamine use.)

A 2010 news report by Dina Rickman in *The Guardian* cites the dangers of ketamine, detailing the story of one girl who began using it when she was eighteen years old and who, two years later, was "wandering the streets, high and covered in her own blood. . . . She was caught in 'K' cramps and the only cure for the cramps was taking more ketamine—trapping her in a vicious cycle of drug abuse and self-harm."[1] Another young man, in a separate article, states, "I got to the point where I was doing it because it was the only real thing that anaesthetized the pain that I was in. I got into a bit of a spiral where you're just looping around and around. The whole image of a snake eating itself comes to mind."[2]

Flash forward to March 2015, when the Chinese government presents their case to the World Health Organization in Vienna, pleading for a worldwide ban on ketamine, even though China is a major producer of the drug, arguing that ketamine is a significant "health hazard" that should be put under international control. The Chinese lose out to representatives from the US, the UK, Peru, and Spain, who assert that "reports of dependence in humans are rare,"[3] which is sheer twaddle based on my own observation of the cruel death-dive dependence that the drug ignites. The Chinese proposal is correct, because ketamine is a real killer that destroys its victims in a particularly swift and insidious way.

Back to January 25, 2013: Ashley's mother comes right over to pick her up. Evidently, Ashley's schizophrenia has made her particularly sensitive to ketamine, which was a lucky thing for both girls, or this might have gone on much longer than it has.

I should have seen this coming. There is always an environmental trigger that causes Jenny to relapse or harm herself, and this time, it is what took place more than three weeks ago.

On December 28, 2012, Jenny is forced to meet privately with the psychiatrist for the defendant in Jenny's suit against the cab company of the driver who hit her in April 2009. This cunning shrink asks Jenny many ruthless questions about her early sexual abuse. Jenny's legal cause of action is traumatic brain injury (TBI)/post-traumatic stress disorder (PTSD), and the defendant is trying to prove that her issues were caused by her having been molested as a young child and not by her being hit by the taxi at a high speed, thrown some twenty feet in the air, and going in and out of six comas. I do not even know how this psychiatrist found out about Jenny's history of early sexual violation. I vigorously protest to Jenny's contingency-fee lawyer both concerning this line of questioning and because I was not allowed to be present in the room when Jenny was interrogated. Her attorney tells me that Jenny had to answer the questions in private.

That evening, Jenny comes home and starts to cut her legs. She looks at me with the eyes of one wanting to be rescued from invisible occupation, aching for me to understand her unspoken bondage but not comprehending it herself, because although she feels she needs to slice herself, she is appalled that she cannot stop. I try to recognize and deal with the fact that she has slashed gashes in her thighs, which are now pouring bright crimson fluid. I am sinking as I watch the red liquid gush out of my daughter's flesh, and I feel as if my own spirit is flooding out with her life's blood. This is beyond my ability to fight at this point, and I have failed to counteract her being overtaken by the impulse to carve and disfigure herself. And the knowledge of that is absolutely terrifying. This is my child, whom I love with all my heart and soul, and what have I done that she feels so badly about herself? Am I responsible for all this, awash in anguish for what she is suffering? Familiar decisions need to be made: antiseptic, Neosporin, and gauze or the ER and stitches?

The next morning, using a large, commercial-sized thumb tack, Jenny punctures two holes in the upper part of one of her ears for cartilage studs and another opening in the side of her nose for a nose ring. Revision had required that Jenny remove each of her piercings while she was there, and for the first time in seven months, she has broken faith with the Revision ethos. In hindsight, it appears that Jenny's decorative self-mutilations have always preceded her drug use, without fail.

It is Sunday, January 27, 2013 (one month following her interrogation by the defendant's psychiatric/legal team), and Jenny is back in Mother of Guidance Hospital, suffering from all the gripping, adverse effects of ketamine use. Evidently, Jenny has landed in a "K-hole," where she is experiencing serious dissociation and murderous depression.

At 11:00 a.m. on Monday, January 28, 2013, Jenny calls me from Mother of Guidance to tell me she is so sorry and she is "never going to do this again." She is crying and sobbing into the phone, so sick from going through withdrawal from "Special K" (ketamine). I drive right over to Mother of Guidance and find her with a fever of 102 degrees. She is so physically ill that she cannot sit up, cannot move her neck (a possible indication of meningitis), has pains in her spine, and wants to vomit. It seems to me that the drugs she has taken must have been cut with something contaminated. The orderly on the floor tells me no in-house medical staff are available today, and this is only a psychiatric hospital in any case, so Jenny "will have to sweat this out." I want to take Jenny by ambulance to Restful Valley Hospital, as I can see that she needs immediate medical attention and that without it, anything could happen. The nurse calls the psychiatrist, Dr. Z, who arrives and tells me, "Jenny was not sick yesterday, so she cannot be sick today." Really? I ask Dr. Z if she wants to know Jenny's symptoms, and Dr. Z replies,

"I do not want to know her symptoms, because I am not a pediatrician," to which I answer (and I am pretty outraged at this point), "Jenny is an almost-eighteen-year-old young woman, and you are a medical doctor who took the Hippocratic Oath, and you are telling me that you are not going to allow me to get my daughter the urgent medical care she requires and that you are making this decision without even hearing her symptoms, which are severe?"

Incredibly, it just seems that at every corner, at most of these hospitals and detox places where I take Jenny, I run into some unethical, dangerous, neglectful, or uncaring situation that I am forced to confront in order to keep Jenny safe.

So I ask for witnesses to our conversation, and Dr. Z calls in a six-foot-five-inch bouncer-looking male assistant in blue scrubs to grab me. I tell him to take his hands off me and not to terrorize me, because I have the right to take my daughter out of Mother of Guidance against medical advice, and they must let me leave with Jenny for Restful Valley Hospital, or I will hold them each liable for whatever happens to her. I then call for a cab and leave with Jenny.

After we arrive at Restful Valley Hospital, the doctors find that Jenny's tonsils are weeping pus, and she has a virulent bacterial infection requiring a high dosage of intravenous antibiotics every four hours, Prednisone to stop her throat from closing, and Motrin for her fever. I bring her soft food and ginger ale and want to remain with her to reassure her. They place us in a large bubble room with the super bright overhead lights that must stay on 24/7. I lie next to Jenny in my dirty, war-torn clothes, with a security guard staring at us all night long through the oversized fishbowl window. Supervision at last!

Later the next day, with Jenny on oral antibiotics, the psychiatrist tries to transfer her back to Mother of Guidance. But readmission there is denied because Dr. Z's paperwork states that Jenny was discharged as "mentally stable," so insurance will not cover her return. In other words, Dr. Z has fabricated documents. But the second in command at Mother of Guidance finally lets Jenny back in.

Now another challenge is lurking. The social worker, Brooke, is back on the floor, and I request for Jenny to see Father K. She does meet with and cry with him, which is a relief for her. Brooke ridicules me for saying that I hope Jenny will work on her issues now, "God willing." The irony is that Brooke has me all wrong, as I am not yet a heartfelt God-believer.

I am only an agnostic, but from what I have seen, I strongly suspect that if Jenny were able to think of herself as a child of God, be persuaded that she is not all alone in this world, and have faith that there is a higher power of love, goodness, and light that is stronger than anything that may seek to prevail against her, then she might be less inclined to do such horrible, self-destructive things to herself. The psychiatrists and the pills they give Jenny have certainly not helped her. Something is clearly missing from their paradigm—something profound that speaks to the core, something spiritual.

According to Jenny, at least 50 percent or more of the children on the adolescent wing come from group foster homes, and they are "dumped" at Mother of Guidance for weeks and even months at a time on a regular basis. The unit always seems inanimate; however, I send Jenny there for detox, depressurization, and fast containment when the demons become too overwhelming. Unlike Jenny, these children have no parents to visit with them, let alone advocate for them. They live in a kind of twilight zone. When I bring Jenny candy, I bring lots for everyone. She tells me that the foster girls say they "love Jenny's mom," and they are also saying that "Brooke is now running around saying to anyone who will listen that Jenny's mother is bad and Jenny is bound to fail at this program." This, of course, is completely unprofessional and inappropriate and makes Jenny feel awful about herself. Brooke then sends a psychiatric report to a local rehab, and predictably, Jenny is rejected.

I quickly realize I must find a rehab for Jenny on my own, without Brooke being aware of my plans. Jenny is, thankfully, accepted into the Rocky Cliffs rehab, located in a suburb of New York City, on February 1, 2013. Rocky Cliffs is for adults, but they allow Jenny to enter their program (even though she is five months shy of eighteen years of age), as I have convinced them that she is a very mature seventeen-year-old who is used to, prefers, and enjoys socializing with people older than herself.

Falling from Rocky Cliffs

Rocky Cliffs (which has less-than-minimal one-on-one therapy but is full of groups) at first seems to be a helpful drug addiction center, and I am grateful that Jenny has been admitted. Although within a few days' time I can sense that Rocky Cliffs is an equal-opportunity exploiter, I initially accept this because I reason that one-sixteenth of a loaf is better than none.

In the first week, during our parents' group meeting in a small, windowless room, the rehab team leader tells us parents that our (adult) children are not well because "our children have not yet reached rock bottom" because we parents are "enablers" who have not permitted our children to reach "rock bottom." I would like to know what their "rock bottom" is, because I have a feeling that Jenny has been there and back a couple of times. I would like them to explain and illustrate what reaching rock bottom is like, how it leads to recovery, and what a parent should do or not do. When asked, their reply is only, "That is personal for every person, and some addicts never get it" (whatever "it" means).

The group leader then states, in response to a question from one parent, that the relapse rate for our children, after rehab, "is 99 percent" (*So why are we here*?), but "We [parents] did not cause it, we cannot control it, and we cannot cure it." (*Again, if that is true, then what are we doing here?*) I am not willing to give in to this hopeless statistic and their useless slogan, so I tell the moderator that what the rehab is really telling us is that it comes down to our quality of life versus the lives of our children—"us or them." One woman pipes up and repeats the worn-out bromide "Well, you have to put the oxygen mask on yourself first, don't you?" Ironically, she is the new stepmother of a young woman attending Rocky Cliffs, and she is attempting to get the biological father to turn his back on his heroin-addicted daughter—and as quickly as possible. The team leader encourages applause for the hackneyed airplane analogy. However, another family nods at me with eyes wide open and recounts how one set of parents with a son who used heroin told him they were "not going to enable him anymore, and he had to leave," whereupon this young man went down the hall, filled with despair, and hung himself. "He was a beautiful boy, a wonderful boy," they say. Yes, and this was another death engineered by the false rubrics of the rehab mill. The ultimate craziness is that one of their addiction counselors, according to Jenny, tells them that at times suicide makes sense and is justified. *Oh, ain't that just great?*

Despite my exposure to the disingenuousness of Rocky Cliffs, I am still shocked and surprised when Jenny is unceremoniously dumped at the two-week mark even though Rocky Cliffs had told me that our insurance would cover her for a thirty-day stay in their facility. At 8:00 p.m., a caller apprises me that the insurance will not pay for another day, "so I must pick Jenny up immediately, first thing in the morning." In addition, they eject Jenny without a discharge plan and tell me that because Jenny is a minor, they are not required to provide one.

Also, Rocky Cliffs (like most of the rehabs that take insurance) seems to place addicts who cannot afford to self-pay in an assembly line, in batches of two weeks "in and out," without bothering to try to fight with insurance companies to allow patients to stay for the usual thirty days. There appears to be a "wink and a nod" between the facilities and the insurance companies that two weeks will be the "compromise number." Therefore, in comparison to the classic eighteen-month addiction inpatient model, everyone who is suffering from a substance abuse disorder and cannot afford to pay $1,000 per day out of pocket receives less than 3 percent of the amount of therapeutic care required, at a minimum, to cure addiction. The two-week rehab stints are an exercise in futility conducted during a temporary stay of execution.

Food for the Gobblers

The victims have become food for the strong, just like wounded caribou. For institutions, systems, and businesses that profit from the mentally injured and/or the addicted, such as rehabs, psychiatric hospitals, and pharmaceutical companies (collectively, "the Gobblers"), the most vulnerable persons are a financial gravy train. It doesn't concern the rehab Gobblers that addicts, who are in the battle of their lives with a possibly terminal illness, will have to leave treatment in two weeks' time, because there are plenty more where they came from.

Drug addiction is a massive epidemic in the United States, so the rehab Gobblers are fully aware that another jammed trainload of drug dependents sits right behind the ones who were just culled, spun, and spit out. Although both the quantity and quality of care are woefully inadequate, the moneymaking contrivance is humming, and the rehab/relapse machine is the Gobblers' God. Not only is there no way that those who are afflicted with substance abuse can be cured in fourteen days, but the residents in rehabs are never given the opportunity to gather themselves unto themselves and to think and center themselves in a meaningful way because they are so distracted and jostled by being thrown into the crowds of groups. They have been using drugs to distance themselves from their own unique inner issues and pain, and now the distraction of addiction is being substituted with the transitory diversion of collected activities and general talk.

They will all have to be re-re-re-re-re-rehabbed, because they are all being set up to re-re-re-re-re-relapse. They are in the rhythm of the dance of death, unless they receive the type and duration of care that they truly need to heal. There will never be a shortage of victims for the Gobblers to dine upon. It is like setting vampires loose in a densely stocked, ever replenishing blood bank.

I come across an online post regarding Rocky Cliffs, stating that all they care about is the money and that if you are lacking even a few dollars, and even after you have paid them in full for months, they will not let you attend one meeting. The individual who posted reported that one of the counselors waxed lyrical about the wealthy lifestyle of the owners, and he found this especially concerning because it was clear that all they cared about was their own financial enrichment.

Re-re-re . . . lapse

It is, regrettably, not surprising that Jenny relapses the day after she is released from Rocky Cliffs. On February 23, 2013, while I am having extensive emergency tests done in Restful Valley Hospital, she abandons me when I pass out from the high dosage of pain medication I have been injected with. Although I do not know it at the time, Jenny has run away to join up with a tough male heroin addict (whom she met at Rocky Cliffs) at a heavy metal concert in Queens. I am released from the hospital in the late afternoon, and Jenny does not come home this Saturday night. Because it is the weekend, the Round Bridge police tell me that no one will be "on the case" until Monday. At 3:00 a.m., I have been up all night wondering where Jenny could be and what she is doing—and I am panicked. I double over, crying from my heart and my gut, as I look at Jenny's baby pictures on the shelf.

It is now Sunday morning, and I call our driver, Olaf, from the city, to come out and be with me. When you don't have a husband in these kinds of emergency situations, you need reliable masculine backup, and Olaf has become a friend to me and to Jenny. Olaf understands that this way, if Jenny gets in touch with me, we can leave immediately to pick her up, because with her, time is always of the essence. "Oh, Olaf, what am I going to do?" I ask. Olaf has calculated that—in all our joint rescue missions for Jenny and trips back and forth many times per week, for weeks on end, to hospitals, rehabs, and therapeutic schools around the country—he has clocked a mileage beyond that of the circumference of the earth with me. I pray, "Please, God, you have never betrayed me," and just then, Jenny telephones from a pay phone, and Olaf and I are on our way to New York City.

Jenny is standing outside in the freezing cold, all alone, on a deserted boulevard in Jamaica, Queens. As we near the destination, Jenny calls again, and I ask her to stay in the phone booth and to keep talking with me, because I know that if she does not, we will never recover her. I hold her in conversation, and we finally reach her. On the car ride back to Round Bridge, she spews her deep hatred for me and tells me that even though what she has just been doing was so extremely dangerous, she regrets that her only option was to return to me because she has nowhere else to stay on a permanent basis.

Jenny falls asleep shortly after we arrive home, and I have to drive her to an Alcoholics Anonymous (AA) meeting tonight. On our way there, she says, again, that she detests Round Bridge for its hypocrisy and snobbery.

After I take Jenny to AA, she wakes me up in the middle of the night and tells me, seriously, that she does not think she is going to get well, as this disease is stronger than her or me. I tell her that she must pray to God for help, while thinking to myself that we have to try prayer—as no one, nor anything else, has helped us, except for Revision. I also know that, according to credible scientific experiments and from personal experience, prayer works. I want to pray over her, but she refuses, sensing that I am just an experimental believer, and I am dismayed by my own lack of authenticity and my own want of sincere and convicted faith.

For some reason, Jenny has asked to sleep in my bed every night, and I sense this is probably a good thing, as I can watch over her. I feel that this keeps her safer. One night, I touch her forehead, whispering, "Jenny?"

She turns her face toward me with an eyes-closed, halfway glance and speaks in a dry, matter-of-fact, but alien voice, "Jenny is not here. There is no Jenny here."

I respond, "Yes, there is. My Jenny is here."

She again replies, with a light smile that hides a confident certainty, "No, Jenny is not here. There is no Jenny here."

I can feel a chill pulse through my body, and later Jenny has no recollection of ever saying this to me. However, I will not be intimidated or tricked—I am her mother, who will fight anything and everything for her, and I stand my ground: "Yes, my Jenny is right here, right here inside, because she is my baby, and I am her mother who loves her, and my Jenny is here."

I am bound to Jenny now, and I cannot go anywhere without her, or she falls apart. Is this a form of "rock bottom"? I try to keep her occupied and provide her with the endorphin boosts that are only stopgap measures against the monster of suicidal depression. Am I "enabling" her? Almost every day, I take her shopping for pretty stuff. I drive her to guitar lessons, and we purchase two blue parakeets in love, who chirp all day. I am in financial skyfall. I am metaphorically slitting my own wrists, overcome by my intense feelings of failure as a mother. I do not know what else to do, but I believe that as of right now, I have no choice but to spend money in order to distract Jenny from wanting to kill herself. And it will turn out that this was my only option.

I stay with her while she crochets, take her to almost every movie that comes out, and watch DVDs with her at home. We cook together and go to arts and crafts stores and painting shops to get supplies for artistic projects at home. However, all these wholesome activities delay but do not forestall the inevitable default into breakdown and reckless self-destruction.

At night, I lock the front door with an inside tumbler lock. I hide all the keys to the medicine cabinet, the car, the door, and the windows. And I take my purse with me when I go to the bathroom. I tape keys and money behind furniture and paintings, and sometimes I put them in pots and pans with the lids on, and I do not always remember where I have hidden everything.

On the surface, this resembles a game of "outsmarting," and it could be for Jenny. No matter what I do or how much I try to prevent danger or set boundaries or chastisements, Jenny is a runaway train. There is no stopping her. What corrections can I give her? This is a girl who has already made four suicide attempts and who subjects herself to countless perils and exploitations when I do not give her money to keep her by my side. The only consequence is jail, which is full of sexual abuses and not the solution to mental illness. But what discipline can I provide that will stop her? I am standing between her and death. She is in the grips of a powerful suicidal ideation, and there is no staunching it. No one has helped me constrain it—all this money and all these therapists, and we have had no real help.

Jenny then has a powerful nightmare that troubles her greatly, and she describes it to me as follows. She is in a garden, like the Garden of Eden, and demons are attacking her and taking her over. The demons write on one of her arms in Latin and other ancient languages and make a certain mark on her other arm. There is a satanic woman dancing in the garden, and the demons tell Jenny that this is the evilest place in the world and that she belongs to them, and they tattoo her with the figure of the malevolent dancing woman. However, when Jenny starts praying to God to stop them, the demons try to prevent her from praying, telling her that prayer will defeat them. She ceases praying, and then she resumes praying to fight them. And then she wakes up.

What Are We Fighting?

In confronting the battle of addiction, one is forced to analyze concepts that one could never dream of considering with such intense examination before: good and evil; God and the devil; angels and demons; spirit, soul, mind, and body; materialism and spirituality; science and love; and the power of prayer. I do not yet know how everything fits together or what I truly believe, and I will only later come to an understanding that spiritual ambivalence, lack of love, and the failure to set forth as our primary goal the aim to achieve virtue and to do good and be good is at the core of Jenny's problem, and my problem, and the world's problem.

What was the sin committed in the Garden of Eden? So much has been discussed, but I believe that, at its core, it was the most primal and mysterious of sins—the loss of innocence. It is the defilement that takes place when the open-hearted spirit of love is rejected and betrayed by those who would destroy it so that the goodness of God can be replaced by the ego's feeling and exercise of power. In short, it is child abuse, and most especially, child sexual abuse. Matthew 18:3 (KJV) says, "Except ye be converted, and become as little children, ye shall not enter into the kingdom of heaven." Our authentic selves and true destiny are linked to our inherited and innate belief in love and God, but they are ruined when despoliation and exploitation result in the desecration of our spiritual identity. And Lilith (a figure in Jewish mythology depicted as a dangerous demon of the night, the first and rebellious wife of Adam, and even as the serpent in the Garden of Eden) is portrayed as a destroyer of children.

Is a sexual abuser possessed of an evil spirit? I would say so. I have come to believe that there is a higher power of pure intelligence, knowledge, goodness, and love, whom I call God, who is pure spirit energy. However, there are those days when I "relapse" into the concrete, "just-do-your-stuff" materialist automaton who reverts to the "rational," secular, academic unbelief on which I was raised. This fallback position seems so much easier, but it is in fact the most difficult locus of all, because it is a place of distraction and denial. It's a place where we *think* we have control and understand all.

Quantum theory tells us we are composed of the same elements as everything else in the universe, only in different forms and aspects. We learn that the particles that compose everything in the universe are both particles and waves. We are body-particle and spirit-wave. Nothing in the universe is wasted: the body returns to the earth, but what about the spirit? Does it join the universal spirit, the higher power?

Increasingly, many psychotherapists are arriving at the conclusion that patients require a therapeutic paradigm that combines both medical and spiritual knowledge and attention.

Psychiatry—in the way it currently treats drug addiction and mental illness—is not working. With an almost exclusive reliance on pharmaceuticals, psychiatry today focuses only on neurological tissue and not on the mind, heart, soul, and spirit of the person, which are crying out for acknowledgment, recognition, cure, and relief. Furthermore, as we have an understanding of approximately only 3 percent of the functioning of the human brain, psychiatry cannot possibly have all the solutions, nor can it claim complete authority in the name of "science" (which in its earlier days justified decades of lobotomies, female hysteria cures, electroshock treatments, and dangerous drugs). But more to the point now, how will psychiatry be paid for catering to spiritual issues? You can't prescribe medication for those. How can the mental health care/rehab system heal a suffering spirit if it refuses to acknowledge the existence of the soul and its crucial need for spiritual love?

On Energy

According to Ralph Bergstresser, an inventor and friend of Nicola Tesla's, Tesla once counseled, "If you want to know the mysteries of the universe, think in terms of energy, frequency, and vibration." Everything in the universe is energy and the transference and transformation of energy: light, heat, kinetic, potential, mechanical wave, chemical, electric, magnetic, nuclear, elastic, gravitational, and so on, and I would add thought and emotion. Thoughts have energy and tremendous power, and they travel as surely as radio waves from sender to intended receiver. In the physical sciences, an energy transfer from one system to another is said to occur when an amount of energy crosses the boundary between them. A thought can have the force of a fist, and love can heal. We are only just beginning to develop the equipment for studying the reality of energy and thought transfer. This was demonstrated by the advance of recent technology in the University of Washington (UW) experiment that achieved the first noninvasive human-to-human brain interface. Here one researcher, Rajesh Rao, was able to send a brain signal via the internet to control the hand motions of a fellow researcher, Andrea Stocco, on the other side of the UW campus.[4]

In common parlance, we speak of the spirits of kindness, love, and generosity and the spirits of cruelty, hate, and avarice. If we are spirits, then we could take on the quality of other spirits, just as Ms. Stocco's mind received Mr. Rao's thoughts, which caused Ms. Stocco's finger to move. We can go as far as speculating that just as wounds open us up to disease, so mental, emotional, psychological, and physical abuse may open us up to active, predatory spirits, to an "energy" of malignant mental and emotional attacks, that remain inside of us. As "far out" as it sounds, is it not possible?

The phenomenon of projection was conceptualized by Freud in his letters to Wilhelm Fliess. Freud considered that collective thoughts, motivations, desires, behaviors, and feelings that cannot be accepted as one's own are dealt with by being "projected" onto others. What he meant is that the one doing the "projecting" is, in fact, perceiving those traits in someone else. Indeed, these intense, undesirable energies adversely impact the energy systems, or spirits, of those into whom they have been projected in the same way that the "thoughts" of Mr. Rao affected the finger of Ms. Stucco in the UW thought transference experiment. "Projective identification," an unconscious defense mechanism widely used by most of us, does just that: the person receiving the projection "identifies" with what is being projected onto him and assumes it as part of himself, behaving and feeling accordingly. This action is largely unconscious in both the sender and the receiver.[5]

In disease, the DNA of a viral entity attacks our healthy DNA, feeding off host cells, on a microscopic level, when our immunity is low. Does a kind of negative, alien energy entity attack our own healthy spirits, resulting in psychic weakness from injury to the self-love shield and a deterioration in the health of the self? Does prayer work because it is such a strong vibration of positive spirit energy that it has the ability to overwhelm and dispel malevolent spirit energy? I am entertaining that possibility, and prayer is a formidable assistant in the healing process, although by no means is it a substitute for clear, well-established, hard science.

Jenny was beautiful, talented, self-confident, and highly intelligent, but the experiences of trauma, bullying, neglect, social rejection, and unkind treatment have led her to be hooked on drugs and have broken her life. And this is where the ruminations of a mother desperate to find an answer lead.

The Runaround

Jenny is next admitted by the Round Bridge CSE to a therapeutic day program in Restful Valley, and I do not understand why the Round Bridge Board of Education did not send her there a year prior. Unfortunately, too much has happened to Jenny, and this placement is too little, too late. Jenny very quickly shows she is unable to keep up with the classwork, because she is sleeping in the halls during school time. As a last-ditch effort, I enroll her in horseback-riding lessons with a wonderful trainer in a nearby town. It makes me feel I am doing something concrete. At first, this seems to help a great deal, as Jenny loves horses and horseback riding and shows a real aptitude, so my hope is that she can have a meaningful experience and develop an attachment or a relationship with the horse, as often happens. I take videos and photos of her riding, which she delights in reviewing with me. These are very hopeful and happy times. However, within two months, Jenny is practically falling off the horse, which she later admits was due to her relapsing onto ketamine. I am in a constant state of tension, calling to find out where she is and when she will be home every day, going out looking for her, picking her up, locking the door once she is in by 10:00 p.m. (which is her school-night curfew), and then staying up with her through much of the night.

In mid-April, Jenny suffers a nasty double concussion to the head in freak accidents. Restful Valley hospital says the CT scans are clear, but a week later Jenny starts to suffer internal distress and becomes suicidal. She is seen at Mother of Guidance, which has no beds and sends Jenny to Clifflake Children's Psychiatric Center (CCPC). This is a state hospital with an ancient, abandoned adult inpatient "insane asylum" (that looks like something out of a Stephen King novel) situated next to the "new" adolescent facility. Once in, it is almost impossible to get your child out of CCPC, especially as the head doctor immediately places every juvenile patient on Medicaid, which pays for stays of months to years at a time, and this keeps his business running. Within one day, Jenny is brutally beaten in the head—again—by a gang member, and I fight with all my might to take Jenny home.

I later discover that earlier that same year, one Clifflake Psychiatric Center adult outpatient engaged in a severe altercation with another patient and killed him by beating him repeatedly with an L-shaped piece of metal, causing blunt force trauma to the cranium.

Once Jenny is home, she starts visiting new friends in Bottle Bay all the time. At a certain point, she becomes distraught, as one of her girlfriends has been amorous with Jenny's first crush, Guillermo. Then tragedy strikes in mid-June 2013 when my aunt passes away in the apartment next door to ours. This overwhelms Jenny. Too many people have died in her short life.

Suicidal Runaway

Two weeks after my aunt's funeral, I am falling asleep, exhausted, while Jenny is in her bedroom. I am barely aware that she comes in to look at me. Something seems odd. I have a feeling she has decoded the padlock to the chain around her bedroom windows that leads to the fire escape. Jenny has never figured out the combination before, but my gut tells me that this time she has. I should act on my presentiment, but instead I pass out from extreme fatigue.

At 11:30 p.m., I am awakened by a phone call from Jenny's friend Olivia, who attends the therapeutic day school with her and lives here in Round Bridge. Olivia is in tears, telling me that Jenny has posted a suicide poem on an online poetry forum and that she has run away, and Olivia is afraid Jenny is going to kill herself. I call Olaf and the Round Bridge police, who call Olivia. I rush over to the police station at 1:00 a.m. and show the suicide poem to the police, and now they are taking this very, very seriously.

Jenny has been bombarding me with mean and provocative put-downs for weeks, and sometimes it is hard not to argue back when being constantly hit by hateful insults that rip open deep wounds. I am pretty worn down. Jenny's biting remarks cause me to feel very bad about myself, and that, combined with all the energy I expend trying to keep her off drugs and monitoring her whereabouts, makes it hard for me to stay vigorous and function as I would like to. I would love to be more Buddha-like, unfailingly calm and impassive, and only reply with never-ending strength, compassion, understanding, and kindness.

The next morning, I wake up with a terrible premonition about all the drugs I can feel Jenny has taken. I don't know why I do what I am about to do, and I know how weird this sounds, but I am following my instincts, I am desperate, and I am not going to question it. It doesn't hurt anyone, right? And it's what I do now, as I'm at the end of the rope and there is nothing to be done.

I place myself prostrate on the living room floor on my stomach, with my arms stretched out in front of me and my legs flat on the slats behind me. I pray for Jenny's life, for God to please save her. Then I lift my face up and then place my face back down, as if I am with Jenny and connected to her, although I am not there physically, wherever she is. Then I vigorously raise my face and my upper torso off the floor, as if I am in Jenny's mind and body, working on waking her up out of a stupor, lifting her up out of unconsciousness, with my own spirit and body lifting Jenny up to consciousness, and then I dive back down to the floor again. As I dive down, I can almost see in my mind's eye that I am diving into an inky black fluid. I go through these motions—up and down, up and down—repeatedly, and I keep saying out loud, over and over again, "Wake up, Jenny! Wake up! Wake up, Jenny! Wake up! Get up, Jenny! Get up! Get up, Jenny! Get up!" I do this while I pray for her life until I feel I have done all I could do.

I go to the police station and give the detectives all the telephone numbers I have gleaned from Jenny's phone records. There is a suspect number in Brooklyn, and I sense that this is the guy we must find. The police discover that his name is Jeff, and they are out to find him while I also try to locate him on my own via a cell-phone check.

I end up with Olaf in a rundown apartment building near a movie theater and a hotel. Jeff might live in this building, and I intend to go door to door. Suddenly, my stomach is hit, as it always is in times of extreme crisis, and I lose my guts against the old white tiles of the workers' bathroom in the bowels of the apartment building, crying hysterically. Jenny's suicide poem was absolutely terrifying, and although I can usually get an intuitive feeling as to what is going on with Jenny, this time, for the first time, my "little voice" is silent, and I cannot receive any sense of what has really happened. I begin praying and pray very hard for Jenny to please be alive—please, Jesus, please.

I do not know it, but only two blocks away, in this very same hour, Jenny is being held at knifepoint, and she barely escapes with her life.

I come out of the front door to where Olaf is waiting for me, and I am paralyzed with fear. While we are in the car, Jenny's friend Valerie, whom Jenny has known since grammar school, telephones me. Valerie meets me in Manhattan and joins me in the car to look for Jenny while calling anybody she thinks Jenny may have contacted. Just having Valerie with me for moral support is a great comfort and seems to create a positive energy. At around 8:00 p.m., Olaf takes me back to Round Bridge, and I stay in touch with the detectives and wait. Finally, at 11:30 p.m., I receive the telephone call that they have Jenny, and they do not sound happy. When Detectives Stone and Guildhall return with her, they look at me gravely and tell me, "This is the worst it has ever been with Jenny," "it cannot get any worse than this," and I "have to make some major changes." I can sense that there are things they are not telling me and that, although they have seen a lot in their years as detectives, whatever Jenny has been involved in has stunned them. I find out that they finally persuaded Jeff, a drug dealer, to guide them to Jenny, who had enough drugs inside her to sink a ship—mostly cocaine and heroin.

The next day, as we sit at the kitchen table, Jenny informs me that she pawned the beautiful amethyst and diamond rings I had gifted to her, which were given to me by my own mother. In three years' time, all our jewelry is gone. Jenny then views me with serious astonishment and says she does not know how she is alive. What does she mean?

"Mom, to tell you the truth, I did not think there was any way that I would wake up the next morning. When I hooked up with Jeff that first night that I ran away to Brooklyn, he gave me so many different kinds of drugs, in such a massive amount, and I swallowed them all at once. When I took them, I thought that there is no way that I am going to ever wake up again and that this is it, 'bye-bye,' I will be dead in the morning. But somehow, this morning, I did wake up. I woke up! And I was so shocked that I woke up. I could not believe it. I could not believe that I woke up and that I was alive. I don't know how it happened. I don't know how I am alive."

As she speaks, I am subvocalizing, "Thank you so much, God, for saving Jenny. Thank you so much. I cannot express the depth of my gratitude."

I recall that, coincidentally, at that exact same time, I was repeatedly and desperately praying and performing my prostrate "Jenny, wake up/Jenny, get up" ritual on the floor of my apartment. How can we explain this phenomenon—the association of my trying to wake Jenny up while I was prone on the floor in Round Bridge with Jenny waking up in Brooklyn, many miles away, after her overdose? Was there a connection made? Did my consciousness connect with hers?

The Guardianship Issue

Jenny goes back to Rocky Cliffs, and the older women with whom she makes friends convince her to allow me to become her legal guardian when she turns eighteen years of age, in one week. My $300-per-hour guardianship attorney, who has been on the guardianship trip with me for the past six months, warns me that the judge may "just let Jenny go," because "that is what they do."

As I sit in the courtroom and listen to the judge's line of questioning, it is crystal clear to me that, notwithstanding all of Jenny's psychiatric hospitalizations, history of PTSD, official governmental disability status, drug addiction, and multiple detective rescues from life-threatening situations, the judge would not have appointed me, or anyone else, as Jenny's guardian had Jenny herself not voluntarily consented to it. In addition, despite my heartfelt requests, no one agrees to be Jenny's co-guardian with me—not one of my relatives, and not even my good attorney friend Steve. My moneyed corporate cousins warn me that I should not take on the responsibility of guardianship, saying that it exposes me to possibly devastating financial and personal liability. I reply that I have to be able to help Jenny because she cannot really help herself. As it will turn out, they are right, and I am right.

When Jenny comes out of Rocky Cliffs for the second time, she immediately relapses once more, this time onto marijuana and Vicodin. In view of all that has happened, and the warnings of Detectives Stone and Guildhall, I decide to make a complete change, as Round Bridge has not worked out. I move Jenny and myself back to the Upper West Side of Manhattan. Who says you can't go home again?

7

FORGOTTEN AND (FINALLY) RECOVERED

Amnesia: I had it and still do. From that abuse I never talk about that befell me when I was three years old. That shocking, murderous assault that marks the end of my childhood, in which my beloved grandmother had been my protector. I still bear the outer scars, and I have tried so hard to hide the inner ones. I lost two years of time, and I cannot tell you what happened in them. Every person who has been violated deserves the restoration of all the stolen parts of themselves.

If you don't have drugs to help you "get away," then your mind will find a way to make you forget that which is too atrocious for you to remember and still stay sane. (My escape was scholarly work and achievement, music, and literature—I was an outstanding student.) You must lose all memory of how the people who hurt you assassinated your innocent soul with a strike of pure malevolence.

Bipolar, schizophrenic, ADHD, ODD, OCD, borderline, addicted, PTSD, neurotic, cutter, suicidal—blah, blah, blah. Perhaps no one is willing to say it, but the only cure for what ails us is love. And the bottom line is that without enough love, which is the only antidote to evil, and without protection and safety from abandonment, betrayal, and abuse—at any age, but especially in the young—we lose our minds. Yes, the answer is active, energetic, selfless, caring, patient, understanding, compassionate, empathic, qualitatively and quantitatively attentive, kindness-filled, warm-hearted, affectionate, altruistic, life-giving, listening, validating, emotionally secure, sharing and connected, guiding, supportive, encouraging, vigilant, safeguarding, dedicated, devoted, ever present, healing *love*. Of course, this presupposes a value system, knowledge of, and desire for goodness and the exercise of virtue. *This does not come in pill form.*

After detectives Stone and Guildhall told me that I needed to make radical changes, following Jenny's disappearance and rescue, I vowed to recast our daily lives entirely. Therefore, at the end of August 2013, in a new effort to make Jenny's sobriety possible and to guide her toward becoming a part of mainstream society, I move us back into New York City, paying extra costs and triple the rent. With my assistance, Jenny obtains employment at a major high-end department store, where she excels in fashion and retail merchandising and loves her job. This is a glowing achievement for Jenny, and she takes great pride in her position there, and still does. In addition, I go with Jenny to enroll in the Bellevue drug outpatient program, where she is fortunate to have an excellent therapist who tells her, "Stay close to Mom, because Mom loves you." I also ferry her back and forth to young people's AA meetings and general AA programs all over Manhattan every evening of the week.

However, within the first week of our arrival, Jenny starts to become ill, throwing up several times per day and seeming markedly lethargic. I am required to pour water over her head, physically raise her from her bed, and help her get dressed in the mornings in order for her to arrive at work on time. Her complexion seems to have developed a green undertone, her speech is slurring, and she wants to sleep all the time. Now, I know what the reader must be thinking, but back then I believed Jenny must have contracted West Nile virus, so I take her to her pediatrician to be tested, but the test comes up negative, and I am more puzzled than ever. Ever since we arrived back in the city, Jenny has been in the company of a former resident of Revision named Kim, who (Jenny and Kim both tell me) goes with her to daily (and sometimes twice daily) AA meetings in Manhattan. Kim had told me that she also thought Jenny had West Nile virus. But even after all we've been through, incredibly, I am still woefully naïve.

On a Sunday afternoon in late September 2013, I receive a call from Jenny, who is crying into the phone. She asks me to come and meet her with her new friend, Lucy, right away, at a restaurant one block over. When I arrive, Jenny tells me that she has relapsed onto heroin, that she started using it when Kim pushed it on her, and that Kim has been dealing her heroin nonstop, every day, for the past four weeks.

I am paralyzed (but able to send Kim a terse goodbye text)—*HEROIN!!??*

Jenny tells me that Lucy convinced her to tell me the truth and that she is "her savior." At Jenny's insistence, Lucy then accompanies me and Jenny to the St. Lukes–Roosevelt Hospital detox program, and Lucy shares with me (in a very caring and moving way) that she lost someone very close to her because of addiction. She adds that, because of this, she is "not going to let anything bad happen to Jenny" and that she is "here for us." I want to believe that Lucy is true of heart and a selfless, good person, although a nagging premonition tells me, "No." However, this is heroin, for Lord's sake, and I am desperate for assistance, so I quell my reservations, because I do not believe I can afford them. Where would Jenny be if Lucy had not persuaded her to come clean about her heroin use? I know that one should always question and reject the free lunch and that if something is too good to be true, it is not true, but I am all alone and in need of help with Jenny. Lucy can see this all too clearly, and she will take full advantage in the coming months.

In accordance with their medical protocol for heroin withdrawal, Bellevue places Jenny on Suboxone, which is difficult to take, as it is very bitter. I lock the Suboxone in a heavy metal filing cabinet, and Lucy visits every day to bolster Jenny to dissolve the

Suboxone square on her tongue and not swallow it prematurely, even though it is so very distasteful that the slow dissolution produces physical shudders. This process is a necessity, and Jenny tells me she will not take her Suboxone unless Lucy is there with her. I do not like this blackmail, but I do not see what else I can do. Jenny begins spending more and more time with Lucy, and spending money on her too, and I can feel the slow tow of someone else entering our lives and beginning to exert too much influence, which may then be able to use for good or for ill. Unfortunately, unless the person is a saint, it is usually for purposes of his or her own, and I hope we will be able to swim to shore before the riptide pulls us under.

Late one evening, after taking her Suboxone for one month, Jenny stares up at the ceiling as she lays on our sofa. Her eyes have taken on a translucent clarity such that it is almost like looking at the surface of a beautiful planet, somewhere light years away. "You know," she tells me, "I think evil forces have been attacking me. I think it's true. That has to be what has caused all of this to happen, over all this time. There is no other explanation." She speaks as if communicating from another realm, and she appears more loving, fragile, and sweet than I have ever seen her. I tell Jenny that there is a God and that Jesus loves her. Jenny starts to cry. I ask her why she is crying, and she tells me, with an expression so pure, searingly honest, and full of deep gratitude that it is palpably and startlingly otherworldly, "I am crying because when I think of what he willingly sacrificed, that someone would do that for me, that he went through all of that for me—it is overwhelming." A moment in time.

However, several months later, in February 2014, Jenny moves into an apartment in a run-down section of Brooklyn with Lucy, who has convinced Jenny to go to court to end my guardianship. And the court, despite Jenny's perilous history and as the guardianship attorney had predicted, just lets Jenny go. Lucy, who is now living off Jenny's disability money, then introduces Jenny to a friend of hers, and what happens to Jenny at the hands of this individual for the next eleven months is almost unrepeatable. Suffice it to say that Jenny is seduced and subjected to the worst forms of mental, personal, psychological, and emotional maltreatment, as well as medical illness and physical injury. Ultimately, on New Year's Day 2015, Jenny runs away from this very abusive relationship, which is a testament to her inner strength. I am so proud of Jenny, and it is indicative of her will to succeed that notwithstanding all the constant harm she has endured, she still manages to achieve her GED with a very high score and maintains her sobriety for one year.

But finally the combination of the acuity and accumulation of traumas, without effective healing intervention, has taken its toll. So to wipe everything out of her mind, Jenny plunges herself for the next eighteen months into the river of Lethe that flows around the cave of Hypnos through the Underworld, where all those who drink from it experience complete forgetfulness: the illegal, underground watering holes of fantasy, electronic dance music, graft, illness, rape, dancing, drugs, and death otherwise known as the "rave scene."

It is now March 2015, and Jenny is living back at home with me in Round Bridge. She has been emotionally destroyed by her experiences over the past year, and she must somehow effect a getaway from the reality of what she has lived through. She feels she needs to escape from herself because it is she now who holds all these horrific memories. So she has submerged herself into the urban underclass of outlaws by attending Brooklyn raves, where the party does not end until the afternoon of the following day and the nonstop use of "Molly"—the nickname for MDMA, or Ecstasy—keeps ravers going. Molly brings about a rapid heartbeat, high blood pressure, and unregulated body temperature, and some of the chemicals lead to prolonged panic attacks, psychosis, and seizures. Then there's also the other popular aforementioned drug ketamine, which, when taken in large quantities, causes the user to become totally unable to exercise proper motor skills or even respond. They are left in a pacified state that renders them essentially vegetables while under its influence.

I never thought Jenny would become involved in raves, as she has always eschewed them in the past, but now she is immersed in "raging." She is well acquainted with most of the DJs, the promoters, the organizers, the vendors, the bouncers, the ravers, and the drug dealers. Tonight, I placed ice packs on Jenny's legs, as well as a topical painkiller, because her knee caps are two eight-inch circumferences of huge, welted, swollen, red, black-and-blue flesh that tell of a massive pooling of blood beneath her skin. Jenny was dancing frenetically on Molly and did not even know that she was severely injuring herself as she kept crashing to the floor, more than fifty times, all night long, seeking attention (love), with all eyes upon her. No one stopped her.

It is now 3:00 a.m., and Jenny has just burst into my room, crying: "Why the hell was I born? Why did you have me? You tried to get pregnant for six years; wasn't that a sign that you were supposed to stop!? . . . I have been through too much. . . . I am never pretty enough, smart enough, or good enough. . . . People turn on me. No one loves me! . . . When I am cutting myself, I actually feel good! I feel so much better. I just wanna tell you, I almost killed myself cutting my arm in the bathroom at Mountain Pass.'"

This is the first time I am hearing this. She continues: "I got a razor and I just started slicing my arm, just butchering myself, trying to kill myself! So many times, I wished that I could die. But the blood started pouring out under the bathroom door, and my roommate started screaming and grabbed me and started sobbing, and she said to me, 'Don't do this to me ever again!' The nurse stitched my arm." The nurse never told me. *Oh, my God, I never knew this.* "I just realized . . . that's why I took all the drugs, . . . and always just tons of drugs all at once—not because I was a drug addict—but because for years I have just been trying to kill myself—hoping I would never wake up again! I cannot take the pain of not being loved anymore."

Jenny always expressed a want and need for love, subconsciously and consciously, and this is "it" in a nutshell. It is right as rain, and very basic and true, and I was not at home to properly mother her, and so many mothers cannot afford to be home with their children anymore. No wonder so many of these kids are going to raves and on drugs.

If only I could go back in time, I would change it all, but I can't. Had Jenny gone for treatment for her PTSD at the exemplary program that had accepted her last year, she might be on her way to wellness now. However, as the court had revoked my guardianship, I could not require that she attend.

She says, "I cannot take the pain anymore of not being loved in the world and of how mean and cruel everyone is. What did I do to deserve all this suffering? I wish that I would not wake up. Every time I overdosed, I hoped that I would not wake up, but then I did wake up."

I mention God to Jenny, and she tells me, "I do not believe in God because of all that I have had to suffer."

My heart is breaking for her, and I feel like my brain is splitting over the enormous amounts of tragic phenomena to be filtered, compassionately listened to, emotionally shared, and carried by me for Jenny. But she cannot yet unburden herself to me because she is so angry at me—and rightfully so.

I tell Jenny that God has kept her alive for a reason and that while trying to do good, I try to measure my life by whom I have helped. I share with her that I ask myself where I have spread some light and that the light is stronger than the darkness. I remind her of all the goodness and kindness she's shown other people and how that makes her a good person because she cares about people. I let Jenny know that I believe that there is a higher power and that we are here to make a better world.

By way of an answer, Jenny tells me that she has been using drugs actively over the past two months, especially MDMA, which is the main ingredient in Ecstasy, the drug that landed her in her first long-term rehab. I am terrified for her health and often wonder if there will ever be an end to this hell, but I never give up hope. I cannot, for I love Jenny, and that love will keep me pushing forever. I also believe in Jenny, and I know how much strength she has inside of her. Over the next months, I encourage Jenny to enroll in a college nursing program, but she finally tells me she is not interested, so she drops out. Then she signs up for a university dance curriculum, which she truly enjoys and where she excels, but sadly, her drug use renders her unable to continue her classes.

When she becomes very ill from multiple respiratory conditions (caused by the contaminated air that fills the illegal, filthy rave warehouses) that require treatment with antibiotics, prednisone, and around-the-clock nebulizer applications, I take care of Jenny 24/7.

Over the next few months, I am forced to endure watching my daughter run back and forth between New York City and Round Bridge, weekend after weekend. The only good thing about Jenny's freedom is that she seems somewhat less afraid to be honest with me and sometimes admits to me when she has gone to extremes. I believe that her being able to speak these truths to me will be helpful to her in the long run, but I also want so badly to be able to prod her back into getting professional help as soon as possible. She does contact me while in the city, and I have an agreement with her that if she doesn't telephone or text me within one day's time, I will call everybody and anybody until I am able to find her. She concedes that there is no reason for her not to reach out to me at least once within a twenty-four-hour period if she's OK. Jenny always does call.

As the months go by, the revelations become more and more appalling. After raging Thursday through Monday, Jenny will tell me all that has gone on throughout the long weekend. One day, she informs me about an experience she had at the underground rave spot she attends weekly, where it was necessary for her to help a boy who fell on top of her while dancing because he was having a seizure. Nobody cried out for help on the inside, and nobody called the police or an ambulance, so Jenny and one male at the venue had to push people back from surrounding the young man, as ravers just wanted to move him out of the way of the dance floor. Once the seizing stopped, Jenny instructed others on what to do because she had seen seizures properly dealt with at all the rehabs she has been to. Then an in-house EMT helped her with the boy's recovery until he was stable enough to be taken home by his friends.

I bend all best efforts to try to set Jenny on a productive path, and a few weeks after the seizure incident, I arrange for her to be hired for a great job at an outdoor camp center that she truly loves in Round Bridge. She stays with me, I wake her up in the mornings, and I drive her back and forth to her place of employment every day so that she can attend a full day's work. Jenny seems to be doing well until, one day, she tells me she's going into the city, on a weekday, for some event that is taking place at the spot she regularly frequents. My intuition tells me not to let her go, and I strongly advise her against it, but she insists, and there's nothing that I can do to stop her.

The next day I receive a call from Jenny, who was supposed to return to Round Bridge the night before. She tells me she has lost her job for not showing up to work because she has been protecting the girlfriend of a promoter who had "beat the shit out of her" inside the venue. I hear the fear in Jenny's voice as she explains that she is currently in the hospital with this girl, who has sustained serious injuries, and I know it is bad. Jenny, who is compassionate, stays with the young woman (who has a one-year-old daughter) and tries to protect her from the boyfriend by hiding out with her in the Bronx apartment of a longtime friend of Jenny's.

. . . Then there will be the time when Jenny relapses onto large amounts of Xanax and Valium because she always likes to deal with her pain by avoiding it completely, by blacking out for hours and enjoying it.

. . . There will be a time when Jenny has used so much Molly that she has severely depleted the serotonin in her body, and the physical effects are excoriating, including panic attacks, fainting, vomiting, blurred vision, and jaw clenching.

. . . Then there will be all the electronic dance music/rave festivals around the country where Jenny gets "messed up," and I will have to pay thousands of dollars to bring her back home repeatedly.

. . . Then there will be the time when the police stop the car that she is in, and she swallows the Molly that her friends are transporting to avoid being arrested on a drug charge, suffering severe aftereffects.

. . . Then Jenny will go on at least thirty "acid trips," some of them very frightening. Jenny's best friend, Cathy, is worried about her and tells me that after doing acid only three times, you are considered certifiably insane. She also tells me about meeting people at a psych hospital in Connecticut who were permanently admitted for being mentally "stuck" in a "bad trip" they could not escape.

. . . And there will be a time when Jenny will end up in our empty bathtub, thinking she has died, on the verge of a psychotic split, and I have to beg her girlfriend to come over to help me try to bring Jenny back to consciousness.

. . . And at her request, I will drive Jenny to an excellent inpatient rehab that at the last minute she will refuse to enter to avoid creating any records of rehab readmission.

. . . Let's not forget the time she is rescued by a friend from several men who are trying to rape her in the women's bathroom of an illegal rave site while Jenny is unconscious from drug use. (Jenny never admitted this to me, but I learned about it from the friend who rescued her, who was also the person she stayed with while she spent weekends in the city.)

. . . Or what about the many times she's had seizures or had to be given mouth-to-mouth resuscitation?

De Tocqueville was correct: "Everybody feels the evil, but no one has the courage or energy enough to seek the cure."[1] Well, we have to seek the cure, because (1) if we do not, then our society as a whole will suffer, and (2) it is the right thing to do.

It is now October 2015, and Jenny announces to me that she is moving to another part of the country with her friend Maggie to get away from the "city life." Every instinct in me is screaming not to let her go, but once again, there is nothing that I can do. It seems Jenny has made up her mind thoroughly, and I'm going to have to watch my child make yet another mistake that almost ends her life.

Within five days of Jenny arriving out of state, she calls me, crying hysterically. Alarm bells go off in my head as I try to persuade her to come back home, but she refuses. She goes on to tell me the story of how on the third day at her new location, she walked in on Maggie smoking crack and shooting heroin, and as Jenny is two years clean from heroin, she could not put up with it anymore. Apparently, Maggie's friend Ethan, who looks like a six-foot-four blonde Viking with piercing blue eyes, has taken pity on and a liking to Jenny and has decided to help her. He expresses how sorry he is for how Maggie has wronged Jenny and tells her that he will drive her to work and back and stay in her hotel room. Essentially, Jenny has a roommate who never leaves her side. For the next three weeks, Jenny avoids talking to me as much as possible, and I know this is a sign that something is very wrong.

On the fourth week, Jenny finally calls me to let me know that a few of her closest friends have just been embroiled in a shooting, with the trigger man dead by suicide and two others barely clinging to life. She also informs me that she was supposed to be at their apartment that same afternoon but had declined to go as she had not been feeling well! Clearly, drugs and alcohol are heavily in the mix again. And Jenny, overwhelmed by her PTSD and being alone, is involved in very hazardous events and making terrible, irrational choices. I again desperately beg Jenny to come home, because I can sense that everything is banking toward personal disaster for her, but she refuses.

One week later, Jenny telephones me from a hospital she has checked herself into. She begins to explain that Ethan had gone through her phone while she was sleeping and found messages between her and her former boyfriend back in New York. When he came to pick her up from work, he was drunk and angry. He yelled at her repeatedly that he was in love with her and that he wanted to marry her. Jenny, who had no capacity to deal with any of this, answered that she didn't love him romantically but was his friend and never meant to hurt him. As the argument continued, Ethan started slowing down the car on a side road in a very dangerous neighborhood. When the speedometer reached about twenty miles an hour, Ethan leaned over, opened the door, and pushed Jenny out of the moving vehicle with all her possessions that he had brought into the car. Ethan then stopped the car, got out, and began dragging Jenny through the streets. Every time Jenny tried to get up, Ethan would knock her down, push her face in the dirt, and kick her. She wouldn't give up fighting, even though no one would come to her rescue. She yelled repeatedly for help, but no one answered her cries for about fifteen minutes until one man emerged from a building, and she begged him for assistance. She was appalled to see that this man was only outdoors to warn them to keep the fighting down to a minimum or someone would call the police, but that was exactly what Jenny wanted. She begged the man to contact the police, but he refused to become involved. Ethan then immediately apologized to Jenny, convincing her to come with him, and they could work things out. Jenny had one of two options: either stay on the street in a run-down, unsafe area where she didn't know anyone or go back to her hotel room with her assailant. She opted for the second choice and allowed him to hold her until he fell asleep. Once she was sure he was sleeping soundly, Jenny packed her belongings and took a cab to a different hotel. Within a day of arriving there, her middle toe was greatly swollen—she could neither move it nor walk. She got to the hospital, and here my daughter is on the phone with me, with the news that her toe almost had to be amputated.

When Ethan had pushed her out of the car, her feet got scraped up by the asphalt on the roadway, thus she contracted cellulitis, a bacterial disease that, if not properly treated, can cause sepsis and eventually death. The doctor told Jenny that if she had waited until the morning, she would have lost her toe, as the infection spreads so fast. I plead with her, once again, that enough is enough, and she must come home, but she won't listen. Jenny feels that if her resettlement does not work out for her, then she will be seen as a failure because she traveled far away to change her life. So out of ego and false pride, Jenny stays despite all the urgent signs pointing her in the direction of an airport with a one-way flight home to New York.

It is four days later, December 11, 2015, and I haven't heard from Jenny in two days. I am so scared for her life that I do not know what to do. I feel sick, as I can sense that something is very, very wrong. At about 10:00 p.m., I receive a phone call from one of her Brooklyn girlfriends, Tracy, who tells me that I must go on Facebook and that Jenny is in terrible peril. Jenny has been kidnapped but has managed to escape with nothing but a Wi-Fi connection to use at a gas station. Her phone had been taken by her abductors. I log on to see my daughter's frantic messages:

"Mom, are you there?"

"Mom, I need your help. Please, you have to answer me. I'm in severe danger."

"Mom."

"Mom!"

I answer Jenny immediately, and she replies. I do not call the police because (1) I do not want to raise an alarm that may wake her captors and (2) I am not sure that I can trust every police officer, as human trafficking is a big business. Instead, I contact a private car service to drive, with all possible speed, to the service station where she's located to bring her to the nearest airport, and her friend Tracy secures her plane ticket back to New York. She is so lucky to have a friend like Tracy.

When I see Jenny at the air terminal, I hardly recognize her. She looks angry and scarred, like she's seen too much. I run to hug her, and she feels so tiny and frail, as if she is all bones, and with seemingly bottomless, burnt-out rings under her eyes. She looks up at me as if she doesn't even know me, and there's nothing but aggression and cutting rage in her voice.

What I learn is that Jenny was drugged, kidnapped, and brutally assailed while recovering from her toe infection, which required her to take Percocet for the severe pain. Jenny's attackers had stayed in the same hotel as Jenny, upstairs from her room. One morning, a conservative-looking and well-dressed woman had come down to offer her orange juice, and Jenny, not thinking clearly from the Percocet, accepted the offer, as she was almost unable to walk to any food store. Her next memory is one that will haunt her for the rest of her life, and I can only pray that this will not send her spiraling down a path she will never recover from.

I bring Jenny home and never leave her side while she undergoes hours of silent screams, the ultimate expression of grief and shock. Jenny finally sobs aloud:

"I guess if I was going to kill myself, I would have killed myself in the last twenty-four hours. I guess I would have done it by now. I had to go somewhere else in my head. I had to pretend that what was happening to me wasn't really happening to me. Almost like I was watching a movie. You can't allow your mind, heart, and soul to stay in your body at a time like that. You just have to send yourself away to a place where no one can find you. Not even you. *How am I still alive?* How can I still be alive? How is it possible? Am I alive? I guess I am alive. Who am I? I don't even know who I am anymore. I am not even me. I do not exist anymore. They had already changed my name. I wasn't a human anymore. I was a number like the ticket on a car."

Banished and Expelled

After hours of raging at me, which I know Jenny needed to do, she thanks me for allowing her to verbally vent her horror and eventually falls asleep. When Jenny awakens in the middle of the night, she has a very loud, explosive abreaction (the reliving of her experiences and the release of all her repressed emotions). The next day, I proactively inform the managing agent of my apartment complex that Jenny was assaulted and almost human trafficked. I apologize for any disturbance caused by her expressing her deep pain after being the victim of this heinous crime.

However, instead of evoking sympathy, her cries provoke the letter I receive two days later from my co-op board, whose head is a member of an exclusive country club. I am put on notice that Jenny can no longer live with me. In their official communication, the board says that Jenny is responsible for what happened to her and indicates that the reasons for her distress are irrelevant. I am told that Jenny must leave my house forever, three days before Christmas, or they will vote for me to have to sell my home immediately. As Judith Herman points out in *Trauma and Recovery*,

"Women discover an appalling disjunction between their actual experience and the social construction of reality. Women learn that . . . they are not only violated but dishonored. They are treated with greater contempt than defeated soldiers. . . . They are blamed for betraying their own moral standards and devising their own defeat."[2]

And so Jenny—an officially disabled, twenty-year-old young woman reacting to having been kidnapped, drugged, and devastated by human traffickers—is forced to leave my home on the orders of heartless self-professed "churchgoing" social arbiters at the exact point in time when she needs her mother the most.

As a result, unable to cope on her own with the psychic obliteration of what she has undergone, Jenny almost kills herself while dissociating on ketamine. Dr. Herman makes clear that "failure to complete the normal process of grieving perpetuates the traumatic reaction."[3] The only person Jenny trusted to grieve with was me. Given the reality of her recent banishment from her home without any compassion, it is understandable that Jenny, like 80 percent of the women who are attacked, refused to go to a hospital or to the police, or even to therapy.

And as I am no longer Jenny's guardian, I can neither stop Jenny from self-harming nor make sure that she goes into treatment. The only thing I can do is try to keep track of her whereabouts and to be ready to help her. I am all she has in the world.

Now it is April 2016, and Jenny has been living in a low-rent area of Queens for the past four months, but she tells me, and my dreams have been informing me, that "death has been stalking [her]" ever since she was almost human trafficked. Jenny says she is very sick and feels as if she is losing her mind because too many bad things have happened to her. She looks skinny but bloated and exhausted, and her lips are blue. She confides in me that she has been having "out-of-body" experiences while riding on the subway, seeing herself sitting across from herself in the same subway car. Finally, Jenny admits to me that she is "dying in the party scene."

In contravention of the board's orders, which I consider to be illegal, I sneak Jenny into my apartment, scoping out hallways, porter's schedules, and foot traffic and then scurrying past residents and workers undetected and hiding in the elevator. At my kitchen table, she admits to me that she desperately needs help against addiction, as she has relapsed, but she will not tell me onto what drug. The deep, shadowy loops beneath Jenny's eyes remind me of an oubliette—of course they do, as an oubliette is a "place of forgetting," a prison cell accessible only from a hole in a high ceiling. Jenny has been trying to erase from her mind everything that has happened to her since the court ended my guardianship of her. However, now this state of forgetting is in danger of becoming a state of permanent oblivion, and it must stop. What can I do? I cannot require that Jenny get the help that she needs.

I am eventually able to persuade Jenny to allow me to take her to the doctor, as she is experiencing severe pain in her abdomen and lower back, and the physician discovers that she has crystals in her urine and kidney stones. Jenny is supposed to follow the appropriate measures to try to dissolve the stones and go to see a specialist, but she does neither and loses her job at the Starbucks located near her apartment in Queens, which she had been so proud of achieving. Her back pain has become so great that she is unable to stand.

Then in mid-May 2016, Jenny calls me from Updale Hospital at midnight. She is in the emergency room and in agony, trying to pass the kidney stones and suffering from a massive kidney infection. She ultimately admits to me that she has been taking copious amounts of ketamine for months. I stay with Jenny all night long and hold her when the excruciating pain knocks her to the floor repeatedly. Then the nurse gives her an antibiotic shot that, Jenny is warned, is the "worst injection in the world," but she is told that she must take it to fight this out-of-control infection. I think to myself, "How bad could it be? Like a flu shot?" Jenny is not faint of heart, but when she is given the shot, she turns chalk white and passes out. I try to bring her home with me, but she will not come until midnight of the next evening. When I go back to where she is living to retrieve her, she tells me she will never use ketamine ever again and breaks down, sobbing.

Love Is the Answer

"Don't you understand? I died a long time ago," Jenny tells me. "You are the only reason I am alive. I hate myself. I want to die. I wish I could die. I am a burden on you. Just let me go. Why won't you just let me go?"

I reply, "You are not a burden. You are a beautiful person, and I love you with all my heart. You mean everything to me, and nothing is of any value to me without you. Nothing that happened to you is your fault. I would take all this pain for you right now, if somehow I could."

"Yes," Jenny answers me. "Love is the answer. It knows no boundaries and no bounds, and it goes through everything and anything. Love is the answer."

I pray now, much more often than before. I try to remember to pray the rosary every morning for Jenny. Dear God, please help us. Please, God.

In June 2016, Jenny insists that she is going to work with a traveling carnival in California, and I know that this will be the end of Jenny. I am fully cognizant that the time has come for me to finally decide what I believe in. The time for my agnosticism is over. I was raised by my father to even sneer at prayer, but no longer, because I am totally desperate, and I sense that this is it. I pray to St. Padre Pio, and to St. Michael the Archangel, to please prevent Jenny from going to California, to somehow, please, stop her. I pray fervently, every day and night, as I know that, given Jenny's stubbornness, nothing but a physical act of God, like a lightning bolt, can put a halt to this madness. Even though this seems like an impossibility, I pray for a powerful, tangible force to reach out and block Jenny from leaving.

The night before she is supposed to depart, Jenny is at a rave going-away party when a very quick, bold, and canny stranger comes up and swiftly rides away on the bike that is holding Jenny's purse, which contains her phone, plane ticket, cash, credit card, ID, Social Security card, and everything Jenny would need to leave. Now she cannot go to California, and she takes this as a sign that she should not go. This is a strike from out of the blue, and I truly believe it is a divine intervention, and from that day on, I keep praying for Jenny. Every day. Consistently and religiously. This was a revelation that opened a whole new way of living for me.

Suddenly, Jenny meets a young man who seems to care about her, and she makes new, nice friends and obtains a part-time job. All at once, stability starts to enter Jenny's life, and her drug use abates. I have always believed that one really heals through positive relationships and that it is the only way to heal. I continue praying, and I will go on praying for her recovery, security, development, release from the past, and most of all, for all things good in her life and for love for Jenny. My most fervent wish is that she will, at last, turn to a higher power, because a belief that God is near to us is all we have in our darkest hours, surrounded by evil and unable to hear a human voice. We must have hope, as it is our only defense against abandonment and desolation. At this point, I know this, but there is still something missing from my own inner sense of true conviction. What is it?

Finally, in August 2016, Jenny telephones me, asking for my help with a crisis she is experiencing in the middle of the night. She says she feels surrounded by darkness and is very afraid. I am there for her, telling her how much I love her and to pray one Our Father and three Hail Marys every morning and every evening. I tell her to pray—as set forth in Psalm 51:10—for a pure heart and a right spirit each day. The next afternoon I receive a text from Jenny saying that she did as I suggested, that everything became very good, and that she was able to have a peaceful night's sleep for the first time in a very long time. And this is when I remember what I had forgotten (when I hid myself away so very many years ago) and recover that precious gift that my grandmother, who loved me so much, had given to me.

Her Faith, My Faith

After struggling to drag Jenny across the landscape of Pandemonium, I had finally found the way out—the invisible signpost made suddenly readable with the pronouncement of the magic words. Having gone through Pandemonium, I had found God.

PART II

"To Shew Forth Goodness"

Since his Word all things produced . . .
To shew forth his goodness, and impart
His good communicable to every soul,
Freely . . . Yet so much bounty is in God.
—John Milton, *Paradise Regained*

8

SPIRITUALITY AND LOVE

NECESSARY FOR PEOPLE AND SOCIETY AND TO COMBAT ADDICTION AND DEPRESSION

Spirituality: Essential to Mental Health

In respect of the great need for spirituality in our lives today, perhaps no one said it better than St. Mother Teresa:

> We can cure physical diseases with medicine, but the only cure for loneliness, despair, and hopelessness is love. There are many in the world who are dying for a piece of bread but there are many more dying for a little love. The poverty in the West is a different kind of poverty—it is not only a poverty of loneliness but also of spirituality. There is a hunger for love, as there is a hunger for God.[1]

Recently, a gentleman in his midforties wanted to share with me two profound dreams that he had, one at the age of six and one five years ago. It was clear that these experiences had moved the core of his being and were very important to him. In each dream (without details of the content), God appeared to him dressed in white attire, first as a young boy and later as a man, at the same age that he was at that time. After experiencing the last dream, he was so deeply affected that he felt compelled to call a childhood friend of his who was also a Methodist minister and asked to be baptized right away—and he was—in his friend's kitchen that very same afternoon. I looked at him and voiced the obvious:

"And everything changed for you right after that, didn't it?"

He answered, "Yes, absolutely, it did. I created a whole new life for myself and have never looked back."

Such is the need for and power of faith in a loving creator. Because once we have knowledge of and trust in a personal, caring higher power, everything we do flows from that center. We may be forced to face the trials and challenges that this earthly realm casts upon all of us, but we continue, with God at our side, and we have no more doubt about how to live our lives in a good and right way. We believe and feel we are loved by God and so want to give this love to our fellow human beings. And we see that we are all here to connect to one another, in and through the exercise of virtue and the sharing of beautiful spirit and consciousness. We hold that life can be wonderful, and we are meant to be happy and productive, functioning as the "I" we were born to be, making a contribution that uplifts others and living in mutually harmonious, close, loving, and loyal relationships and families.

In addition, for a society, it may be said that the collective belief in a supreme being of goodness unites its people with a sense of support and validation and a reason to live, because it encompasses the joined and exhilarating conviction that good is there, we can attain it, and it will endow us. The cultural inclusion of this principle as a widely held persuasion also requires that ordinary citizens, politicians, business and professional persons, and institutions strive for what is honorable and humane—so that we can expect their conformity to a universally accepted standard of truthfulness, equity, and ethical effect and intent. (This pretty much described America, despite its flaws, up until the latter half of the twentieth century, before the Vietnam War, the Cultural Revolution, and the takeover of American democracy by the corporate capitalist lobbying industry.)

But spirituality is rarely promoted in our present culture. Here, advertisers, marketers, and power brokers across all media and information networks, keen for political dominance and expert in the art of scaring and brainwashing the masses, bend us to identify ourselves solely by our acquisition of their "stuff" and to fear ostracization and marginalization if we do not. They want us to lack any center other than our own brittle ego, because a belief in God—a spiritual identity and especially weekly religious practice—is the surest opponent of materialism and would cut into their profits. Spirituality fosters the nonmaterialistic ideals and the true and abiding happiness that come with caring and meaningful personal interconnection, along with the realization of the veritable internal self or soul that does not seek to prove its worth through external prestige procurements and personal fame, but rather seeks to glorify God. The pure self only wants to express and give back from the internal God-self core—the heart—in the spirit of love and truth and for the common welfare and cheer, the gifts (talents, abilities, intellect, and unique individual spirit) bestowed on him or her at birth.

Yet trapped in the closed-circuit rational consumerism of our present society, our young people are reduced to deriving their self-esteem from their possession (or lack) of heartless, extraneous factors: money, notoriety, prestige, influence, social standing, and cosmetic physical perfection. So their inner selves are buried. There is scant acknowledgment of a higher power and therefore the absence of a call to virtue, with very little healthy self-love or genuine love for others. The aftermath is interrelations that are often untrustworthy—either nonexistent or unstable, narcissistic or usurious—where almost everyone and everything seems fake. This is quite a contrast to the affinities of a hundred years ago, where oftentimes young people fell in love, married their high school sweethearts, and stayed happily together for the rest of their lives. We have witnessed the near destruction of the institution of the American family (because nurturance of the young becomes a luxury that one cannot afford, where time is money and money is God) while hedonism reigns as a distraction from the truth of our lack of individual and societal soul. And all this (along with the socioeconomic and democratic failure that befalls a nation lacking a moral compass) leads to despair and to the plagues of drug abuse, mental illness, and societal violence—and at younger and younger ages. Indeed, as noted in chapter 5, reporter Karen Weintraub cites Dr. Carl Bell, a community psychiatrist and clinical professor emeritus at the University of Illinois at Chicago: "Until recently, he doesn't remember seeing children younger than 13 who were suicidal or severely depressed. '*I don't know what happened, but now I see it all the time*.'" Dr. Bell offers that he would like to send his inner-city patients to social services and treatment, but they are essentially not present in the areas he works in.[2]

In discussing the psychic-health function of spirituality, British psychiatrist Larry Culliford offers an incisive comparison to our use of the internet when he analogizes that every person has an individual soul that is like the personal setting on a computer that is connected to a wider spiritual nexus. And from this spiritual internet we receive messages that indicate that there is a right versus a wrong way of living our lives.[3]

Dr. Abraham Verghese, professor of theory and practice of medicine at Stanford and 2016 recipient of the National Humanities Medal asserts the critical importance of spirituality in the healing process, citing the findings of various studies noting that spirituality protects against depression and suicide in children and lowers the experience of life stressors. In his view, spirituality is "a globally acknowledged concept that involves belief and allegiance to an all-powerful force usually called God . . . and involves ways in which people fulfill what they hold to be the purpose of their lives, a search for the meaning of life and a sense of connectedness to the universe."[4] He finds that this sphere of deep human consciousness fosters virtue, as it encourages behavior that is loving, truthful, compassionate, and hopeful.

The crucial need to incorporate spirituality into society as well as medical and psychiatric care is similarly advanced by the renowned psychiatrist Nancy Coover Andreasen in her 1996 editorial in the *American Journal of Psychiatry*, in which she asserts that the loss of the soul in our civilization may cause depression, addiction, violence, and obsessions, and so it is incumbent upon psychiatrists to urge those in the medical field to return spirituality to medical practice, as it is necessary for the mental health of individuals.[5]

Addressing the collapse of our culture, renowned social critic, author of numerous books, and professor at the University of the Arts in Pennsylvania, Dr. Camille Paglia commented on June 20, 2017,

"I have been saying for twenty-five years that people need religion. . . . Secular humanism is on the skids, because secular humanism has no spirituality to it."

In this regard and following up on the insights of Drs. Andreasen and Verghese and our own experience, it is our belief that, on an individual basis, an effective antidrug and mental distress (dual-diagnosis) therapeutic model should include spirituality and effective psychotherapy joined together in a dynamic experience of one-on-one psycho-spiritual treatment. Such therapy would treat a human being as body *and soul*, with true and gentle caring coupled with resolute devotion. This would help individuals work through past traumas and bridge the breaches in their psyches until they can reconstitute themselves with a new, strong, self-loving, and self-confident identity, moving forward with love, hope, and faith in themselves and others—and truly healed.

In addition, as a part of this therapeutic paradigm and to augment our ability to save lives, we suggest providing the option of supplemental pastoral counseling in all addiction and mental health residential and outpatient treatment centers, as well as the establishment of no-cost, street-level, multidenominational psycho-spiritual listening posts available to the public at large and instituted at various churches, synagogues, temples, and mosques. The foregoing measures can be implemented as a means of affording desperately sought-after human solace, as well as practical and spiritual help. It really behooves us to seek the achievement of these proposals as set forth in chapter 10 of this book.

But this is not everything that is required, because as Dr. Andreasen has pointed out, we must infuse soul back into civilization as well, for the individual functions at his best only within a milieu that observes and fosters human values. And this is achieved when the culture (guided by the leadership of the nation) acknowledges spirituality and cultivates virtue via the methods detailed in chapter 11.

The Individual's Hunger for Spirituality

Our True Craving

Recently, I spoke with a wonderful friend of Jenny's who had just returned from Halcyon Headland, where he had been diagnosed as bipolar, tried various medications, and was also being treated for substance abuse. He told me that he was finally confronting the fact that he had been numbing himself with drugs and alcohol instead of facing his problems. He said that he was taking it one day at a time but was still overwhelmed and depressed, and he did not feel that he was "bipolar" but rather felt that he was suffering from a lifetime of trauma.

"I wish," he added pensively, "that I could believe in God." And with more verve, he continued: "I want to believe in God so badly, . . . but I'm confused because everyone around us, everywhere you go, no one will even let you say the name of God. Not in school, certainly not in a psych hospital, not at work, and not even in general society. . . . I really want to believe . . . so badly. When I am all alone, I want to know that there is someone there for me who is in my corner and who truly wants me to make it, someone who is rooting for me, who loves me unconditionally—God. They say that I cannot prove it—but it is a feeling, and I can feel it, and the feeling is real. My friend's father told me that there were almost no people with mental illness when he was growing up but that now we are overwhelmed by the number of people with psychiatric diagnoses. Why? He says it's because the whole society has changed, and many feel it's not politically correct to say they believe in God anymore."

In my discussions with many of Jenny's friends who have been to numerous mental hospital wards and rehabs but who are still suffering from addiction and depression, I found this same longing to believe in a personal higher power who will never betray them, and by whom they feel beloved, watched over, and even championed and forgiven, so that they can forgive themselves and others. Because then we are never alone, and from that beneficence so many positive things flow that brighten our lives. But the amazing and gladdening reality is that the spirit of God is the only thing that never changes and is always there at every age for us all—no fees, no bills, no social skills required, but lots to be gained.

In recognition of this widespread need for spirituality, despite it being excluded from almost all institutional medical and psychotherapeutic treatment models, Alcoholics Anonymous (AA) emphasizes the importance of faith in a loving higher power as a source of recovery, as set forth in statement number two of their Twelve Traditions:

"For our group purpose—there is but one ultimate authority—a loving God as He may express himself in our group conscience. Our leaders are but trusted servants; they do not govern."

Many hospital psychiatrists refer in-facility alcoholics to AA, knowing that spirituality is a cornerstone of the program, because AA is free of charge, and such patients often cannot afford to enter inpatient rehab or private, one-on-one outpatient therapy.

Interestingly, a MSNBC broadcast of some two years ago on the topic of drug addiction, focusing on the valid and urgent need to fund the opiate antidotes methadone and naloxone, also mentioned an interview with an addict in his twenties who was two years clean from OxyContin use. He had traveled thousands of miles to reach South Florida in search of the one program that had succeeded in freeing him from his dependence on this form of heroin—and it was a faith-based program.

Also, a young man named AJ, the son of a justice of the Supreme Court of New Jersey, who now runs his own treatment center, spoke about the life-saving importance of turning to a higher power in combatting substance abuse. Addressing President Donald J. Trump at the president's hosting of an Opioid Drug Abuse Listening Session on March 29, 2017, AJ stated the following:

> **AJ:** I grew up in a little town in South Jersey. It is a picturesque town, really good schools. I was a good student, I was an athlete. I found alcohol and other drugs and I was probably well on my way to having an issue, *but then I found OxyContin*. My dad got in an accident and I decided that it would be a good idea to try it and that's really where my story started. . . . When I did my first one, I remember doing it and thinking, "This is how I want to live the rest of my life." . . . *I was always searching for something outside of myself that would make me feel better*. People always think the drug is the problem and to some extent its accessibility is—but addiction is a disease that I always had and just had to be unlocked and that is what I feel OxyContin did for me.
>
> And when that happened, you know, now I am a brother and a son and . . . I own a treatment center . . .
>
> And I love it and am so happy I went that route . . .
>
> I really enjoy what I do helping other alcoholics and addicts . . .
>
> I don't drink or do any drugs . . .
>
> I was a thief and a liar, and I ended up homeless . . . my parents did not want me home . . . I was living out of my car. And then I ended up going to a long-term treatment center . . . I accepted what I was . . . that I was an addict . . . and I would rather die than live with that, so I left . . . *my plan was to kill myself* . . . and I was not able to get home.
>
> *So, I surrendered . . . and a lot of people do not believe this part of the story . . . and whatever someone's conception of God or a Higher Power is—I got on my knees on a shuttle back to*

treatment and I hadn't used, and I said "God—either please just let me die" (because my plan was to shoot myself) . . .

"Let me die or just let me get this" and I swear to you that that obsession . . . to use was lifted that day . . . and my goal now in life is to help another alcoholic and addict . . . and I think back then I would have rather died than have this disease . . . but now . . . a normal person can be miserable and be angry and resentful and that's just how they live their life, but me if I get angry, resentful, miserable. I will drink, do dope, heroin and I will die . . . I am not allowed to be miserable . . . I have to try to get the most out of life . . . normal people don't have that . . . they won't die if they don't do that.

I am grateful I am what I am.

PRESIDENT TRUMP: How did you get off it? Did you go to a center or something?

AJ: I did . . . I went to the mountains in Arizona to this place . . . I was only coming off opiates . . . and it was this tall guy . . . he said you don't need detox . . . you will feel like you are going to die but you won't . . . and I detoxed cold-turkey . . .

It is 20 times worse than the flu, but the anxiety is the worst part . . . the suicidal ideation . . . It took 2 weeks . . . then the mental obsession came . . . and I wanted to use so badly . . . but I had accepted what I was, and I knew that I couldn't . . . *I wanted the obsession to stop . . . I wanted my brain to stop yelling at me to pick up . . . and I did not want to be that person anymore.*

So, I figured I would kill myself and it would stop . . . but . . . I was not able to get on a plane to get home to get what I needed to end my life . . . so I got on my knees and prayed—and that was really the beginning.[6]

And in a very similar story, peer support specialist Bobby Brazell told *Fox News*, "I've tried many ways myself to get clean, but it was not until I asked God to help me. . . . I was in detox and I asked God either let me die right now or help me live a life free of drugs and that was when I got clean."[7]

In a report on the apex of the narcotics epidemic in West Virginia, Travis Lowe, pastor of the Crossroads Church in Bluefield, West Virginia, with a former career in banking, notes that dismal socioeconomics has resulted in a failed family structure that can no longer support the church—and vice versa. Pastor Lowe asserts,

"Our educated elites have mocked the church and traditional morality for half a century, but it is those same elites who are more likely to attend church and to get married before having children than their poorer less educated peers."[8]

Pastor Lowe argues against the "leave 'em lie, let 'em die" mentality toward drug addicts, so his church works to (1) create employment opportunities that assist families in staying together, (2) encourage teen entrepreneurship, and (3) teach local organic farming to young people, both as an acquired skill and as a means to supply food at home. All this helps to curtail substance abuse. The church has rolled up its sleeves to feed people in both a spiritual and a hands-on educational/economic/jobs way in order to fight and conquer this reign of drug addiction—something that I believe all churches should do now. Then there is Pastor Robbie Gaines, who established a branch of the Highland Fellowship Church in West Virginia, working with local children's services to provide needed material aid. Mr. Gaines states that people "feel they lack purpose and hope, but we believe in a God who restores hope."[9]

During a recent trip to China, my collaborator on this book, Dr. Anna Badini, met an American family also traveling—middle-age parents and a daughter with her husband—who struck her with their kind, helpful, optimistic, truly loving, and intimate connectedness among themselves and toward others. They all had a sense of purpose, a palpable centeredness in a meaningful life, and joy. During a conversation, she learned that they all work together and asked the elder father if he had grandchildren. He responded, "I have twenty-four." With his minister son-in-law, this gentleman had started a school with twenty-four students from his community whom he thinks of as his own grandchildren, where prayers are said in the morning prior to class and at the end of the day, and where human values, morality, and ethical conduct are practiced and taught. He said, "Something has to be done, . . . so I am doing my bit." For the new scholastic year, the student count had already reached forty. That is one example of how an individual can contribute to the amelioration of our society.

My Lack of Manna

When you go to St. Patrick's Cathedral in New York City, no matter your religious affiliation, or even the absence of one, you feel that you are ushered into an elevated and other-dimensional place. The world is pounding on the streets outside, with frenetic commerce, taxis jostling for position, melting asphalt, and gobs of people rushing by on hard, glittering pavement. However, once you enter the basilica and the great doors close behind you, all the outside (and materialism with its sensory assault) fades away, and you pass into another reality of peace and spirituality. You breathe a sigh of respite and relief, suddenly surrounded by tranquility and benevolence. You feel (as many have since medieval times) that you have found sanctuary and protection from the onslaught without and that there is safety and succor here. Now, I know that the cathedral is a concrete metaphor for that inner security and outward defense that spirituality can provide, although prior to the Renaissance, it was a place of actual physical inviolability from any temporal power, where a serf who remained inside for one year and one day was thereafter a free man.

Uncanny, some ten years ago, upon my first return to St. Patrick's Cathedral in perhaps half a decade, and still in my agnostic phase, Jenny and I met a woman at the basin of the church stoup who told us she was filling bottles with holy water to take to her daughter's bedroom. She was overcome with panic and desperation, and even though we were total strangers, she divulged to us that her daughter was a drug addict who was completely out of control and that every program she had been to had not helped her. I was shocked and horrified—*drug addiction*.

At that time, this was a concept foreign to me that implied a life lost and a shadow existence. I told this woman that I wished her daughter well, and I tried to reassure her. The surface strata of me thought that this situation would never be an element of *my* life, but another, deeper layer intuited that I had just been touched by something vaporous, and I had an odd feeling about this jarring encounter. *I realize now that it was a warning*. I could say that this was fate tapping me on the shoulder. Here I was in this consecrated environment, yet how was I nourishing my own heart and soul and that of my child—without our own "manna," our necessary spiritual food? Where were my humility and incorporated belief in something greater than myself? They were nowhere, and I was left without the inner wisdom that I would need to prevent what was about to befall my own child. I was ensconced in assuming we were safe and that I and Jenny were not this woman and her daughter, and I had secretly mused that the "aqua sacra" was not going to help them.

However, as stated by the sixteenth-century English poet and cleric John Donne in his *Meditation XVII*, "Any man's death diminishes me, because I am involved in Mankind; And therefore never send to know for whom the bell tolls; It tolls for thee."

I have since learned that we are all connected, all of us who are composed of the same elements as everything else in creation, who are part of the same world and involved in the same quantum dynamics. But then I had yet to comprehend that without conviction in a loving creator, I would be psychically immunodeficient, unprepared for spiritual assault when it hit me and my daughter, and I would never see it coming. And drug addiction is a formidable attack on one's being—it destroys any belief that one is truly loved and matters, so it assails one's self-love, the connection to one's own soul and to others, one's sense of identity or that there is a good and right way of being, doing, and living in this world.

That feeling of safety, benevolence, and protection could extend outside the cathedral if our culture and society were more truly spiritual, with all that it entails.

Saving Us from Spiritual Starvation

Prior to my struggle to save Jenny, if you had said to me that I must be spiritual and have faith in a loving higher power, I would have politely resisted. I questioned whether a belief in a transcendent being might be little more than the fantasy construct of the unenlightened, the "opium of the masses," as Karl Marx put it. After all—that is what all the "smart people" said, so I passively fell in line with the views of the academically respectable materialists who ruled the corridors of power in the Philistine, earthbound state. But I did this at my own peril and that of my child, as we were starving on the meals of mere materialism. All the signs of gross malnutrition were there, but I could not even recognize the ailment. Because the truth was that rational secularism was the real opium, inducing people to live a false reality, existing on illusion while thirsting and starving for the spiritual waters and sustenance that would save them but that they were inanely told did not exist.

Nonetheless, it finally became clear to me, as I blindly fought to rescue Jenny, that I was going to have to come to terms with the underlying truth and that I could no longer turn my back on the reality of a creator. There was nowhere else to go for help, because no one was addressing the soul issue. And when my love for my daughter cracked my heart wide open and brought me, prostrate and weeping, crashing to my knees before God and praying, theretofore impossible and wonderful changes occurred.

So I came to fully understand that we are impaired without expanding beyond our external, urbane concerns to an internal faith in a higher reality of infinite meaning and love and all that it entails in our affiliations with others and the conduct of our lives.

Because the profound truth is that we are souls embodied, and our psyches absolutely require the sustenance of spiritual love.

The Individual's Hunger for Altruistic Love

The Life of the Soul

In the movie *The Devil's Advocate*, the devil is attempting to seize the soul of the protagonist by completely seducing him into a professionally venal lifestyle as a top Manhattan criminal defense attorney when our hero asks him, "What about love?" The devil answers, "Vastly overrated." (Of course, this is the evasive response of our current society, wherein consumerism, ego, sex, and power are the things we are induced to covet.) As the devil knows, altruistic love (not materialism) is life to the soul and critical to realizing the creative best that man can offer. When deprived of this God-essence, the soul is without its strength, its good spiritual center, and its core belief in what is right. Hence the person is rendered spiritually passive to be manipulated and used by exploiters, as they will.

To love (and to be loved)—whether we are aware of it or not, or even if we would deny it—is the true and universal need and desire. And altruistic/spiritual devotion is one's channeling of God's spirit, truly loving ourselves and others, bringing optimism and joy, understanding, appreciation, acceptance, blessings, caring, liveliness, and elevated and enriching oneness. This is the experience we all yearn for in our relationships—an extramundane, pure, and heartfelt connection untinged by self-serving emotions and desires that is deeply dedicated but leaves its recipients free, only wishing them to be healthy and happy and not expecting anything in return. Such love is concerned for the beloved before oneself, absent any motivations of self-gain. It will run into the breach with passionate assistance and self-sacrifice to rescue another from distress. Finally, it can mean giving all that one has when necessary to save the life of another—an offering demanded of so many whose close ones suffer from the afflictions of drug addiction and mental illness.

I find that an essential element of love is quite simply "being with" the soul of another as we carry that other in our hearts. It is "being with" God; it is "being with someone" in need of recognition, aid, and attention; it is a therapist "being with" her client rather than merely cognitively analyzing and categorizing her. It is a physician "being with" a patient rather than just treating her mechanically and without permitting his or her own spirit and caring self to be part of the treatment interaction; it is a priest "being with" his individual parishioner as a sympathetic listener and an emissary of God's beneficence and forgiveness rather than just a lecturer from a podium or an institutional fund raiser. It is a national culture "being with" the youth and the wider citizenry of its people by fostering shared virtues and justice in its institutions and overall society for the realization of the full potential of every man, woman, and child. Most especially, it is a parent "being with" his or her child in supportive and nurturing togetherness.

And this aspect of love addresses the most central cause of drug addiction and suicide, which is the pain of loneliness, of having no one at our side "to be with" us, who truly cares about us and who we can trust in today's world of disconnection. In this regard, one only has to view the postings of young people in the hardcore music scene who acknowledge, grieve, and decry the increasing fatalities of friends and acquaintances who are suffering from acute depression and dying from addiction and suicide. These concerned and caring individuals stress the importance of letting others know that they are loved, and that people are there to listen and to help them through their pain with compassion.

Finally, just being told "I love you" or "God loves you" is such a healing and saving elixir for a person whose spirit is thirsting and parched from the lack of this vital essence. At times, it can even mean the difference between life and death.

We, all of us and our entire society, need to allow ourselves to learn how to connect to each other with love again.

The All-Important Nutrient in Child-Rearing

It has been said that "neurotics" feel they have not been loved sufficiently—so are we all neurotic? How deeply we experience this lack seems to determine how much psychic distress we suffer, how well we function in the world, and how much happiness we can achieve. Such is the power of love.

In terms of ideal child-rearing, it is universally acknowledged that when a child feels truly cherished by her parent, that child feels lovable, feels valued as she is listened to, is visibly delighted in, and is allowed the freedom to express herself. She knows that when a certain limit is reached, the parent will intervene to correct, set boundaries, and protect her, firmly but with a kind and understanding gesture. That is a blessed child, because a great value has been instilled in her. She is confident that the parent is "there," certain in the parent's *love*; she *trusts* and has *faith* in the way the parent guides and safeguards her and is securely *hopeful* that she will grow to be who she is meant to be as a person—an expression of her honest self. That child internalizes the parent's own feelings and loving guidance toward her, has certainty in her choice of what is good and right in life (conscience and healthy activity), and is more likely to be generous, understanding, and warmhearted to others and herself as her parent has been to her. This child will feel free to reveal and share her feelings of pain, vulnerability, confusion, anger, or whatever they may be within a relationship and space of secure attachment and will be helped to handle these emotions by a sensitive, nonjudgmental, and compassionate parent in a healthy and caring way. And when acting out in a rage, as small children will do, the good parent will get down on the child's level and say to her, "You are upset, but tell me with words" and help her verbalize her problem. Such a child will grow to be and feel like a vital part of her involved family, able to move on and move out toward life as a responsible adult, capable of loving with confidence. Also, in contradistinction to our impersonal handling of children who are regularly thrown cursory robotic behavioral commands by stressed-out parents on the run, such a child has not only been given "quality time" but also experienced a significant and free-flowing quantity of parental involvement—a fulfilling amount and spaces of time of parental *attention* and affection. This dedicated nurturing of the child's soul will accompany her through the most crucial stages of development that form the building blocks of one's personality for life.

And let us not forget the key importance of the extended family of yore, with its ample cousins, aunts, uncles, grandparents, and even great-grandparents. Prior to the advent of our post–World War II, super competitive, high-tech, egoist, "lone-tiger" society, it was generally expected that children, after receiving their graduate education or trade certification, would work and settle in the same environs where their parents resided and where they grew up. This was to foster the loving sharing, safety and succor of the family as a whole—especially the very young and the elderly. This humanized each person and cultivated the qualities of understanding, empathy, and caring. They were surround by a protective "tribe" that relished in the recounting of family history and stories, watched out for each other, defended each other, and gathered together on the lawn at the Fourth of July barbecue or around the Thanksgiving table. But this enriching and supportive structure has been ripped to shreds, and it needs to be reinstated and/or recreated by churches, synagogues, temples, and mosques, as set forth in chapter 10 of this book.

Some believe that a profusion of psychiatric afflictions—from "attention-deficit disorder" (named for its symptom, but perhaps fittingly so for its probable cause: a deficit of interested focus, tenderness, and parental attention) even to the so-called personality disorders—result from either a lack of parental attention, or the wrong kind of parental attention, or both, which can be experienced as traumatic neglect and cruelty. This makes it impossible for children to form healthy attachments, and I suspect it is the reason many young people act out, seeking the attention they needed and never received by going from one person and situation to another in a kind of frenzy. Or they might be acting out that early, chaotic, out-of-control, unattended experience that was so frightening to them as children—and may still be—while seeking inner fulfillment through drugs. By contrast, a child who has felt loved and has a trusting relationship with her parents is not self-destructive but wants to please them, to make them proud, and to have a meaningful life.

Here I recall Dr. Verghese's findings that the mother's spirituality, partaking of the mother-child bond, is beneficial in many ways.

I always bemoaned the fact that we mothers were exhorted to take classes in the Lamaze breathing techniques, and much else concerning prechildbirth, while we never received any information on what to do once the baby arrived! And because we live in a society with fewer large, extended families and with more first-time mothers of advanced age whose own mothers may have died, this much-needed knowledge, guidance, and support is available to an increasingly shrinking number.

And regrettably, some mothers feel like emotionally impoverished children themselves, repeating their own pasts and their own unhappy childhood experiences—all they know. It has been said, and it is worth reiterating, that all parents should feel unashamed and free to ask for help with their own unmet needs and unhappiness. Because if a certain aspect of their own development was neglected or damaged, it will not correct itself by itself; it will be part of and determine the quality of their relationships, as each new relationship will fall prey to the mistakes of the unhealthy old one. Therefore, parents' heartfelt seeking of the therapy they require—so that they can give their child and themselves the caring and closeness that everyone so desperately needs—is an act of deep love. The happiness and equanimity of the parents, especially in the earliest years of life, is key to the health and happiness of the child.

However, ironically, the ability of parents to achieve this happiness and to dispense affection and attention to their children has been negatively impacted by several factors.

Society: Drained of Love

> To Educate a Man in Mind and not in Morals *is to educate a menace to society.*
>
> —President Theodore Roosevelt

Our society is composed, but not exclusively, of our entertainment/mass media and internet, as well as our institutions and systems of education, governance, health, and our economy. And indications are that our current epidemic of young people tormented by lack of love and turning to drug addiction and suffering mental illness is, in large part, a direct result of

- our societal deprivation of higher-level, or spiritual, content, bringing about
- the consequential collapse of the American family and middle class, caused, in large part, by
- the eradication of America's founding belief in a creator, leading to the abandonment of individual moral duty, the abdication of political power and democratic will, and the loss of economic prosperity.

A Society Deprived of Spiritual Content

It is not surprising that the statistics are overwhelming concerning our deluge of social ills since the 1960s, when (in a radical departure from our 325-year educational practice) prayer was removed from the schools, religion was amputated from culture, and the "sexual revolution"—along with what Camille Paglia has called a replacement "belief system" of "politicized visions of sexuality"—took off and took over. Since 1962, the US Census Bureau noted a 150 percent increase in the criminal arrest of teens, the National Center of Health Services reported teen suicide in ages fifteen to nineteen was up 450 percent, the National Institute on Drug Abuse documented that illegal drug activity was up 6,000 percent, the US Department of Health and Human

Services cited that child abuse cases were up 2,300 percent, and the US Department of Commerce recounted that divorce was up 350 percent.[10] Also, during the 1960–2015 period, according to the Pew Research Center, the percentage of all children living in traditional two-parent households in their first marriage declined from 73 percent to 46 percent, the percentage in remarried (one or both) two-parent households went from 14 to 15 percent, while the percentage of all children living in single-parent households increased from 9 percent to a whopping 34 percent, with 5 percent of children living with no parent at home.[11] All these figures speak to a dramatic correlation, which suggests a probable role in causation. Nor have our public schools continued to provide our children with an education in either ethics or civics.

Quite interestingly, British evolutionary biologist, resolute atheist, and author of *The God Delusion*, Richard Dawkins, has rethought his position. As reported in 2017 by Breitbart's Thomas Williams, Dawkins now tells us, "I think that it is an important part of our culture to know about the Bible," and he reportedly believes British children should have a religious education and be familiar with the Bible. He declares, "I have mixed feelings about the decline of Christianity, in so far as it might be a bulwark against something worse."[12] And that "something worse" is succumbing to the oppressions of totalitarian ideologies, where a nation has relinquished the spiritual components of a free society.

This spiritual deficiency has deprived our young people of faith in something more than the uninspiring potluck buffet of life and left them stranded and nauseated, without meaningful direction. They no longer trust and share that there is a loving higher power that brings a sense of confidence, fulfillment, wholesome activity, spiritual beauty, hopeful spirit, and heartening being-with others—of all that feeds the soul. Something had to fill the spiritual and moral void and quell that unnamed hunger, so idolatry of wealth, celebrity, and social strata became our only culturally approved credo and form of worship and the sole and brutal yardstick of our worth.

Yet, inconceivably, all this has been permitted to happen, notwithstanding that, throughout history, society's encouragement of noble belief and spirit has been recognized as the key element for engendering the physical, mental, emotional, civic, economic, and spiritual well-being of its people, as well as inspiring magnificent expressions in art, architecture, and music.

However, when a benevolent faith and beneficent human ideals are not promoted by society, they become nonexistent. And without worthy mind-sets, messages, and mores, toxic ones will lead to the demise of a salutary and democratic quality of life, as exemplified by the fate of the corrupted old Roman Empire, once a proud and strong Republic, and as we see today in the deterioration of the American family and middle class.

The Deterioration of the American Family and Middle Class

A family that looks to impart love, protection, solid standards, self-discipline, integrity, spiritual-mindedness, and laudable structured behavior to their children is the essential nucleus from which stems the future of the country. But parental instruction and discipline need the support of society in the form of a continuation and reinforcement of that moral training, conscience, and spirituality in the school system and as an important function in our nation. Otherwise, its effect as a social contribution is diluted or trivialized and cannot be sustained. Now parents are fighting against a culture that not only does not bolster them but is countermanding and delegitimizing their efforts by condoning and actively pushing unhealthy and immoral practices, ethoses, and false values. So within this context and with parents feeling overwhelmed, like a snake in the grass, the "anything goes" lifestyle ultimately desensitizes and defeats adults as well as their children.

Indeed, the HuffPost's Judith Johnson reports (citing the work of Nancy Jo Sales in her book *American Girls: Social Media and the Secret Lives of Teenagers*) that "70% of teens have smart phones, thus access to the internet, therefore to pornography. Most teens are on the phone all the time—in school, in bed at night, walking to the bathroom, while you are trying to talk to them and while trying to do their homework. They are in instant access with one another, living in a perpetual state of staccato interruptions." Furthermore, "There are virtually no enforceable or societal parental controls short of depriving a child of a phone, resulting in their rejection from real and virtual friends."[13] Also, we know that if parents take the phone away, they will fan the flames of hatred toward them, leading to alienation and, because of the perils of the current environment, leaving children with no way to contact their mother or father, and quickly, should they be in danger. And it should be noted that online pornography is a multibillion-dollar industry. A 2017 article entitled "How Many People Are Watching Porn Right Now? (Hint: It's a Lot)" points out that "in 2016 alone, Pornhub got 23 BILLION visits. That's 729 people a second, or 64 million a day—nearly equal to the population of the United Kingdom." Tragically, and indicative of what our young people may be watching, "the most popular search term in the whole site was 'step mom' for the second year in a row. That's right, incest-themed porn."[14] Ms. Johnson notes that a teenager's capacity to form judgments and control impulses and emotions is underdeveloped. But the area of the brain that seeks immediate pleasure and reward is fairly well developed. She adds, "Throw in raging hormones, and we have the perfect recipe for instant gratification, thrill seeking, and impulse behaviors far outweighing careful consideration of potential consequences. As a result, teens are more susceptible to becoming addicted to nicotine, drugs, cellphone use and engaging in rebellious and dangerous behaviors." And "the approval of their friends is increasing and eclipsing the value to them of parental approval."[15] In addition, "research shows teens are extremely deficient in face-to-face communication skills. What else are they missing out on in terms of personal growth and development, social skills, and academic discipline and learning? What about their stress levels?"[16] In this regard, "This is a gold mine for the technology and pornography industries who financially benefit [because] every click equals more money for them. . . . Kids are addicted to accumulating 'likes' on social media, and the more sexualized their visual content, the more 'likes' they get. If that's not child pornography, I don't know what is!"[17]

We also have the latest Tide pod challenges, where teens admit that they are swallowing Tide detergent pods and posting their videos online in an effort to accumulate the greatest number of hits, "Why take your doctor prescribed meds when you can take Proctor & Gamble's, administering to yourself the ultimate cure, death on your own terms?"[18]

Social media has boomed into the largest and most profitable part of a teenager's life, where nothing at all is hidden from them and where temptation to partake in destructive activities is ever present.

Who does not know about video games and the huge impact they have on young people's lives? Not only are video games used to train soldiers to kill, but one report asserts that by age eighteen, kids have "killed" more than one hundred thousand people in video games and other online media. It was conceded that it is impossible to determine the exact number, but it was agreed that "their virtual personas do a lot of killing," and in many cases, the tally is much higher than one hundred thousand.[19] In the UK, young programmer Philipp Budeikin, the creator of an online "suicide game," told law enforcement that his victims were "happy to die" and that "there are people—and there is biological waste." He received love letters from teenage girls who were not receiving enough love and attention at home, the very kind of young people who were susceptible to his "game."[20]

In addition to the overwhelming cultural challenges cited above, the interior strength of the family as a unit and a positive force for the nurturance and safeguarding of offspring has been seriously and dangerously reduced in many cases. This is because most mothers can no longer afford to remain out of the labor force to raise their children while, not coincidentally, they are most often shamed for wanting to do so. One of the reasons for this phenomenon is likely that, over the last fifty years, we have witnessed the substantial decline of the middle class of all ethnicities. A 2015 article published by the Pew Research Center provided statistics showing that the middle class is no longer the majority in the overall population, with both the lower and upper classes having expanded to collectively surpass it, while the middle-class share of aggregate incomes has plunged from 62 percent to 43 percent.[21] And a 2016 article by Richard Florida cites a study by Sean Reardon and Kendra Bischoff, which states that "the share of American families living in middle-class neighborhoods fell from nearly two-thirds (65 percent) in 1970 to 40 percent in 2012."[22] Not very democratic, and notwithstanding that a growing middle class is the most effective means by which people can rise out of poverty. And when economic deficiency is coupled with anti-stay-at-home-mother social attitudes, both mother and father, and certainly single mothers, are now often forced to work more than two jobs just to make ends meet. So, who is "minding" the children? The answer is often abusive and/or neglectful and indifferent hired "caretakers," popular social entertainment, drug dealers, internet child sex predators, and ultimately those who profit from the capture and sale of human beings.

Millions of America's sons and daughters are sent to daycare centers from infancy through early grammar school. Most of these young ones are being raised en masse by strangers, in a room that often smells, frequently located in a strip-mall storefront, with harsh lighting, and supervised by overstressed employees making at or near minimum wage. A 2017 report by Elissa Strauss mentions a study that found that of more than a thousand parents surveyed nationwide, one third reported difficulty finding childcare: "just 13 percent of 2-year-olds who are cared for outside their homes are in settings rated as high quality." One couple in California called more than seventy centers before finding one that could care for their baby, and this center ultimately placed him on his stomach, and he died from SIDS.[23]

The result of our national failure to value and prioritize home-site parenting has exposed our young people to great risk. They have often been left undefended—without vigilant parental protection, from ever-present predatory or overworked or inattentive custodians and strangers who, in many cases have caused deep-seated soul wounds that lead to psychic trauma and, later, to compulsive self-medication. In addition, our youths have at the same time been deprived of warmhearted parental affection, attention, and strong, proper guidance that form the core of healthy parental attachment, self-love, and confidence—an appropriate early developmental base that forges a powerful shield against depression and the self-destructive temptations of drug addiction and other self-harming activities later in life.

However, even those families who can afford to have one parent stay home will still have difficulty in rearing healthy and happy children—absent necessary reforms (discussed in chapter 11) to a society that presently encourages murderous competition and licentiousness, and in which almost all persons might be deemed addicted to their cellular phones, the internet, and television, where a heartless and destructive philosophy is purveyed. And as already noted, it is nearly impossible to prevent teenagers or, increasingly, young children from being exposed to corrupt persons and practices, taunting and bullying on their computers or mobile devices.

The root cause of this consequential dismemberment of what one might call the "eighth sacrament" of parenthood is the abdication of our solemn duty, political power, and democratic will brought about, to a significant extent, through our loss of belief in a creator.

The Loss of Our Founders' Belief in a Creator

I do not believe that it is "proselytizing" to point out that the Declaration of Independence reads as follows: "We hold these Truths to be self-evident, that all Men are created equal, that they are endowed by *their Creator* with certain unalienable Rights, that among these are Life, Liberty and the Pursuit of Happiness—that to secure these Rights, Governments are instituted among Men" (emphasis mine). The "Creator" is set forth in our primary founding document as the sine qua non, the irrefutable origin of all our "inalienable rights" (not transferable), not just those to "Life, Liberty and the Pursuit of Happiness."

The Declaration reads like both a prayer and a vow that was taken (their "Lives," "Fortunes," and "sacred Honor," and those of their families, submitted as ransom), with the implication that, as with any hallowed promise, its breach will destroy that which is constituted upon it. Their very serious and upfront affirmation of a belief in a higher power (in numerous instances throughout) was not a quaint expression of provincial times, as historical revisionists have attempted falsely to assert. They purposefully set out their faith in the "Supreme Judge of the world" as the keystone of our national identity. So it is impossible to divorce either the Constitution or our nation from its declared reason for being: an avouched belief in God.

For more than 350 years, the acknowledgment of a loving higher power was an important element of the substance of our culture, the golden thread that held together the moral fabric of our society, and a motivation for each individual to achieve a beneficent and honorable life.

It is well known that nature will not tolerate a vacuum. And we also agree that those brilliant men who "brought forth, upon this continent, a new nation" were keen students of history, of the rise and fall of empires, of just and perverse systems of ruling, and of human nature. So why (other than as their true belief) did they call upon their "Creator" as the grounds for the adoption of a brave, new egalitarian government, one such as the world had never seen? Because their erudition had taught them only too well that *either God is the measure of all things or man and mammon/wealth are the measure of all things, and man without God is a beast.* They knew that without deference to the affirmations of a transcendent source, man has unchecked behavior, with no required praise of virtue. I cite the leader of our American Revolution and our first president, General George Washington, in his Farewell Address: "Of all the dispositions and habits which lead to political prosperity, religion and morality are indispensable supports. In vain would that man claim the tribute of patriotism, who should labor to subvert *these great pillars of human happiness*, these firmest props of the duties of men and citizens . . . A volume could not trace all their connections with private and public felicity." He further asserted that: "Reason and experience both forbid us to expect that national morality can prevail in exclusion of religious principle." These are prophetic words indeed, and they are predictive of the drug/suicide epidemic and all its accompanying evils, which are only getting worse.

Believe or don't believe, but many a recalcitrant atheist (like Richard Dawkins) will concede that benevolent religious components are a force for political, social, and economic good. In this regard, Patrick Fagan, former Deputy Assistant Secretary for Family and Community Policy under President George H. W. Bush, asserts that regular religious practice (where there is sincere internal religious belief not simply exercised for outward public purposes) has the following benefits:

1. Strengthens the family unit
2. Is the most important predictor of marital stability
3. Helps poor persons move out of poverty
4. Contributes to the formation of personal moral criteria and sound moral judgment
5. Inoculates individuals against suicide, drug abuse, out-of-wedlock births, crime, and divorce
6. Encourages beneficial mental health and greater self-esteem
7. Helps repair the damage caused by alcoholism, drug addiction, and marital breakdown and is a major source of strength and recovery
8. Is good for physical health, increasing longevity, and improving one's chances of recovery from illness[24]

Our founders realized, as Alexis de Tocqueville later pointed out, that "liberty cannot be established without morality, nor morality without faith."[25] Perhaps they foresaw that through the rabid obsession with materialism that would overtake a democratic society lacking a belief in the immortality of the soul and higher-reaching principles, citizens would no longer wish to devote the time required to engage in the responsibilities of political participation, nor would they feel a moral obligation to do so. In this regard, author Carson Holloway points out that these citizens would see and feel that informed and active civic involvement requires some effort on their part and cuts into their exclusive individual pursuit of coinage and worldly climb. As a result, they would hand over their citizen tasks to a (likely) not-so-benign select few, who would then decide their lives, codes, and culture for them—but it would not be in the best interests of themselves and their children.[26] Ironically, it would result in their loss of economic prosperity—the very thing they forwent their political freedoms to obtain—and so they would only have to work longer and harder than ever to try to stay on the wheel, lest its spokes impale them.

Now we may reflect upon how and why we, the citizenry, abdicated our democratic representation to a shady syndicate of corporate lobbyists funded in the billions of dollars. Although the average citizen has little time, it is the 24/7 mission of these highly paid artificial persuaders to ensure that our nation's laws (the tax code, in particular), rules, regulations, and administrative and executive orders serve to advantage only a very slim layer of political/financial elect and their industries, such as Big Pharma and banking (now "too big to fail"). Through lobbyists' relentless, organized, and concentrated involvement in all layers of government and bureaucracy, the wealth (power) of the nation has been transferred from the former middle class to the top 1 percent of the population. In her 2015 article, Katie Sanders concludes that Bernie Sanders's statement that 99 percent of "new" income is going to the top 1 percent is "mostly true" when one refers to "pre-tax, pre-transfer income growth during the economic recovery from 2009–13."[27]

Furthermore, without a communal faith in a higher power, the national pursuit of noble principles, and shared moral absolutes, a people easily may be divided and conquered, one faction played against the other. As such, they will be unable to coalesce in order to maintain their private and collective liberties and to defeat undemocratic challenges from both within and without. What is worse, they will most likely not even perceive these threats to their self-determination, quality of life, and ultimately even life itself. Overwhelmed and confused, they will abdicate their responsibility to rule themselves. Having an innate human (yes, religious) need to believe in something "higher," they will hand their political power over either to the "it" of the "all-knowing" system or to an outwardly benevolent but functionally malignant human, cult of personality, or substitute god or goddess whom they may worship. *And this willing renouncement of their individual citizen duties is perilous.*

Holloway makes the vital points that for de Tocqueville, "nothing has such a striking power to turn Americans away from their pursuit of gain as religion" and that over the long march of history, American democracy and upward mobility were only made possible as an outgrowth of the religious precept that all people are equal *according to God*, regardless of ethnicity, gender, social status or wealth: "There is neither slave nor free." He also notes that de Tocqueville sees religious principle as a bulwark against a possible tyranny of the majority, and this needs to be carefully deliberated upon. In addition, Dennis Prager, in his article "How Do You Know What's Right and Wrong?," highlights the acute danger to freedoms we take for granted when we assume they just sprouted out of nowhere and can never be removed. He notes that if a people do not share a belief in a higher power, then "good and evil, right and wrong, don't objectively exist," "people arrive at moral truth according to how they feel,"[28] and feelings are changeable. We cannot hold on to a thing if we disconnect it from its source: water from a stream, medicine from its chemical components, equality *from the Creator.*

Hence, absent a shared spirituality and obsessed with materialism, a citizenry will eventually slide into states of indifference, demoralization, desensitization, cowardice, and division. These malignant manifestations must then result in practices of injustice, decadence, corruption, and criminality, which will lead to conditions of poverty and servitude (of which drug addiction is one form), the incapacity of will, and the eventual loss of quality of life, liberties, and ability to pursue happiness—the loss of their unalienable rights. And why else, in addition to the foregoing domino effect, will this occur?

Because we hold our souls in our oaths.

Since we vouched that man's equality and rights flowed from our announced belief in the truth of a supreme being, when we no longer honor our promise, we, therefore, become separated from these very same rights and equality. They and we are no longer protected, and they are no longer unalienable because we have alienated ourselves from their source. We renounce them. We breach our original vows, our foundation cracks, and the walls come tumbling down.

To sum it all up, De Tocqueville states,

"Despotism may govern without faith, but liberty cannot. Religion is much more necessary in the republic which they set forth in glowing colors than the monarchy which they attack; and it is more needed in democratic republics than in any others."[29]

He then poses the question, "*What can be done with a people which is its own master, if it be not submissive to the Divinity?*"[30]

It is no coincidence that in our present time—when we have almost succeeded in completely cutting ourselves off from our spiritual roots—we have a degeneration of family life, the rise of a parallel structure of despoiled systems that stand behind their specious "clean" facades, and a generation of youth that is desiccated and dying on the vine. As St. Augustine wrote, "Evil is the absence of good."[31] And what has happened to our children, to the integrity of the family and the health of society, since we absented spirituality, love, and their virtues from our nation?

Regarding the loss of our ability to pursue our constitutional right to happiness, during a 2017 interview, author, actor, and comedian Russell Brand, who has newly authored the book *Recovery: Freedom from Our Addictions*, said that he believes happiness to be a constitutional right and that we have confused happiness with pleasure, because pleasure is something that is sold to you, whereas happiness can't be bought. But in today's culture, "we have been turned from citizens into consumers and addiction is merely the amplification of this phenomena."[32]

I believe that happiness is in the center of our souls, and it comes alive when we live our lives with love, faith, and hope in our interrelations with others, with our world at large, including our planet, and in all that we do. And when we listen to our own souls and do what we feel is right, following our inner intuition and essential passion, then we will feel true to who we really are, to who we were meant to be, and to the expression of the gifts that we were born with and that we are intended to realize for the benefit of all.

So how do we restore our young people, our families, our communities, our institutions, our culture, and our nation to health, goodness, and happiness? How do we save ourselves?

We begin, unafraid, by choosing, first, to push back with our belief in a higher power, human values, and morality and, second, to hold fast to the giving of time and spiritual love in our families, in our communities, and in our relations with others—on our own—as individual persons.

9

THE PERSONAL EXPERIENCE OF SPIRITUAL LOVE

AND THE COSTS OF ITS ABSENCE

The question is, How specifically do we employ love and spirituality, unified in the experience of spiritual love, to restore ourselves and our society to health?

In this chapter, I will explain the operation and benefits of spiritual love on a personal level and give examples of the singular price of failure. This is important as, for each one of us who constitute society, such understanding and embracing are key to improving our world, person by person, and to demanding and effecting their inclusion in our culture. Individually, we can begin by being more considerate and more loving and helpful toward others, because goodwill and good deeds have the power to connect people positively. And from that springs the confidence to exchange ideas and work actively to change our national leadership, institutions, and industries for the better via the methods set forth in the next two chapters.

The following quote from the apostle St. John makes a clear point: "No man hath seen God at any time. If we love one another, God dwelleth in us, and his love is perfected in us . . . God is love; and he that dwelleth in love dwelleth in God, and God in him" (1 John 4:12, 16, KJV).

When Personal Acts Are Healing

Compassionate Feeling and Action: The Curative Connection

Compassion is a palpable, loving, emotional response based on empathy that was traditionally viewed as the impetus for the desire to heal others with medical intervention. That feeling of wanting to assist someone who is suffering then becomes the energy for active caring and strengthens the curative bond between the benefactor and the recipient. Compassionate acts and attitudes are uplifting and may include good and supportive over-the-phone and in-person sympathetic listening and conversation, as well as tangible, concrete aid—food, shelter, clothing, money, employment, health services. The Bible notes that before Jesus preaches and seeks to heal the hungry multitude, he feeds them.

A compassionate person is also kind, and kindness has often been described as "more than deeds. It is an attitude, an expression, a look, a touch." I agree: it is the gaze and the extension of (and these words need to be read slowly and considered) undiluted benevolence, empathy, acknowledgment, and gentleness, along with the something extra that "touches" and salves the wounds and uplifts another person.

I don't believe that compassion toward others is just a "genial thought" that we might entertain when we feel pious or magnanimous; I view it more as our moral duty to our fellow human beings, as part of a keen awareness of the interdependence of all people and things. It is not biased or prejudiced; it is extended to others despite their imperfections and blameful as they might be, just as in the New Testament the curative power of compassion is linked to the forgiveness of sins.

How can it be applied in our daily lives, especially to help those who are suffering from inner psychic torment and compulsive substance abuse? I have found that in the case of individuals who have undergone traumatic experiences, our attempts to be helpful are oftentimes met with anger, hostility, blame, resentment, disrespect, and even severe dislike, as their hurts are so deep and their emotions in such disarray that it is difficult for them trust and believe that anyone can help them with no strings attached. The spontaneous reaction of many of us to such unpleasantness is often to return that animosity, offense, and defensiveness in kind—and even abandon the suffering individual. But in such circumstances, how we relate to the afflicted person can be crucial; hence our actions should be considered and carefully weighed. That is, our compassion must have muscle so that we may have the strength to persist in our efforts to meliorate and not fall into the trap of our own counter-resentment and/or lack of heartfelt commitment, being overcome by our own "compassion fatigue." Our focus must be solely on restoring the other with, as Father Gabriel Amorth has noted, "listening, acceptance, consoling and reassurance."[1] When we are struck by hurtful and destructive expressions, that is when we need to approach the individual without judgment and in the spirit of love. This is our only way to soften the heart of the aggrieved person, who is usually suffering from intense feelings of rejection—by showing them the approval and open-hearted caring they so desperately yearn for. What I believe is that we must not react; rather, we must remain calm and "hear" or "read" the despair, fear, and heartbreak "between the lines" and say that we understand, we are sorry for it, and we wish to help.

It may take much time, patience, and dedication (in addition to psychotherapy and/or the help of a religious representative, such as a priest, minister, rabbi, or imam), as our attempts may be disbelieved, tested, and repelled over and over again before things get better. In certain situations, this is the only chance we (both they and ourselves) have.

By way of illustration, there were times when Jenny was straining with maintaining sobriety and would come to see me "loaded for bear."

Jenny would begin, "Ugggh, I can't stand being here! I can't stand being around you! Do you think I would be here if I had anywhere else to go!?"

Instead of responding defensively to insults, I remained centered in a zone of charity, felt deep compassion for all she has endured, and replied, "What is going on, Jenny, honey"?

She would answer, "What is going on? What is *going on*!? What do you think is going on? My life is a mess, and it is all your fault!"

At such times, I think about how I will answer, validating how she must truly feel and offering hope (because much of what she is saying is usually correct): "Jenny, honey, I know how frustrated and desperate you must feel. I am so sorry for everything I did that was wrong, and I have been trying so hard to make it up to you. You have been forced to pay for things that were not your fault and were not of your making. I was not there for you then, but I am here now. I love you, and I am here for you, and I want to help you in any and every way I can. You did not deserve any of all the things that happened to you—no one would have. And I am so very sorry. But I am here now. And I am here just to listen to what you want to say."

And on most occasions, Jenny has responded positively to an openhearted approach and said,

"Forgive me, please. I should not talk to you that way. You do not deserve it."

So bitterness and destruction do not win, and the progress begins toward inner realization and healthy change—for both of us.

Faith: Acquiring Strength and Identity

If e'er when faith had fallen asleep,
I heard a voice "believe no more"
And heard an ever-breaking shore
That tumbled in the Godless deep;

A warmth within the breast would melt
The freezing reason's colder part,
And like a man in wrath the heart
Stood up and answered: "I have felt."

—Alfred, Lord Tennyson, *In Memoriam A. H. H.*

According to the Bible, "Faith . . . worketh by love" (Galatians 5:6) This is because faith is the absolute, unquestioning knowledge of the existence, love, and support of a higher power of goodness and love.

It has been said that "we are twice armed if we fight with faith," meaning that not only do we have our own force, but we have that of God, in whom we have a certain trust. And we are confident that when everything seems insurmountable, we can "give our problems over to God"—that is, we can stop struggling to control the outcomes while we pray, hope, and strive to do our best.

Ultimately, we are what we believe in, and we know that traumatized and addicted youths lack a real and positive sense of selfhood. They lack self-confidence, assurance in a supreme being, and constructive objectives. They lack faith, purpose, and a vision for their future.

Many of the young people I met at Halcyon Headland were suffering from devastating and crushing unhappiness underneath their addictions. When they were ready to be discharged, they felt discouraged from returning to anything better than what they had experienced and left: a tough, cruel world instead of a consistent, loving, welcoming embrace. Our youths are afflicted not only with depression but with the spiritual oppression that exists in our child-abuse society, where they feel a void of God, bereft of benevolent human values while subjected to early sexualization, objectification, and various kinds of exploitation. They have been robbed of their innocence and peace of mind and forced to perceive themselves to be without healthy options, leaving them feeling defeated and despairing, even turning to criminality. Under such circumstances, there is hardly anyone or anything to have faith in. Love is nearly absent in their world, so God is very hard to find.

This is lamentable because just as God is the only thing that is always there and never changes, so belief in a higher power of goodness and love is always available to us. And faith leads to the experience of hope, strength, and an individual sense of enthusiastic being—"this is what I know to be true"—that stands firm and impregnable. Faith is the one thing no one can tamper with: "This is who I am; I own it." It allows us to no longer be a nobody, a "shadow," but a living being with an internal, invincible sense of our core substance, of our own identity. It enables us to assert our own integrity with a sure knowledge of the healthy path we want to follow in our daily lives and to carry on, with the presence of God, no matter what obstacles life or other people throw in our path.

Lack of self-confidence means a lifetime of constant anxiety about not being able, good enough, or strong enough to accomplish anything meaningful or be accepted and welcomed by others. That is a sad, frustrating, self-punishing, unhappy, and lonely existence. The inner certainty that one can rely on oneself, that one is desirable, acceptable, and welcome in the eyes of the world, is acquired in early childhood. But when that developmental step has gone awry, faith can give one a real and beautiful second chance.

In talking to youths from many backgrounds, I find that most are yearning to experience the collective joy that comes from the communal recognition of spirituality. When I spoke with two young men who were recent immigrants from Central and South America, they independently expressed their belief that rehab/mental health programs in various locales should bring in the support of religious organizations within those same communities as part of in-facility treatment and as a source of outpatient support. They voiced their opinion that the merging of psychotherapy and religion—of the clinical knowledge and behavioral insights of psychology with faith and denominational assistance—would be a powerful, healing combination. And in describing this prospect, they expressed feelings of optimism, good cheer, and friendliness. This is a longing ready to burst forth.

In the past, Jenny so yearned for the faith that eluded her, and she told me with deep sorrow that "faith is a blessing," but one that had not yet been bestowed upon her. I recall friends of my grandmother admitting to her that they envied her great faith in God. As Judith Herman states in *Trauma and Recovery*, the patient recovering from complex PTSD must find "a new sustaining faith."[2]

With love and faith, optimism for the prospect of a better tomorrow is possible and provides a reason for living in the pursuit of an achievable happiness.

Prayer: The Way to Healing Energy

For me, prayer is earnest communication to a spiritual plane that, unlike any other, alters my experience and my state of being. For some, prayer is born of faith, and for others, it is born of hope in faith—and both are valid.

Out of my desperation to save my daughter, I cried out to God, and I discovered that when I pray for those in dire need of mediation and positive transformation—if I pray with all my mind, heart, soul, and strength, and with pure love—then it can be a powerful force for good. I saw that it can work to release others from the tribulations that hold them in their suffering and bondage. And in what I understood as the miraculous granting of my invocations, I have felt the depths of gratitude for God's mercy and the gift of love returned. I have found, empirically, that prayer is a vital weapon—both a sword and a shield—in the battle against evil. And there are times when it is our only armament.

As I was prostrate, praying for Jenny's life, I had to plead, as have many other atheists or agnostics with addicted children, "Dear God, please save my child," not simply "Jenny, be well." When staring into the face of death, in my experience, most of us will cry out to divinity. We instinctively reach up to something beyond ourselves, because we know that we alone, limited and flawed as we are, cannot rescue and redeem the person we love. In that moment (if we are going to be honest), many a "nonbeliever" will either acknowledge or be willing to hope for the existence of a supernatural reality, an unparalleled force, an all-encompassing energy, the puissance and all-knowing intelligence, "God," as we intuitively pray.

I have known numerous incidences of the incredible power of prayer, of which I will name a few. Once, as I prayed, Jenny was categorically stopped from going on a self-destructive trip to California (as described in chapter 7). Another time, my intense prayers (as set forth in chapter 6, while I placed myself prone on my bedroom floor) seemed to have lifted her from an overdose after she ingested many times more than a fatal number of narcotics. A third time, to pull Jenny out of deep terror, I asked her to pray, and she experienced a change of spirit and a restoration of wellness. When my mother prayed the Hail Mary over me while I was overcome with deep depression as a young woman, the oppressive atmosphere suddenly lifted away, and all the darkness evaporated. And there have been so many instances in which I prayed to find Jenny only to become informed of her whereabouts, almost instantaneously, through the intercession of Good Samaritans who seemed to have arrived out of the blue, or to have Jenny herself reach out to me in such crucial moments. I will never forget praying for her almost impossible escape from the human traffickers who were holding her captive in a far-away state, as move by move, she was somehow able to slip from their clutches on her own in a seemingly impossible getaway. Jenny later told me that only the power of God could have saved her because there was no way that everything would have fallen in place to enable her escape with all the odds against her if God had not intervened. Most saliently, when I prayed for Jenny to come out of her coma, as described in chapter 2, shortly thereafter a neurologist appeared, using the driving knuckle-rub to the sternum, and Jenny woke up. I continue praying daily for Jenny's healing, and I watch as, step by step, positive improvements take place.

I never give up on prayer. It is the rock of my spirituality and that to which I dedicate my first waking minutes and several moments throughout each day.

As noted by Mahatma Gandhi in *The Story of My Experiments with Truth*, "When every hope is gone, when helpers fail, and comforts flee, I find that help arrives somehow, from I know not where. Supplication, worship and prayer are no superstition; they are acts more real than the acts of eating, drinking, sitting or walking. It is no exaggeration to say that they alone are real, all else is unreal."[3]

The 2016 Galanter study reports that prayer assists people who have achieved sobriety in Alcoholics Anonymous (AA) by reducing their cravings for alcohol, and MRI scans show a markedly different image in the brains of subjects who prayed versus those who did not.[4] Also, Dr. Harold G. Koenig of Duke University notes that studies have shown that prayer can forestall people from becoming ill, and if they do fall ill, it can assist them in recovery. He cites an exhaustive analysis of more than 1,500 reputable studies showing that individuals who pray have superior mental and physical well-being. This includes a study in the *Southern Medical Journal* demonstrating that prayer helped improve the conditions of patients with hearing and visual impairments. Dr. Koenig adds that people with devout religious practices cope better with stress, "have more hope . . . commit suicide less often . . . [and] have stronger immune systems [and] lower blood pressure."[5]

The *American Journal of Public Health* studied nearly two thousand Californians for five years and found that those who attended religious services were 36 percent less likely to die during that period than those who did not. Most significantly, the power of prayer had a positive effect on those who were prayed for and never told. In this regard, research conducted at San Francisco General Hospital observed the impact of prayer on 393 cardiac patients. Although 50 percent were prayed for by individuals whom they did not know personally, these same patients had less difficulty, experienced fewer cases of pneumonia, and needed fewer pharmaceuticals.[6] Professor Leslie Francis of the University of Bangor, Wales, has studied thirty-one experiments on the effectiveness of prayer. These trials took a group of hundreds of patients recovering from heart surgery. One group was prayed for (without their knowledge), and the other was not. "The findings," according to

Professor Francis, "were staggering. Studies show that patients in hospital who are being prayed for (even when they do not know) are more likely to recover."[7]

In his excellent book *Recovery: Freedom from Our Addictions*, Russell Brand discusses Step 7 of the AA program, which includes the following prayer:

> My Creator,
>
> I am now willing that You should have all of me, good and bad. I now pray that you remove every single defect of character that stands between me and my usefulness to You and my fellows. Grant me strength as I go out from here to do Your bidding.

I believe this prayer is profoundly powerful and transformative. It incorporates humility and faith in and reconciliation with a higher power and is a giving of oneself up to God. Also, it beseeches the Creator for strength to do his will and to be of service to others in right action, because changing old habits, negative thought processes, and destructive behaviors can be very difficult. But with this new "north star," one is now on course, liberated and motivated to be the very best one can be and was meant to be. One's harmful past, whatever it may have been, no longer has a hold on the individual, and the exaltation of one's own ego by external material means as a way of compensating for feelings of rejection and insecurity is no longer what one seeks to do. One is no longer imprisoned by "having to prove oneself" to anyone. One is free to be and live as his or her real self.

One of my deepest regrets is that I failed to instill in Jenny a sense of spirituality. I believe that if I had shown her, from a very young age, a strong but humble faith in the reality of a loving higher power and the vital importance of abiding daily prayer, then both she and I would not have suffered from such spiritual destitution, awful grief, and the ravages of drug addiction.

Forgiveness and Self-Forgiveness, Bursting Out of Hate

Forgiveness comes from the Old English *forgiefan*, meaning "to give up, completely," and it is a literal translation of the Latin word *perdonare*, meaning "to give completely, without reservation." In other words, despite what others have done to us, we abandon feelings of revenge, no longer holding on to the destructive and self-destructive energy of resentment and hate or demanding payment of debt for wrongdoing toward us.

I will speak of the role of forgiveness in more detail in the next chapter. However, while editing this section, a 2012 email somehow found its way into my inbox. The email was from Sari, a close and beloved friend of Jenny's who passed away at the age of twenty-eight after taking a psychiatric pharmaceutical without the prescribing facility informing her of its contraindication to another medication. Sari was one of the most beautiful souls I have ever known. She was constantly caring for others, even for those who had hurt her, and she valiantly struggled and ultimately succeeded in winning her battle against opioid dependency despite so many life obstacles. I am including Sari's email to me, written just after both she and Jenny had exited the same rehab, because it is clear to me that although Sari died in the spring of 2017, she has sent her communication to us from heaven, where she is, and wants us all to hear it. Her message is that if we are truly to be restored, we must understand the reasonableness of the ultimate healing of forgiveness:

> Dear Vivian:
>
> God wants us to be happy. Vivian . . . my parents weren't prizes, and I could hate them if I chose to. They were both VERY abusive, both of them. Andrew [the counselor at Rocky Cliffs, described in chapter 6, who told Jenny's group that in some cases suicide was fine] even said to me, "It's OK to hate them." BUT I CANNOT. I CHOOSE LOVE AND FORGIVENESS INSTEAD. But no one even apologized to me or begged me for it. The fact of the

matter is forgiveness is the most freeing thing we can ever do for ourselves and for the people we love. That was Jesus' true message. As long as we harbor resentments and hates, we will always be in the dark. Our job is to truly live as Jesus wants us to . . . IT IS TO FORGIVE OTHERS AND OURSELVES. He wants that for us. That was the gift he gave us. I may be new to religion, and it may seem that maybe I shouldn't talk about what Jesus wants for us. But I am confident that I get it. Jesus doesn't ask us to suffer. How some organized religions speak of the true message, forgiveness, is a shame. We need to be easier on ourselves. I pray for you, my friend. I pray for your daughter.

Love,
Sari

I do believe that God heard Sari's loving prayers, because as Jenny herself has said to me recently, in a moment of great insight and healing, "The key to everything and to being well is forgiveness. We have to forgive others, because they also have each suffered in their childhoods in ways we do not even know and maybe even more horribly than we can imagine. And whatever they have done to us, we also have done similar or maybe even worse things to other people. They have said or done things that hurt me or others out of their own hurt and pain, just as I have said or done because of my own hurt and pain. So we must forgive them. We all must forgive each other."

What If Spiritual Love Is Absent?

A Cautionary Tale

I have seen everything unravel when someone is under powerful psychic attack, without the experience of being truly loved, and deprived of spirituality.

Suicidality can emerge from the most unbearable and engulfing sense of emotional exile and despair—a complete lack of self-confidence; an emotion and belief that one is totally incapable of leading a normal life, unloved, unlovable, and utterly isolated without significant caring or support; a feeling that life is futile, senseless, and meaningless and that there is no worthwhile future for oneself in this world; and sometimes, an uncontainable rage is turned against those feelings in oneself. In many cases, the victim felt unwanted from a very young age, solitary and disdained, which leads to an internalized state of nearly complete self-rejection and suicidal ideation, even as early as grammar school. The experience is a sense of doom—that one's fate is sealed and one has irrevocably been set up for an evil destiny, that "the fix is in."

And there is the burden of not permitting the inner agony to show. With all these negative thoughts about oneself, often such a person attempts to keep tormenting feelings at bay by erecting a false scaffolding of outward success, achievement, beauty, or popularity. That's why many who have known such a person are completely shocked and incredulous when he or she commits suicide.

This fragile external structure can last as a "false self" for a long time but then collapse under the weight of new hardships that cause the individual to crumble while in the company of others or totally withdraw from human contact. When facing the abyss without human support, knowing that one is not alone because there is a loving God who is always present can make all the difference.

That said, not everyone has achieved this kind of belief, so it is essential that we reach out to suffering others *in time* and in person with caring and reliable assistance, for the truth is that without love, we lose our minds.

For example, I grew up in the 1960s in a suburb of New York City, where my mother's best friend was a beautiful lady nicknamed Ellie. Unfortunately, Ellie's very wealthy husband was a misogynist who called her stupid in front of company and their children and demeaned her at every opportunity. He was rich, powerful, glamorous, and popular; he knew how to handle people; and he mistreated Ellie. Feeling insecure, she took up social drinking, and soon she turned to it privately for uplift, ending up a severe alcoholic. Over the years, I watched her slow but sure demise, and by the time I reached my eighteenth birthday, Ellie was dead.

As the verbal abuse continued, and as her youthful beauty started to fade with age, Ellie had become sicker and sicker. The doctors started removing one organ after another from her body: first her appendix, then her gallbladder, her spleen, and part of her lower intestine. She had a hysterectomy and then a pancreatic operation. It all seemed unnecessary and beyond bizarre. This was an era when doctors were "surgery happy" and when slews of children had their tonsils removed at the smallest sign of infection. Still, I wondered, *how were the physicians justifying this?* Ellie went along with or requested all these surgeries, which struck me as an ingrained (and incorrect) belief that she was bad, and her badness had to be taken out like the rot from a rotten apple. It also seemed like a desperate cry for love and an effort to obtain at least some pity from her husband.

Ellie next ended up in the offices of psychiatrists who (in consultation with her husband) told her in no uncertain terms that her problem was her jealousy of her own daughter. Why this insensitive and blameful attitude? Why did they not help her resolve her depression with empathy and compassion? Ellie's husband placed her in the hands of these same psychiatrists, who had started giving her electroshock treatments—their final protocol to manage her severe depression. On the heels of one of those procedures, I came to visit her while she was isolated in her bedroom, hearing her "friends," her husband, and her daughter in the living room chatting about life and about what a "drama queen" she was.

Ellie looked at me and said,

"Vivian, aren't you afraid to see me? Aren't you afraid to come in my bedroom? Everyone else is afraid to see me."

"No, Ellie. I want to see you. I came to see you." I remember thinking that her seclusion was wrong, demeaning, and terribly detrimental to her. "Why would I be afraid of you?"

She sighed. "Oh, Viv. I am a bad person. I am jealous of your mother because she has a career and I don't go to work. I have nothing of my own. I don't do anything. Sometimes, I look at the furniture, and it slants, and I look at the walls, and they slant. I am crazy. Don't you know that I am crazy? Everyone says that I am crazy."

I considered what I was going to say to Ellie, and then I answered her honestly.

"Ellie, you are not a bad person; you are a good person. All of us feel jealous of someone else at some point in time. That is true of everybody, not just you, and it does not make you a bad person. As for not working, you are very talented at a lot of things, especially interior decorating, and you can get a job in that field when you want to, I am sure, and you would be great at it! As for the furniture and the walls slanting, do not worry about that. Sometimes, they look that way to me too."

Ellie stared at me wide eyed, grabbed me, and started to sob as I held her in my arms. She begged me,

"Oh, Viv, please don't go! Now you are going away to school. [I was going out of state for college.] You are the only person I can talk to. You are the only person who is not afraid to touch me, who I can cry with. I can cry with you. I can talk to you. You understand. You can help me. You are going away, and then you won't be here to help me. What am I going to do without you?"

Then Ellie confronted me with terror in her eyes and pleaded with great earnestness and conviction: "Vivian, get me a priest. Only a priest can help me. Vivian, get me a priest." This was startling, as Ellie had never been overtly religious in any way, but her sincerity and seriousness were overwhelming.

I went into the room where her husband was talking to my mother, and I told them both that Ellie was urgently asking to see a priest. They dismissed her request as "not serious" and as evidence of her "theatricality," and they replied that she was "just seeking attention, like always."

I answered, "No, Ellie really wants to see a priest. We need to get her a priest."

I was countermanded by her imperious husband and my mother, both telling me to "mind my own business." The next day, I left to go away to school.

The morning after I arrived, I received the phone call telling me that Ellie had gotten up in the middle of the night and used her hospital walker to throw herself off the eighth-floor balcony of her deluxe condominium. Her beautiful, petite body lay in a smashed and broken heap on the concrete porch of her ground-floor neighbor. Ellie was dead.

I blamed myself. I should have insisted on bringing a priest to her. I should have gone out immediately, searched, and found one on my own. I realized that Ellie had been desperately looking for empathy from an incorruptible ally, to be heard and seen as a real person, and for hope and for the pure kindness and gentle love that a priest would tell her existed and came to her from a higher power.

As in the case of Ernest Hemingway (who also committed suicide following electroshock therapy) and so many other people who gave up on life, the psychiatrists had given her no sympathy and no medicine for the soul. In a cruel and unjust twisting of reality and most probably to deny their own culpability, her family and "friends" condemned Ellie for her own suicide and labeled her as a "bad, selfish person" for taking her own life. The truth of the matter is that Ellie was a very good, lively, and courageous woman in spite of her insecurities who, in the past, had risked her own life to somehow save her husband's, and against all odds. He showed no gratitude, and the others were all privately envious of her, feeling she possessed everything material that they did not have and would have wanted. What a tragedy it was that they did not have the inner goodness, as well as the capacity for deeper spiritual understanding, that could have reached Ellie.

She was seeking caring, acceptance, and compassion from another human being, someone with whom she could share her deepest emotions of rejection, sadness, isolation, and rage, and her feeling of being unloved, that were drowning her; someone to whom she could just let out these feelings and who would receive them in a sympathetic, empathic, and sheltering way; a person to whom she could safely attach who would embrace her and be there for her in a genuinely reliable and encouraging relationship. She was also looking for faith in a higher power that would provide a source of unconditional spiritual love, support, strength, and alliance, a validation of her worth as a person, and a reason to hope and to live; however, at that point in time, she could not contact God on her own. She needed human help, but she was all alone, surrounded by insensitivity.

The Failed Mental Health and Rehab System

In the four decades since Ellie's passing, not much has changed. Every establishment to which I took Jenny (except for Revision and Heliotrope), demanded the complete exclusion of religion, any mention of a higher power, or any interest in spirituality. These institutions were robotic in practice and therefore failed to reach and mend the broken hearts and restore wholeness to the traumatized souls of the young people who vainly went to these places in search of true understanding and healing. Many of them, like Ellie, did not survive.

In these organizations, recovery is attempted with the dispensation of more drugs to counterbalance the drugs of addiction and the forced intake of usually ineffective and even harmful antipsychotic medications said to address the (often incorrect) diagnosis du jour, along with some recycled, generic and general remediation lectures. These patients are "talked at" in the prefabricated language that is part of their impersonal "treatment," which taken altogether comprises an iron-like template stamped upon each patient with industrial dispatch.

Thus Jenny has raged to me when infuriated by how she and her friends were *mis*treated by the mental health/rehab "system,"

"All that happens in these rehabs and psych wards is that I and most others ended up being abused and learning about more drugs, where to get them, and exposed to the worst sorts of behaviors! And on top of all that, having to go from one to the other 'cause of the lack of real treatment and the harm they do, we lost any education or vocational training or chance to be taught how to be responsible and organize our lives—and we're still stuck adolescents! We landed nowhere. Sick with lack of accomplishment when everyone your age has already graduated from college and has careers, not having learned the skills to make a life for yourself and hating yourself for it! That's extremely depressing and makes you want to keep using drugs!

"And the pills don't work! And these places deny it because they and the pharmaceutical companies are making too much money shoveling these useless meds down everyone's throats! Who knows what sawdust or pulverized garbage is in this stuff? No one really knows! And the so-called placebo effect can only last for so long! If you confront them with the truth, as I tried to do, you become a problem because you are getting in the way of their profit machine. So they label you with a destructive diagnosis like 'sociopathic' and try to break you down and break down your terrified parents, who don't know what to do. They break our mind and spirit so badly that they not only back us into a corner, but they get us to willingly walk into that corner on our own! The only drug they gave me that was effective was Seroquel—because it knocks you out so completely that you can't do anything wrong, and you don't feel the pain. But once you wake up, all your problems and your pain are still there. These places are all totally soulless!"

How is that for building self-confidence and self-esteem, without which a person is a shadow?

First and foremost, these facilities fail because the underlying emotional/psychic/spiritual *causes* of the drug addiction and the mental distress, personal and unique to each individual, are seldom acknowledged; they are not connected to or worked through in a meaningful, empathic, private, therapeutic way. These young people are not given anything that confirms and touches them as unique individuals—as distinct souls.

Nor are the patients given the option of exploring a belief in a personal, loving creator of caring and goodness who is more powerful than our problems and our pasts. So they are left feeling isolated in their anguish and without the assistance of spirituality as a source of hope, love, and restoration.

I believe it is time to consciously and purposefully unite medicine, psychiatry, psychotherapy, and spirituality so that others no longer may suffer the unjust fate of Ellie and so many of Jenny's friends. We must make a commitment to achieving a paradigm that truly works.

What follows in the next two chapters is meant to start this conversation and lead to the establishment of a solution on a personal and societal basis.

10

A NEW THERAPEUTIC PARADIGM

RESTORING THE INDIVIDUAL SOUL

Individual Psycho-Spiritual Therapy

Healing the Soul With Love

St. Padre Pio of Pietrelcina gave a powerful invocation for the role of love and spirituality in the healing process:

> You too, doctors, you came to the world as I did with a mission to accomplish. Take note: I speak to you of duties when everyone talks about rights. . . . You have the mission of curing the sick, but if you do not bring love to the bedside of the patient, I do not think the medicine will be of much use. . . . Love cannot do without words. How can you express it if not with words that relieve the patient spiritually? Bring God to the patient. He will be worth more than any other cure.[1]

This was acknowledged by Jenny's good friend Darcy:

"I spent about a week at Halcyon Headland, and it was good that I went there, but I still feel shaky. I am trying so hard to make it. I am working on painting in oils, and it is pretty. It is keeping me occupied."

I could see her pain and her struggle. What words could I speak to help her? I felt inhibited from saying what I was about to say, but it was all I could think of that might make a difference, and I believe it to be true:

"Remember, Darcy, you are a child of God. And He loves you . . . I do believe that. I hope it is all right that I have said that to you."

She looked at me with astonishment as the light of a wish for faith and hope moved across her face:

"No. You are right. Thank you so much for saying that. People need to hear that. We need to hear it. It needs to be said, and it is never said. People need to hear it."

With regard to psychotherapeutic healing, Armand—a psychologist—was fond of saying that the solution to helping his patients was simple:

"Just love. Just reach out with love."

Jenny herself, has stated,

"Yes, love is the answer. It knows no boundaries and no bounds and goes through everything and anything. Mom, love is the answer."

And psychiatrist Dr. Karl Menninger is often quoted as having said,

"Love cures people—both the ones who give it and the ones who receive it."

A similar understanding was presented in a little-known writing in the early half of the twentieth century by the American psychoanalyst Izette De Forest, pupil of the famous Hungarian analyst Sándor Ferenczi. Dr. De Forest pointed out the role of trauma in the phenomenon of splitting the True Self (or Soul) and the necessity of "the redemption of the individual by active love" to help him or her regain the power to love. I have personally found that many people in search of healing are oftentimes seeking their first "lost love," which broke their heart, destroyed their self-love, severed their connection to their inborn selves, and may even have extinguished their belief in God and other people. That heartbreak most likely was caused either by unwitting or deliberate parental betrayal in the forms of neglect and abuse or by family circumstances that may have been interpreted as rejection, such as the absence of an ill parent or the invisibility of stressed-out mothers and fathers working excessive hours in a cruel economy. Or they may have undergone another crisis of faith, such as that experienced in wartime and/or when an individual is subjected to instances of extreme inhumanity outside the family, such as sex and human trafficking, rape, physical assault, and mental and emotional injury.

So what is the place of spirituality, the soul, and love in the therapeutic method? While all the evidence affirms their vital importance and we know that the humans have yearned for loving spirituality throughout time, nonetheless, this factor has been orthodoxically excluded from the therapeutic paradigm. This dismissal has occurred despite our excessive reliance on impersonal groups and preprogrammed management at the expense of individual psychotherapy, electroshock and the former use of lobotomies, and pills, all of which have been abysmal failures—and all performed in the name of "science." Of course these methods have failed; we are dealing with people's individual souls, not mere neurological circuitry, and science is oftentimes wrong and still very limited. And when I mention "spirituality," I do not intend any specific religion.

Psychotherapy—derived from the ancient Greek word *psyche*, meaning "soul," and therefore translated as "soul" therapy—is capable of healing a human soul. But in order to do so, psychiatry and medicine must first admit to the existence of the soul within each person and then include it in the focus of his or her care.

I believe the soul is the immortal, spiritual, animating kernel of life. I understand it to be the core of one's self-identity and authenticity. When we say "with my heart and soul," everyone knows that we mean with the innermost part of the self, the container of love and one's essence. And I truly believe that loving relationships provide life to the soul.

In the words of Dr. Abraham Verghese, "Physicians should never forget that the patient has 'two hearts' one that is the subject of tests, and one that holds the patient's soul . . . Find a way to communicate to patients: 'I carry your heart.'"[2] Doctor and patient are in a caring human relationship wherein the doctor must feel a love and a responsibility for the patient and desire to see the heart and soul, as well as the body, healthy and well. The body and soul are interlinked—they are all you, and doctors must want to treat the whole person.

In a psychotherapy that acknowledges and addresses the existence of the soul, which I will herein call "soul therapy," the physician/therapist experiences the other's pain, identifies with the other's emotions and ordeals, and feels that he or she is the other's guardian and "life-guard" within the therapeutic relationship. But "group," as was essentially exclusively relied upon in the facilities Jenny attended, cannot "touch" the inner being, the soul, and the anguish that is suffered in silence by the individual patient, because "group," by its very nature, precludes a private, loving, one-on-one relationship and the confidentiality essential for total honesty, individual insight, retrieval of personal trauma, working-through, and healing. However, if conducted properly, group meetings may be a useful adjunct to one-on-one therapy, in that they facilitate the person feeling a part of a number of similarly afflicted peers and not singled out.

As Dr. Verghese so astutely observed, those suffering from illness and trauma also experience a sense of very personal spiritual violation, of "Why?" and "Why me?" Indeed, Jenny has asked me, "Why did all this happen to *me*? Why was I singled out for cruelty, annihilation, and injustice? Do I even belong on this earth in which people always reject me, mistreat me, and see me as so strange and different from everyone else? Why is there no love for me, and why do I never belong? I don't want to live in this world anymore, where I am not wanted and where others only constantly use and hurt me and are so mean and cold-hearted."

What more appropriate place than a treatment facility for dispensing spiritual love, understanding, and acceptance as an integral part of therapy? It should be a means, a way in which cure is delivered, not an afterthought, a consideration, a nod of acknowledgment, a concession, or an element to be sprinkled on a serving of treatment. Altruistic love and treatment should be synonymous. How does one achieve this?

I venture to say, primarily through a universal belief engendered by training institutions, medical facilities, psychotherapeutic organizations, and individual practitioners, that those in the healing professions and we the public at large are all united in our dedication to stamp out illness, promote health, and heal. And essential to that goal is the acknowledgement of the existence and central importance of the soul and its vibrancy in preserving the physical and emotional welfare of the individual, knowing that its own vitality is maintained by receiving altruistic/spiritual love, enabling one to develop a cardinal core of self-love, which is the key to all recovery. Hence it is up to all of us (doctors, therapists, patients, everyone) to speak up and make known what is needed and lacking in our health care system. Then it may be achieved by the organization, physician, and therapist recognizing that they are truly treating the whole person, including the patient's inner "self" or soul.

Altruistic love as part of a cure can be achieved by every caretaker reminding oneself, before meeting with every patient, that this is an awesome and sacred responsibility that demands that one be both humble and pure of heart, loving and seeking to impart human caring as well as diagnostic and treatment skill. Therapy is a dynamic engagement, and spiritual love is the essential ingredient that makes it truly healing.

Dr. Gabor Maté has worked extensively and compassionately with addicts on the lower east side of Vancouver, and interestingly, although a self-described atheist, he seems to be a "work in progress." At a national conference of Eastern Orthodox clergy and laity, Dr. Maté spoke about the spiritual components of addiction, using "The God-Shaped Hole" as the title of his two lectures, saying that he believes in "divine law" but struggles with the concept of a "divine law giver"; however, he added, "If you believe the

10 Commandments are random, try breaking one." Maté told those at the conference, "If an addict can feel loved, their brain can relax, and they can accept the possibility of salvation beyond addiction." Maté stresses the need to face the traumas of the past rather than sedating them and quotes Thomas Hora in saying, "All problems are psychological, all solutions are spiritual."[3]

An Example of Soul Therapy

There was a time when spirituality as part of therapy worked a miracle in my own life. Although I had once been an excellent student, I was failing my freshman year in a Catholic, all-girls high school and considering heroin use (which in those days meant only elastic bands and needles). My father had sent me to Catholic school "for discipline" (although, with my mother's permission, he had already "drilled" me into the ground), not for theological inculcation, as he was a staunch anti-Catholic and stalwart atheist.

As fate would have it, I went to speak to a visiting young educational guidance counselor who was also a priest. Serendipitously, I later discovered that he had been friends with my beloved maternal grandmother, who passed away when I was eight years old. In his thoughtful and empathic manner, he made me feel I could trust him, as I perceived that he truly wanted to help. I did not exactly reveal the abuse in my home, but I intimated that I was struggling and in great personal anguish. He listened to me with concentrated interest and caring, and I could see that he felt my pain and was sorry for it. I related to him what I thought: "I am no longer a good student, but if someone just told me that I could succeed in my coursework, that they believed I could do it, then I could do it. If only someone would tell me they believe I can." I later realized that I was seeking someone who could tell me honestly if I was of some value as a person when it seemed to me that every message I received was a rejection of who I was.

He then looked at me like my ally in a war against injustice and said to me, with a confidence that felt like a benediction, "I believe that you can do it. I believe you can." I walked out the door, and almost overnight, I became a straight-A student. He gave me faith in myself, and his words, combined with his sincere interest, loving connectedness, and honest encouragement, seemed to contain a potent, healing energy and grace that formed a protective shield around me. His entire attention and concern were focused on me, on my emotions, and on what I had to say. He "saw" me, was "with me," and I felt understood, real, meaningful, and validated. This enabled me to move forward, with hope, despite the constant injuries that I was subjected to in my abode. He accepted me and valued me, "loser" that I was, and let me know that I was important enough to be heard and believed. I felt that he was telling me that we are all equal, and I came away with a feeling of self-love for the first time since my grandmother had died.

He did not "classify me"; nor did he try to "fix it all" with pills or send me for group therapy. Instead, he spoke to me privately, personally, and individually, and I felt that he had truly acknowledged my inner self and that he had, in a way, held my soul in his hands and helped me with altruistic/spiritual love.

His visit to our school was only for one day, but I often wonder how different my life would have been if I had the privilege of meeting with him on an ongoing basis.

An Ideal Form of Soul Therapy

It should be pointed out, before proceeding any further, that many exceptional psychodynamically trained therapists do practice what we refer to as "soul therapy," in that they intuitively convey the highest caliber of humanity and trustworthiness because of good training and who they are as people in their conduct of psychotherapy. What is described below is what we consider excellent therapy, and we describe it in detail so that everyone may be assured that it exists and can request it.

In successful soul therapy, the patient would experience unconditional positive esteem within a therapeutic dynamic of mutual equality, approval, and respect. Here the stance of the therapist would be (while always correct and professional), first and foremost, that of a lovingly sympathetic ally and friend who has compassion for the patient's suffering and who seeks to help the patient carefully identify and release its cause, with the goal of alleviating his inner torment, enabling him to connect to his original self and empowering him to rebuild his life. Of vital consequence, the therapist would be completely nonjudgmental, gentle, and kind, listening with full, heartfelt attention and sincere interest. This approach would allow the patient to feel protected while disclosing the external and internal experiences that troubled him, what they have meant and how they have affected him; his often strong and unwarranted self-condemnation and self-limiting beliefs; his frank affects; and his sense of rejection, unworthiness, and futility. This is difficult but very rewarding work and is hardly ever completed within a short period of time. Frequently, initially the patient might report what has been on his mind currently and how he has reacted to recent people and events. Then gradually he may be willing and able to disclose crucial previous ordeals that have left their painful mark.

Of great importance is the patient's ability to express and share her true *feelings* of vulnerability, grief, loneliness, unbelonging, shame, and anger to someone who can guide her and with whom she feels safe. Because these *emotions* have a somatic intensity and are steeping the individual in a psychic-physical agony, she may be overwhelmed by them. They impede her ability to think clearly and to act in her own enlightened self-interest, so they must be released and lovingly accepted, understood and validated by the person to whom they have been expressed.

There is the danger of deep depression, panic attacks, and immobility when a person begins to revisit her past and handle the extreme anguish and feelings of hopelessness, devastation, and doom linked to encounters of early devaluation, different incidences of abuse, and denials of love. Therefore, much care needs to be exercised in the likelihood of such an eventuality. In such cases, as the interaction continues, it is best to caution against any potentially dangerous or self-harming behaviors and treat her with ample amounts of reassurance, raising her self-esteem by pointing out all her positive qualities and accomplishments, and with the therapist's own optimism, liking for her, and belief in her shining through. The therapist will also be sure to communicate that other people have overcome their traumatic pasts and have gotten well and that she can too, thus enabling the patient to begin to feel self-confidence and see the possibility of a meaningful future.

Hope begins to emerge after a sensitive and truly caring person comprehends, values, and *identifies* with the patient's experiences and expresses deep appreciation of the wrongs and crippling occurrences he has endured. It is healing for the therapist to tell the patient "I am so sorry that this happened to you" and that these maltreatments were not his fault, he did not cause them, and he not deserve them—that no one would. This usually helps the patient feel free and secure enough to explore more fully and make important connections between his traumatic episodes, perceptions, and patterns of behavior—of feeling, thinking, and reacting—that he lives by. As a result, the patient hears his own story in a way that makes it feel part of his reality and true, not unreal and "crazy." In good time, the patient may be able to understand his own actions and attitudes and what defense and self-soothing mechanisms he has adopted and how they have been tripping up his health and progress. Then he may see that he does not need the old patterns anymore and be willing to let them go and adopt new and salutary ways of thinking and feeling about himself and others and of interacting with the world. He is open and has the capacity to learn to change and to grow. He might feel, perhaps for the first time, genuine self-worth and dare to conceive a positive and even blossoming life for himself.

This therapeutic avenue would allow a distressed individual to gain conscious control of the devastating incidents of yesterday rather than permitting them to continue their unconscious, hidden, and destructive mastery over his very fate. In the end, one must learn to manage one's own circumstances and past or be managed by them.

Such psychodynamic treatment would be best introduced gradually in a hospital or rehab, at least during its commencement phase, for the security of the patient whose anxiety, depression, and urge to "use" will rise during the process due to the dredging up of psychic injuries.

When this type of psychotherapy is not available in the inpatient hospital or rehab (although it should be), then the patient should be referred accordingly. We as a nation should work to make sure that such quality therapy, over a necessary length of time, is covered by affordable health insurance.

Ultimately, for the patient who has been subjected to multiple traumas, some too horrible to repeat without the passage of much time, and fearing that neither she nor anyone could ever recover, it is important to realize that by focusing on and dedicating time and energy to achieving ever more positive endeavors and with good relationships, the effects of these traumas will fade away. New and rewarding experiences will take their place, redefine the person, strengthen her sense of self and identity, and promote self-expression and the realization of her God-given potential. So it is helpful to recall the words of 1 John 4:4 (NIV, italics mine): "You, dear children, are from God and have overcome them (*the evil of the traumas, no matter how many or how great*), because the one who is in you (*God and God's pure love, goodness and power to heal*) is greater than the one who in in the world (*the evil in the world*)."

Places for Psycho-Spiritual Support

Psycho-Spiritual Listening Posts

Through all my encounters and observations, I have come to understand that what everyone struggling with emotional trauma and/or addiction needs is a healer to listen with concern and empathy, providing personal human support while helping to clarify and point to a good course of action and a life direction.

In olden times, in the Catholic tradition, one could speak to a parish priest regarding issues that were tormenting the soul and leading one down a road of injury to oneself and others. This dynamic listening relief was readily available under an agreement of absolute confidentiality and was totally free of charge (like Alcoholics Anonymous [AA]), which made it extramundane and liberating, as there were no financial gains or obligations. Oftentimes people came away feeling understood, receiving sympathy and magnanimity, calmed of their fears, given relief from anxiety, and set upon a useful way of coping with their circumstances and problems. This rendered them better able to forgive themselves and others, as they were encouraged to live again.

Forgiving oneself and others is generally not adequately emphasized as a necessary element of love and spirituality, as well as of health. And it bears stressing that when we resent without seeking a resolution, we carry the burdensome weight and the contagious negativity of that bundle of vengefulness, hostility, and bitterness. When we decide that nothing more can be done but to let it go, we forgive (not approve), give up the debt that demands rancor, and set ourselves free from heart-fossilizing and soul-poisoning resentments, which leaves us free to focus on and be who we truly are.

This is not an easy thing to do while holding on to a calcified way of seeing and experiencing a situation, and it cannot be forced, but it can be approached with reason. It takes experiencing gratitude for the good things in our lives, having an understanding of and empathy for the offender (when we consider his or her past), and being honest enough to admit that we, likewise, have committed qualitatively similar wrongdoings for which we also need to be forgiven.

The benefits of forgiveness have been documented. Mayo Clinic, on Healthy Living, lists a number of rewards that can easily be understood when we consider their interrelationship:

1. Lower blood pressure
2. Reduced stress

3. Less hostility (e.g., picking fights, road rage)
4. Lower heart rate
5. Fewer symptoms of depression (i.e., it gives us healing and grace and can replace depression with a sense of compassion)
6. Relief from anxiety
7. Less chronic pain
8. Better relationships and friendships
9. Greater spiritual well-being
10. Improved psychological well-being[4]

With respect to listening posts, in contradistinction to traditional psychotherapy or analysis, the priest adopted the posture of a trusted human being who was an instrument in the service of the person in crisis, who listened on behalf of God and was a transmitter of God's compassion, grace, and guidance. He acted as a truthful but loving dispenser of advice and assistance looking to heal the souls of individuals and restore them to personal and spiritual health. This allowed one to come away feeling like a loved child of God, known and capable of abandoning vindictive ideas and destructive behaviors and embarking on a remedial path.

Many persons today consult with a priest not only in private as a caring advisor but also in a special kind of listening post: the confessional. Here, the sole focus is voluntarily to speak out one's hurts, hates, wrongdoings, and negative aspects while asking for absolution. To undergo confession is a great act of honesty and humility, an admission of a desire to restore one's relationship to God, self, and others by making amends to those one has wronged and changing for the better, thereafter feeling atonement—or "at-one"-ment. Confession (to an AA mentor, physician, or cleric) is incorporated in the twelve steps of AA and is the basis of psychotherapy, although the latter alone has (with the exception of pastoral counselors) excised a higher power from the process. It is important to point out that confession is only a positive experience when the confessor listens empathically, with love and understanding, offering instruction with the goal of healing. It is counterproductive if the confessor responds in an unloving way—with harshness and/or shaming, causing the confessed to feel bad about themselves—and/or demands conformity to doctrine.

To differentiate forgiveness and absolution, forgiveness occurs between ourselves and others, but absolution is a divine engagement by which our guilt is wiped away by God himself through the blessing of a priest. Absolution incorporates forgiveness, but it involves revealing to a priest both the misdeeds we have committed and our sorrow for them as offenses to love itself—to God. Then the priest may grant us God's pardon and absolution.

I have met so many young people—young women, especially—who want to speak with good, religious persons whom they see as representatives of God on earth. A therapist may not be enough in some circumstances. Some of the soul-wounded are seeking the ministrations of a person who carries a "blessed authority" and who will hear them and remit their guilty thoughts, words, and deeds on behalf of a higher power, because without absolution and the self-forgiveness that comes with it, they continue to condemn themselves as deserving of punishment, which they exact in self-cutting, drugs, abusive relationships, and general self-sabotage in all areas of their life. Without a divine pardon, they feel that they must "pay the price."

It has been said that frequent confession imparts five benefits:

1. It helps one better know oneself.
2. It helps one overcome vice.
3. It brings peace and serenity.
4. It helps one become more morally good.
5. It helps the will grow stronger.

In days gone by, nonconfessional "listening posts" or "sanctuary stations" were available to anyone at all. It did not take long and costly therapy, and some people felt relieved within one to four visits, knowing that they could always return, should they wish to. One cannot help but wonder how many tragedies could be averted—homicides, suicides, and other acts of harm and self-harm—were such listening posts readily available in society today.

Many persons to whom I have spoken think it would be wonderful if churches and other religious institutions would establish such "listening posts" available throughout the day and into the evenings. People could come, without the imposition of a fee, to pour out their troubles and know that they will be heard and that someone will try to help and counsel them with loving care. Ideally, the listeners would be members of religious affiliations of various faiths who are also trained in psychodynamics, or they might also include well-educated, kindly intentioned, retired or semiretired lay or religious members of the population, with schooling in spiritual and secular guidance skills, who have much to give in terms of time and experience. They would also be able to refer people for emergency assistance or to quality places of inpatient treatment and physical refuge when such is advisable—for instance, for battered women suffering from Stockholm syndrome, for addicts who cannot withdraw from alcohol or opiates on their own, and for those who may be on the verge of a complete psychotic break.

I believe that the establishment of listening posts could save many lives. Thereafter, those who have attended may want to engage a mental health care professional, but at least they will have a place to go for human succor until they can find and afford a truly good therapist, should they still want or need one.

Spiritual Extended Families

Another potential contribution of the various denominations could be the creation of spiritual extended families. We live in a society with a plethora of single mothers; small nuclear two-parent households where both mother and father are exhausted and worried, working twelve- to eighteen-hour days, and isolated; and even abandoned grandparents and elderly. Would it not be wonderful if churches, synagogues, mosques, and temples throughout the country announced and invited persons and families to participate in establishing spiritual extended families, where persons in these categories in the community could form groups of ten to fifteen individuals and be introduced to one another, facilitating the mutual exchange and sharing of help, assistance, companionship, and worship and engaging in projects together (arts and crafts, baking, gardening, agriculture, feeding the homeless, working to build shelters, reading to children, etc.) that serve the religious center and/or those in the wider community?

And with respect to the tremendous potential of a spiritual extended family for children in particular, Dr. Anna Badini writes,

> I am reminded of my childhood in Italy just after World War II, where people had suffered much destruction, upheaval, loss, and poverty. We, girls went to the "nunnery" (convent) after school to play, do homework, learn to sew, sing, and play games under the supervision and guidance of Sister Maria. We prayed and sang hymns. It was a serene place, filled with kindness, caring, and fun. The boys went to the "oratory," where the priest or a monk played ball with them. I don't know what else they did there, but I recall time to go home. These children would leave the buildings with smiles on their faces, proud, well disposed toward a "broken" world. They had received special and focused attention from someone who was not rushed or distracted by more important things. They had been heard and given responses. They felt valued.

The Place of Religion or a Higher Power in Treatment: The Contributions of Alcoholics Anonymous and Pastoral Counseling

I would like to emphasize that suggesting or facilitating spirituality or religion should never resemble or be experienced as an attempt at "converting." It is not about forcing an argument or point of view or saying that one person is better than another. That would be mistrusted and easily rejected. My aim is to start a very important discussion, raise the reader's awareness of what is possible, and tell our story as a means of elucidation.

However, note that we are facing a tidal wave of an epidemic, and the methods used (by the antispiritual, secular "system" over the last fifty years) have failed completely. Therefore, turning once again to the support of religion and spirituality certainly could not hurt us, and there is a plethora of evidence to indicate that it may have a significant, if not decisive, curative impact.

As noted by Drs. Andreasen, Verghese, and others, it is time for therapists and therapeutic institutions to abandon their traditional and biased dissidence toward spirituality and instead admit that it is an important component in medical and psychiatric healing and that religious involvement (i.e., institutionalized spirituality) may be beneficial to some patients. In fact, various forms of exposure to spirituality (e.g., Alcoholics Anonymous, Narcotics Anonymous, religious services, faith-based addiction programs) could be gently offered or suggested as an adjunct to private therapeutic care.

On the beneficial value of spirituality in the treatment of addiction, the Blue Book of Alcoholics Anonymous asserts,

"What often takes place in a few months could seldom have been accomplished by years of self-discipline. With few exceptions, our members find that they have tapped an unsuspected inner resource which they presently identify with their own conception of a power greater than themselves . . . the essence of spiritual experience. Our more religious members call it 'God consciousness.'"

Alcoholics Anonymous assigns a "sponsor" to each member who is available to speak or meet with a member in need of a "listening post" and advice.

Likewise, I believe that with open-mindedness and with a recognition of the needs of diverse patients and persons, ministers, rabbis, priests, and imams should be readily available in hospitals, rehab, and psychiatric facilities, and schools for those patients/students who wish to supplement standard therapy with loving spiritual help. But in the past, mental health facilities and academic institutions have considered the addition of a spiritual element as a threat to psychotherapy/rational secularism, an intrusion to be avoided.

Recently there has been an increase in the number of pastoral counselors, who are psychologically trained persons of all faiths, who provide spiritual and therapy services.

Glenn Williams, a pastoral counselor in Kentucky and chair of the Kentucky Association of Pastoral Counselors, has said, "On a feeling level, people want a safe place to ponder tons of questions that come begging in hard times: 'Where is God? Why did this happen? Is it karma? What purpose does this suffering serve?'"[5] And in a 2005 *Washington Post* article, Allison Buckholtz speaks of the increased desire for therapy that includes spirituality.[6]

Although the Affordable Care Act has allowed more people to receive Medicaid to cover the cost of mental health care, the number of social workers in clinics has been spread very thin, such that people suffering from severe depression may have to wait for weeks to see a therapist. The use of pastoral counselors to serve in both inpatient and outpatient drug treatment programs, mental hospitals and clinics, and schools should allow patients and students in crisis to be seen in a more timely manner and make psycho-spiritual therapy available to those who so desperately wish it. This can be especially helpful in the treatment of addiction and recovery, just as it can be very beneficial in the therapeutic care of the victims of trauma.

11

A NEW PARADIGM FOR AMERICAN SOCIETY

SPECIFIC PROPOSALS TO OVERCOME THE EPIDEMIC

Imperative: A Monumental Commitment

On August 16, 2015, the office of the president designated 2.5 million dollars to create an agency director to combat heroin addiction in the Northeast. This fiscal disbursement constituted a portion of the 13.4 million dollars targeted to "areas with high intensity drug trafficking."[1] This is good thinking; however, the total outlay would fund only eighteen souls to attend a facility like Beautiful Shore for eighteen months, the required stay for effective drug rehabilitation.

The enormity of our current narcotics epidemic calls for a commitment to a national emergency equivalent to the World War II Manhattan Project (our four-year race to outpace Germany in the development of the nuclear bomb). Additionally, one might say it is a constitutional imperative for our federal authority to do so. Logically, as a citizenry enters into a national social contract with the main purpose of defending its people, it would follow that if our government is failing to uphold this fundamental obligation, then it is in breach of its central promise and is no government at all.

How to Battle the Drug/Suicide Epidemic

If we were struck with the incursion and contagion of a killer virus, our government would absolutely find a way to halt its spread, discover a cure, and develop a vaccine against it. And drug addiction/death by suicide, likewise, is the invasion of a malefic pestilence that is readily communicable.

Therefore, we should adopt and conduct strict, strong federal measures to vigorously repulse and repress drug importation, manufacture, and marketing, most especially when operated by drug lords and cartels. To halt the supply of drugs, we should proceed in the same manner and with the same urgent dispatch that we would employ to enact successful and decisive protocols aimed at extinguishing a lethal biologic pathogen overspreading our nation.

To prevent overdose, we should effect the national availability of Naloxone (an opioid antagonist designed to rapidly reverse opioid overdose) over the counter without a prescription so that parents and loved ones may have this life-saving medication on hand. Furthermore, they should be instructed by schools and pharmacies as to the proper dose and use of Naloxone either as a liquid for injection or as a nasal spray (known as Narcan), as well as regarding the proper protocol for safeguarding an addict after he or she receives Naloxone until emergency services arrive.

Simultaneously, it is imperative that we develop a truly successful, dual-diagnosis, recovery treatment paradigm for drug addiction and mental health—*essentially a "cure" with a less than 15 percent to 20 percent recidivism rate*—to curtail the consumption of and demand for drugs. As such, individuals suffering from drug addiction should be offered free access to high-caliber, sanitary, and safe inpatient and subsequent halfway house and outpatient treatment-and-recovery programs. And these should provide the new federal prototype, which may include providing medications that help facilitate opioid withdrawal, such as Methadone and Suboxone. Also, these programs should admit patients for a significant length of time, allowing them to achieve valid and permanent healing. In addition, every locale would benefit by establishing "safe stations" (like those developed in Manchester, New Hampshire) where community fire departments furnish potentially lifesaving emergency centers, open 24/7, 365 days per year, providing addicts with instant help by sending them directly to substance disorder treatment centers.[2] This approach is far more beneficial than going to hospital emergency rooms, where addicts will be ejected, usually in less than twelve hours, and put back on the streets to do more drugs and perhaps finally perish.

Furthermore, as prevention programs are crucial to developing a strong resistance to drug addiction, our federal government should require the inclusion of a powerful antidrug educational curriculum in the school system nationwide. This would include talks and lectures by former addicts, along with informational classes (beginning in grammar school) on the manifold mental, emotional, physical, career, relationship, and often life-ending destruction caused by even using drugs a single time. Students must be told that once they start, it will be almost impossible to stop, and their lives will be full of struggle and pain.

Also, the high school level should include security measures such as drug-sniffing dogs and entry/exit surveillance cameras and guards. Detectives have informed me that these measures drastically curtailed the use of drugs in certain New York City suburbs in the late 1970s but have since been abandoned. (Upscale environs do not want to admit they have a drug problem, which could negatively impact property values in their communities.)

And it is time to install in high schools and colleges (and/or readily available nearby) daily Narcotics Anonymous (NA) and Alcoholics Anonymous (AA) meetings specifically designated for young people. In addition, schools should employ in-school one-on-one therapists who specialize in the treatment of personal and family trauma, pastoral counselors (for spiritual as well as psychological support), and dialectical behavioral therapy (DBT) programs that teach mindfulness techniques to aid students in adopting calm reactions and positive solutions to the stresses and challenges of daily life.

Beginning in preschool, institutions of learning and pediatricians should be encouraged to identify and recommend empathic mental health intervention for traumatized children (childhood trauma being one of the surest indicators of later suicidality and drug and alcohol abuse). Not only do the children need therapeutic help, but their parents, who are in a state of stress and confusion, also need to be embraced by the therapeutic "arm" and understood, supported, and given guidance on how to help their child and address the situation as well as their own upheaval and issues.

As an adjunct to intervention and to lessen the need for it, I believe it is vital for mothers and fathers to be offered the opportunity to be enrolled voluntarily in interactive parenting classes, free of charge, from birth through the age of sixteen. This would help prevent children who have not sufficiently mastered a developmental task from dragging that maladjusted behavior into a dysfunctional adulthood. Harkening back to the proposals set forth in chapter 10, the various faiths have much to contribute by establishing listening posts and other programs, such as spiritual extended families, to combat addiction and suicidal depression. In this respect, it would behoove the administration to appoint a national panel composed of government officials, clergy, and mental health experts. Churches could largely fund instruction for the training of spiritual advisors who can also serve as counselors in the areas of substance abuse and mental health. And these members can coalesce for the development of meaningful and effective community programs that address the issues of addiction and depression; further the wholesome education, guidance, and development of children; and provide advice and support for parents and families.

Another avenue of drug resistance would be government-sponsored research into the development of a heroin addiction vaccine.

All these solutions may seem unaffordable, but with the astronomical cost of drug abuse in the United States—estimated at $1 trillion annually and including—the billions spent on the prison system, addiction treatment, and mental health, along with lost earnings and the ballooning socioeconomic cost, "an ounce of prevention is worth a pound of cure."[3]

In view of all the foregoing, we suggest the following.

Twenty Proposed Elements of a Successful Dual-Diagnosis Inpatient Program

We have analyzed, in depth, the many factors involved in achieving successful methods for treating drug addiction, mental distress, and trauma throughout this book. The following is a summary of some proposed components of a paradigm for healing young people (ages 10–30) and providing them with needed supports and something to live for.

1. **Detox from opioids, benzodiazepines, and alcohol**, with the use of Methadone or Suboxone to facilitate opioid withdrawal over a prescribed period of time, where indicated.
2. **One-on-one in-facility psychodynamic psychotherapy**. Provide psychotherapy incorporating the concept of soul therapy and altruistic love with a focus on the true discovery and treatment of trauma and post-traumatic stress disorder (PTSD). These sessions should be conducted at least twice weekly, in forty-five-minute periods, with properly trained, compassionate, identifying, and credentialed psychotherapists. Such therapy is vital to reach and address the underlying emotional issues, negative beliefs, anxieties, and fears particular to each patient. Also, where indicated, the use of eye movement desensitization and reprocessing (EMDR) is recommended to aid in reducing the impact of traumatic material.
3. **Weekly one-on-one private therapy for family members, friends, and significant others**. Design sessions to help

individuals recognize any problems of their own that might be contributing to the patient's self-sabotaging activities and better understand the patient's feelings, beliefs, fears, and struggles and how to help them and communicate more lovingly and effectively.

4. **Constructive weekly private therapy with the patient and his or her family members, friends, and significant others present**. Encourage the patient and his or her loved ones to forge bonds of trust and affection and heal any resentments and counterproductive patterns and behaviors.
5. **Daily in-house Alcoholics Anonymous (AA) and Narcotics Anonymous (NA) meetings.** Provide support groups using these proven recovery methods.
6. **Addiction education**. Offer information concerning the neurology of addiction and all aspects of addiction in general, including how it impacts the various organs of the body and dental health, both near-term and long-term.
7. **Nutrition education**. Teach individuals about proper nutrition and what foods are good for you, and provide patients with a diet that reflects both.
8. **Relapse advocacy**. Teach patients that if they relapse, they should continue their regular recovery routine and "get back on the horse." If you have $100,000 in your bank account and you are missing $10, will you throw out the $100,000, because of the missing $10? Obviously not. So do not throw away all your good work. Keep going and keep pushing to get clean. Do not allow one slipup to slip you up.
9. **Mindfulness and dialectical behavioral therapy (DBT)**. Provide in-house instruction in the rudiments of mindfulness and the proper conduct of DBT as a help to withstand addiction urges when they arise.
10. **Pastoral counseling and religious activity**. Provide the option to receive, as a supplement to biweekly psychotherapy, additional pastoral counseling and private meetings with members of various faiths on a weekly basis, and as often as

requested, along with the opportunity to attend weekly if not daily religious services.

11. **Relaxation techniques**. Give individuals the option of practicing yoga, meditation, and other forms of relaxation and self-calming techniques.
12. **Exercise**. Offer daily scheduled exercise classes, participation in group sports, and daily access to nature and the outdoors as a means of cleansing and renewal.
13. **Pet therapy**. Give each patient the opportunity to be assigned a pet to care for and bond with.
14. **Ongoing, at-level education.** Provide education appropriate to each person's academic standing (including classes in civics, ethics, and human values/virtues) on the high school or undergraduate level. One should be able to earn a degree upon completion and have the opportunity to continue higher education. Also offer job interview training and job securement prior to discharge.
15. **Classes in the creative arts**. Offer exposure to and the chance to be involved in expressive arts, including listening to all types of music and having the opportunity to study voice and learn to play a variety of musical instruments from truly qualified teachers with real and serious tutelage. This is to allow the possibility of discovering a career in music or the joy of singing and/or playing an instrument as a fulfilling avocation. The same applies to instruction in the visual arts, graphics, and dance. Give people something to be sober for, as tragically, some people feel they are all alone in this world (or truly may be).
16. **Training for a trade**. Provide the option of taking professional trade classes in vocational/apprenticeship training and working toward completing certification and licensing where required. Upon release from the facility, arrange positions of employment at supportive work environments.
17. **Medications for diagnosed conditions**. Deliver nonaddictive antianxiety medications, as appropriate, as well as the possibility of using medical marijuana for the treatment of

PTSD and antipsychotic medications (*but only* if the patient agrees that the medications truly help). All such conversations should be a matter of written record, with the patient's review and written signature thereto.

18. **Safety and protocols**. Apply strict safety measures and require stringent adherence in following all medical protocols within the facility.
19. **Legal and medical rights**. Advise patients of their legal and medical rights, along with their right to review their official medical records.
20. **Comprehensive discharge planning**. Create a plan that includes, but is not limited to, the assignment of (1) AA/NA sponsors; (2) out-patient, one-on-one psychotherapists; (3) religious contacts and local pastoral counselors (as arranged by faith representatives within the facility); and (4) psychiatric centers that provide private psychiatric care and group instruction in DBT as well as updated information concerning the locations of AA/NA meetings. Schedule weekly outpatient follow-up for one year by an appointed sponsor from the inpatient facility.

Teaching and Practicing Human Values and Virtue

Even with a successful personal and institutional therapeutic paradigm in place, it will be difficult for an individual to continue any improvement once released from the pod of medical care if the larger environment fosters the contagions of drug addiction and mental distress. We live in a society that no longer teaches or culturally promotes human values and morality, because over time we have lost their roots—our understanding of the true necessity for them (as set forth in chapter 8). So to combat our current drug/suicide epidemic, we need a radical reinvestment in these worthy ideals and principles that existed prior to the mid-1960s and have been especially lacking over the past two decades.

Among the causes to which we attribute the suffering from drug addiction, extreme depression, and an existential chasm is the fact that we have allowed a society to evolve that does not revere, impart, and reinforce the practice of virtue in our personal activities, in our relations to one another, and in our systems, institutions, and government.

Is this why, experiencing their impoverished souls as emptiness, our young people are attempting to constitute themselves—unsuccessfully—with unwholesome elements they think can make them feel good: soulless consumerism and materialism, hedonism to feed the senses, drugs, partying, video gaming, and internet preoccupation?

Yes, hedonism (the opposite of virtue) is the essence of the "feel-good" culture after all: Do what "feels good" and you'll be happy. Aren't you entitled to it? Do anything that makes you feel good. Why stop? Push the envelope and feel even better. And at that point, who cares about anyone else? Isn't it one's right to do as one prefers? There are no "fairness" rules; there are no "requirements" other than to just do whatever you want. The choice is yours, and it's your right! Therefore, it is all fine and justified.

But the tragedy is that this is a false feel-good because these sensually stimulating diversions and rationalizations are not effective—quite the opposite. They are superficial and fleeting; they do not cure the emotional pain of spiritual emptiness in the soul and are ultimately demoralizing and even dangerous. Initially they create a pleasurable "high" and the illusion that one does not need anyone and that one has control, and ironically, that is when the proverbial bubble bursts and one encounters enormous letdown and disillusionment. One finds oneself alone again, and the old feelings return: nonbelonging, meaninglessness, bleakness, desperation, and never-ending unhappiness. This is what "pleasure" yields as opposed to the "happiness" of which Russell Brand speaks.

A New Curriculum for Public Schools

I believe it is vital that human values, morality, and the exercise of virtue be acclaimed in society and taught in our schools once again. Furthermore, I believe nondenominational prayer composed of the religious essentials supportive of a democratic republic and/or moments of silence during the school day for prayer or reflection should be returned to our educational system for the reasons explained in chapter 8. Also, we should encourage philosophical classroom discussions about a creator/higher power and teach about the beliefs of the major religions.

In respect to the importance of classes in virtue, Dr. Mohan Debbarma, head of the Department of Philosophy at Tripura University in India, expresses that "human society may not significantly sustain without human values. . . . And a human values crisis is a known fact of modern society."[4]

Dr. Debbarma points out that human oneness can be achieved only through adherence to human values such as truth, kindness, benevolence, peace, love, dignity, respect, forgiveness, and so on. One might add to these the following virtues (*virtue* defined in the Catechism of the Catholic Church as "a habitual and firm disposition to do the good") to be taught in a grammar school and high school curriculum: faith, hope, charity, chastity, temperance, diligence, patience, compassion, humility, justice, goodness, courage, fortitude, and prudence. Dr. Debbarma also notes the deadly consequences of our current society, where an individual "seems to be valued on the basis of only material things and one's position, and a person without money is not honored by anybody . . . where human beings have become the means for the rich to earn money." He opines that one of the primary causes of crime is "the lack of virtuous people," and he is another person who argues for an educational system providing instruction in values.[5]

Additionally, I believe that our institutions of learning should tutor students, once again, in civics, with an emphasis on the importance of a citizenry that actively monitors legislation, curtails if not eliminates the activities of lobbyists, and dedicates itself to the preservation of democracy. In addition, they should be taught the importance of consideration for others through classes in ethics and morals. Most importantly, these expressions and actions that we would encourage should be represented by the teachers' own practice of those behaviors toward others. We are all in this together.

Mahatma Gandhi gave us a simple but incisive analysis and implied recommendation named the "Seven Dangers to Human Virtue":

1. Wealth without work
2. Pleasure without conscience
3. Knowledge without character
4. Business without ethics
5. Science without humanity
6. Religion without sacrifice
7. Politics without principle[6]

Young people in high school should be offered classes on morality and responsibility as virtues.

With all the struggles and dangers that befall children born out of wedlock and raised by single moms, kids need to be warned and scared into responsibility when it comes to sex and pregnancy. Yes, provide access to condoms, but also stress abstinence before marriage and teach that young men and women should treat themselves and each other with consideration and respect. Also, teach that true love and monogamy are the way to fulfilling, supportive, and happy partnerships that sustain us through the challenges of the decades, including illness and financial adversity, and enable us to build loving families and joyful lives.

Furthermore, in order to have an informed citizenry with the ability to think critically, we need a truly egalitarian approach to education in which the curriculum and teachers are of a comparable caliber in every locale in the nation. And we should return to the study of the Great Books series, reading the finest works of literature, philosophy, and political thought, geared to the precollege level, in every high school in the country. Classes should teach geography, world history, the causes and components of the rise and fall of empires, the clash of good and evil in humankind, and the struggle over time to achieve American democracy today.

One might think that if our system were more illuminating, qualitative, and absorbing that students might feel more involved and proud of their work, be more inspired and motivated, and have a higher sense of self-esteem. And as a bonus, there would be much less time and opportunity for or interest in social media, online pornography, and some of the other ills previously discussed.

As an example, I can cite the experiences of numerous parents with children at various universities with demanding curricula: the students work very hard, have little free time, and are tired but very happy, proud of their accomplishments, and appreciative of their learning. And they have no time to get into trouble.

I also believe it is a fundamental spiritually fulfilling and civilizing influence for all students to be exposed to classical music, arts, and the performing arts. Here they may discover talents and a joy they thought only belonged to the "elites" and could never be a part of their world; they might learn that they have been born with more innate abilities that are yet to be developed. But for this interest and gift to be realized, they must have exposure and opportunity.

Proposals for Reforms in Mental Hospitals, Rehabilitation Centers, Therapeutic Schools, and Insurance Coverage

Many patients have died as the result of being released from psychiatric centers or rehabs within scant time periods because insurance companies refused to pay for further inpatient treatment. Therefore, it should be unacceptable for insurance companies to discontinue in-facility coverage for psychiatric patients within three to five days or even two to three weeks after admission. The effective therapeutic protocol of the late 1970s required that people afflicted with mental conditions be allowed to remain in a hospital for up to one year, with significant, compassionate one-on-one therapy, until they were actually cured, and addicts entered residential rehab for no fewer than eighteen months. These paradigms worked. Therefore, insurance companies should be required to cover inpatient rehab or mental hospital stays of at least nine months to one year. And mental hospitals and rehab centers have been complicit in not vociferously and vigorously protesting the current lack of proper and adequate care.

Furthermore, the data indicate that many health insurers have ignored the federal Mental Health Parity and Addiction Equity Act of 2008 (the "Parity Act") in that they force patients and the parents of patients to pay out of pocket for treatment for mental health and substance abuse in comparison to other conditions. The findings of a national study are as follows:

"In 2015, behavioral care was four to six times more likely to be provided out-of-network than medical or surgical care. Insurers paid primary care providers 20 percent more for the same types of care than they paid addiction and mental health care experts." Meanwhile, state statistics vary widely; for example, "in New Jersey, 45 percent of office visits for behavioral health care were out-of-network. In Washington D.C., it was 63 percent."[7]

This is disgusting when one considers our nationwide epidemic and the fatality statistics. We must demand immediate compliance with the Parity Act and punitive measures against those who have failed to comply.

Mental hospitals, rehabs, and therapeutic schools (collectively, "treatment centers") should receive stiff monetary penalties for any single incident of a breach of medical protocol that might cost the life of a patient or cause severe regression, whether such harm results or not. The failure to strictly follow medical rules should never be tolerated, and when discovered, it should be penalized severely as a deterrent.

In addition, all treatment centers should provide respectful, caring and dutiful therapists and administrators, all trained in CPR and the proper administration of life-saving medications, with excellent academic and clinical education and experience.

The health care providers on site should be of a total number that is optimal for ministering to the number of patients in the facility. Furthermore, each center should have highly trained 24-hour medical staff, on hand regular maintenance pharmaceuticals and emergency antiopiate overdose medications, crisis asthma medicines and treatments, as well as streamlined procedures in place for immediate access to nearby quality emergency services and trauma centers.

The preadmission explanation of insurance coverage by treatment centers to patients and parents of patients should be both verbal and written. If the health care company fails to pay in accordance with the treatment center's representations, then the treatment center should be required to honor its (mis)representations. This would put an end to the bait-and-switch practices by which dishonest treatment centers lure in patients, promising that their stays will be covered and only later informing them (after one week or so) that the insurance will not remit, and they have an accounting of some $12,000 with a three- to five-day notice requirement that adds another $3,000 to $5,000 to the bill.

Treatment centers should not be permitted to ask any patient, parent, guardian, or other family member to sign away any of their rights or make any sort of promise that relieves the treatment center of liability; nor should anyone be pressured into any kind of psychiatric or other kind of treatment.

Firm consequences should be imposed upon any treatment center that (1) fails to forward the mail or emails of patients, immediately, as requested by a patient, (2) neglects to inform a patient's family/significant others when he or she is unwell, suffering distress, or has been attacked or injured within a facility by anybody, including staff, whether the patient has requested such notification or not, and/or (3) prevents a patient from contacting his or her family/significant others, for any or no reason, immediately upon asking. Significantly, any treatment center that does not attend immediately, thoroughly, and correctly to the medical illness, injury, or crisis of a patient should be subject to punishment, regardless whether any damage was ultimately suffered by the patient.

These practical suggestions are but a few proposals and only point to a direction for change. Assuredly many others will have numerous additional recommendations.

The Support of Marriage and Family

As discussed throughout the book, we need to acknowledge that the swift rise in drug addiction and suicidality parallels the rapid decline of both the nuclear family and the extended family in the United States. Therefore, it is vital that we, as a culture, recognize the necessity to support the survival of the married, two-parent household by creating a tax structure and social milieu that will encourage wedlock and permit one working adult to support a family of two children in a financially sustainable and wholesome manner while a spouse remains at home to raise them. Also, the plight of single parents needs to be addressed with humane after-school community and denominational child-assistance projects in a fiscally helpful way. Parenthood needs to be valued by our society and supported, and the concept of the extended family must be encouraged and promoted.

Additional family empowerment and hope will come through the establishment of programs that foster socioeconomic mobility, moving out of poverty and into a growing and thriving middle class. And this comes only with equal opportunity and excellence of education in every locale, vocational training that includes certification and licensure, resultant jobs, and the sense of accomplishment and stability provided thereby. When individuals and families are productively engaged in activities that enable them to envision and create a meaningful and secure future, they are not as likely to develop addictions or remain stressed and depressed. To this end, the implementation of charter schools (including parochial schools), trade and career apprenticeships, and free or highly affordable community and state colleges should be a part of the solution here as it is in other developed countries. Also, we should have programs to retrain adults in trades and careers for which there is both near and long-term demand, such as IT, various aspects of the health care field, and other areas.

No Incarceration of Low-Level Offender Drug Addicts

The majority of drug addicts are people in unendurable mental, emotional, psychological, and sometimes also physical pain, who are using illegal substances to try to relieve it. They are most often the suffering victims of early childhood trauma, sexual abuse (especially in the case of female addicts), psychical anguish, and/or the product of devastating socioeconomics. And they are regularly abused a second time by a failed mental health care system and then frequently a third time by our brutal industrial prison complex. In this regard, our country's addict imprisonment/penal system business is extremely costly to tax payers financially and soul-crushing to so many parents who may not see their locked-away children for another ten to twenty to thirty years. And let us not forget the unconscionable divide between the sentencing of black and white youths in this country, and from one geographical location to another. And the pain of trauma, without compassionate and truly healing intervention, only leads to more and worse forms of trauma. But we are smarter and better than that, and it does not have to be this way.

No one wants to be a drug addict. It makes no sense to send people to jail for their illness and traumatization. Instead of paying $40 billion per year on arresting and incarcerating low-level offender addicts (not to mention the $49 billion spent yearly on foreign aid, in some cases to countries that are major drug exporters), let's use this money to place these people in truly effective long-term treatment programs of healing, provide them with an education and/or trade, and give them jobs. Therefore, judges should have the option of considering each individual and his or her unique story, medical and psychiatric conditions, and overall circumstances rather than being forced to adhere to mandatory minimum sentencing. Also, the prison terms of those already incarcerated should be subject to case review, with an examination of their personal history, and reduced where appropriate. They should also be given the opportunity to meet with pastoral counselors on a daily basis. Furthermore, after an individual's time is served, his prison record should be wiped clean. Logically, if his incarceration account must follow him everywhere for the rest of his life, it will be nearly impossible for him to find meaningful employment and live a happy, fulfilling, and productive life. And this will set him up to fail again, as it will cause despair, leading him back to addiction and even to crime to feed his self-medication, or as the only way to make a living.

No Discrimination

To guard against anyone—including co-op boards, employers, condo boards, landlords, schools, businesses, and so on—who discriminates or administers organizational rules in an unequal manner to any person who is disabled, the victim of rape or any other form of abuse, or suffering from drug addiction (as long as he or she is not proven to be dealing drugs or using drugs for which he or she has no medical prescription), there needs to be a strongly monitored system that requires an immediate end to such discriminatory actions and imposes stiff fines as punishment.

Confronting a Culture of Corruption

The deaths of our young people also are occurring because of a culture of corruption, as illustrated in many instances throughout this book (such as kickbacks for referrals to treatment facilities and political manipulation by the lobbying industry). All this generates inaction, which engenders hopelessness and defeatism.

An additional example of a kickback system is the money allegedly paid to flop house landlords for sending their tenants (mostly drug addicts and alcoholics packed in bunches of six into one filthy, bug-infested room) to designated drug treatment facilities located in the various boroughs of New York City. The proprietors of these flop houses demand that these vulnerable and indigent residents (many sincerely striving for sobriety) relapse so that they will test positive for drugs or alcohol. Thus they will be entered for group treatment sessions in facilities that will receive their Medicaid funding. They must provide the landlord with slips of attendance or he will not get paid his "referral fee," and if they refuse, he will throw them out on the street. He gets his kickback, or these poor souls get kicked out. Evidently, the practice is widespread.[8]

With respect to confronting the lobbying industry, John Lavitt asks on "TheFix.com," "Why Are the Government and Big Pharma Ignoring the Heroin Addiction Vaccine? Is it because there's No Profit in Saving Junkies?"[9]

Nonetheless, one sign of encouragement is the recent lawsuit brought by the state of Ohio, filed May 31, 2017, against five major drug companies for "fueling the opioid epidemic."[10] The total human devastation has finally made it almost impossible to ignore the corruption any longer. One can only hope that this is the opening salvo in a full-out fight against the stranglehold of lobbying in America. It is a battle that we must win to take back our democratic power and save the lives of our children and others.

Spirituality, Virtue, and Changing the Culture

In September 2011, *New York Times* columnist David Brooks wrote about the lack of a concept of morality among youth. Brooks reported on the findings of a research team, led by Notre Dame sociologist Christian Smith, who were shocked at discovering that there was an almost complete absence of moral thinking among the young people whom they interviewed.[11] Was this surprising? We are social animals, we exist in a collective cytoplasm, and we thrive or die based on the quality of our shared, expressed beliefs and actions.

By way of contrast, at the Catholic school I attended, we were exhorted to engage in a nightly "examination of conscience" and instructed to ask ourselves how we could improve as individuals the next day. We would resolve to improve our inner souls and our outward behaviors and make amends and contribute to a better world. As noted by the second-century scholar and theologian Origen of Alexandria, "Conscience is the chamber of justice." However, according to the National Catholic Educational Association, US Catholic school enrollment reached its peak in the early 1960s, when there were more than 5.2 million students in almost thirteen thousand schools across the nation. In 2016–17, US Catholic school enrollment was 1,878,824 students, with only 6,429 Catholic schools—a sharp drop off, especially when considering the rapid growth in the overall population.[12] Morality is taught in Catholic schools today, but to much fewer students, and when there is a much greater need.

We require a society that encourages principled mores, spirituality, and conscience—one that urges us to realize our individual potentials so that we may pursue worthy purposes and be led to making our unique contributions toward fulfilling and loving lives for ourselves, our families, and society in general, resulting in happiness.

Furthermore, as we work toward and expect an improved national culture, each family must contribute by adopting a more responsible family state of being that includes loving ways, attention, empathy, communication, thoughtful guidance, and respect, along with the aim of being and doing what is virtuous and good.

If we allow our culture and families to exist without strong moral guidelines—to be an amorphous place called America, where many feel that life is meaningless because almost anything goes and nobody cares enough to stand guard, correct wrongdoings, and do the right thing for everyone—it will not survive. It will crumble from within and will fall prey to outside evil and determined forces that are waiting to take over weak and unguarded entities. Like deadly viruses and cancers, they will easily infiltrate and appropriate with their own sick agendas. Then no one will have any rights, and no one's freedoms will be protected.

To turn the tide and prevent this from happening, we need to rekindle our faith in the Creator and our dedication to the founding human values that established our nation and demanded each individual's conscientious political participation as the safeguard of our liberties. We need to evolve spiritually and truly relate to one another with charity, understanding, active compassion, and positive encouragement. This is our challenge and our basic duty for our children, for our country, and for humanity.

afterword

WHERE WE ARE NOW

IN JENNY'S OWN WORDS

It is the beginning of February 2017, and January was a brutal month, on so many levels, for so many people. I am on the phone with Jenny, who has just called me from her $700-per-month, bedbug-infested, small room in a rundown, leaning beach house in tri-state land. In addition to her wildly dangerous and decadent flatmates (whom even Jenny and her raver friends find very scary), some shadowy, unnamed "residents" pay just to sleep on a floor-level plastic couch in the kitchen and silently disappear in the morning, while others live in the attic with the roll-down ladder. They sell whatever they can and do what they have to do to survive. The city is full of "Fantines."

Reminiscent of her expressions of shock, fear, and powerlessness over the increasing number of acquaintances dying last year at this same time, Jenny calls me, very upset, in the early morning hours: "Listen, Mom . . . too many losses . . . I have never seen anything like this before. We lost nine people last week, two in a car crash and seven from overdoses." Jenny is speaking about her circle of New York raver and heavy metal friends.

It started the week before, when Jenny had telephoned me at 2 a.m., sobbing that a lovely twenty-year-old friend of hers, James, who lived in the suburbs, had passed away from a Xanax overdose. His mother had entered his room in the morning, only to find her son not just resting in his bed but dead in his sleep. Horrible.

"I know how it happened," Jenny told me. "The dealers sell the Xanax like six in a batch or it is not worth it for them to drop it off to you, and you build up a tolerance, and then you swallow too many all at once. He took too much. He was the sweetest guy, and so young." Jenny was completely shaken and, I had sensed, in peril. I am fully aware that Jenny uses street Xanax in addition to marijuana in an effort to manage her overwhelming anxiety; however, she tells me that she buys only one Xanax at a time and that her dealer will do that because he is dropping off marijuana in the same delivery. I hope that she is telling me the truth, but I can never be sure, and street Xanax is cheaper than marijuana. Also, I warn Jenny that much of the street Xanax is now laced with Fentanyl, which is fifty times more potent than heroin, and sometimes Carfentanil, which is even more powerful than Fentanyl. I tell her that Xanax users are dying after taking only one or two pills, unaware that it is contaminated with these extremely powerful opioids.

And part of the addiction problem that is not being addressed is that psychiatrists are prescribing loads of Xanax and Klonopin to young people, on a constant basis, for treatment of ever-accelerating anxiety (sometimes ninety pills in one prescription), which increases the risk of accidental or intentional fatality. Then patients become heavily addicted to these pills, which they take in greater and greater numbers and oftentimes mix with alcohol. By contrast, I have never heard of anyone overdosing on marijuana, and it may be considered that with so many teens and young people suffering from debilitating angst in our stress-ridden society, the use of marijuana may be preferable and safer. The best solution, of course, would be the development of nonaddictive antianxiety medications that could be delivered in a manner that precludes overdose.

I have illustrated throughout this book the impossibility of my stopping Jenny from doing what she is doing once my guardianship was taken away. I can only reach out to her on a daily basis via text and be available to her with my love, in her hours of need, to help her and save her from destruction.

When Jenny had called me to tell me about Miguel, I had felt that she was in copycat peril, so I stayed on the phone with her from 2 a.m. to 6 a.m., and throughout much of that same day, trying to cheer her up and distract her. Two days later, I was informed that a high school senior had died of a heroin overdose in Round Bridge but that the town was trying not to let the story get around. Indeed, there seemed to be nothing reported in the papers or on the internet. At this same time, there had been two suicides in a nearby county, one following the other, in parroting syndrome, within a fortnight. Both young men had attended the same prep school and threw themselves in front of their commuter train line. On the phone now, I make sure not to tell Jenny about the recent heroin overdose in Round Bridge or about the two suicides.

Jenny is in a panic and is desperate for answers: "Mom, what is going on? Why is this happening? There is something wrong out there; there is something very dark out there. It's very dark. This is the worst I have ever seen it. What's going on? Why is this happening to everyone around me? What is wrong with me? Why? Why?"

I think about it and I wonder if I should tell Jenny my honest opinion, and I decide that I will, even if she does not like my answer:

"It is happening because no one believes in God anymore. Values and morality are just old words. Spirituality is absent from our lives. And by God, I do not mean the doctrinaire God of organized religions, social conformity, punitive judgment, and dogmatic rules and prescriptions. By God, I mean the feeling of the spirit of God—goodness—that you experience when awestruck by indescribable beauty in nature, the smile of a newly born baby, the purity of newly fallen, glistening snow . . .

"There is no longer a commonly valued way to be or a way to live that is upheld by society and culture as being a respectable and honorable way, a dependable way to aspire to, made up of truth and not deception and make-believe, a way to live that is beneficent, worthy, loving, and ethical. At this point in my life, I believe that the right way of being and living involves love of family and friends and benevolence toward others, built upon a loving trust in a higher power of pure spirit that suffuses our lives, before which we are humble as we strive to improve ourselves and our lot. It implies having healthy goals and aspirations to be more virtuous and loving—understanding, generous, kind, compassionate, honest—more grateful, joyful, and appreciative while being present in the moments of our life. I am sure this sounds like just an almost meaningless and impossible list of adjectives, but can we imagine a person who might be described in this way? At one time, many people fit the description. This is absent from our lives today. Everyone is running or scurrying . . ." Jenny, for once, is not interrupting and is listening—somewhat dismayed, but listening.

"Also, a world in which people feel free to be themselves and are not subject to the stress of vain uberachievement and rivalry, not slaves to selfie perfectionism, appearances, and money-making conformity. Free of feeling that no one wants to know the real person who may be vulnerable, sensitive, different, and sweet. Not a cold-blooded competitor, not a warrior . . . but just a nice person who wants to live a nice life."

But There Is More

I receive a text from Jenny at 2:30 a.m., three days later. She writes that she is too agitated to fall asleep. I try calling her, knowing that she needs to talk, but she does not want to speak on the phone and will only communicate via text messages.

JENNY: I can't fall asleep. I have no pot. My anxiety is out of control. Idk what to do, like I feel so unsettled. I only slept four hours today. This sucks!. . . . I'm just trying to hold on until I get to you in a few days. It's cold outside . . . This is very strenuous. Especially with my lungs. I'm just really messed up. I have anxiety, like, really bad.

ME: You should come out and stay with me first thing in the morning . . . It will all be OK, things are getting better, and God willing, you can build a new life and have a new start.

JENNY: Mom, I start breaking down without anything to calm me down. I've been smoking pot every day for the last nine months. When I don't have it, I get nervous . . . I act like a traumatized person . . . I can't function normally, and I get nervous and scared . . . I don't trust anyone . . . I was crazy when I was younger . . . I was, and the psychiatrists say that once you are crazy, you can never get well . . . but it's not true because I fought my way back . . . but I can't feel, or the feelings will overcome me . . . the traumas will overcome me . . . I worry that I have been through too much . . . But I was not really crazy. It was all the trauma, and that is different.

ME: Jenny, honey, you will heal and get better . . . I understand how you feel.

JENNY: I know you understand, Mom. You are the only person I can talk to . . . no one else wants to listen . . . This world is so cruel . . . I know that you live in constant pain . . . I know the pain that you live in . . . I can't be calm. I'm weird, Mom. And my lungs are being destroyed.

ME: You need to tell me what is making you so anxious.

JENNY: And I don't talk to anyone about anything I feel ever . . . Bcuz it doesn't serve me good . . . But I can't make them go away without distractions . . . I can't make the nightmares go away. I can't make my head stop from filling with such great sadness . . . unless I'm completely mildly calmed down.

ME: I understand, I do . . . You can know that I love you so much . . . and want to hear everything you have to say.

JENNY: I've gotten myself to be completely normal . . . But only if I can shut the traumas off . . . Sometimes when you go through too much . . . you can't just make them stop.

ME: Yes, and you need to be able to shut them down until you can modulate them . . . and with exercise, activities, therapy, and interim antianxiety medication and other forms of help, you will be able to.

JENNY: It's hard. I'm trying so hard. Nobody realizes how hard I work on being normal. And now it's coming down to a point where it's a sick game of "would you rather breathe or face your anxiety?" And it's really breaking me down . . . And I'm scared. And I don't feel like I'm allowed to be scared . . . And feeling scared makes me more scared . . . Mom, you don't get it . . . What if there's just no way to make them stop?

ME: There is a way . . . and in the meantime, you need help . . .

JENNY: Everything makes me nervous. Nobody realizes how scared I really am. I don't let myself feel anymore. And I can't take it. I'm losing it.

ME: You need to come out here and stay with me if you want to, even before I am able to sell this place. I don't give a damn about the board. You come first.

JENNY: It's really hard to keep it together all the time. I can't ever tell in my life who wants me for what . . . You're the only person that loves me. You're the only person I trust. The more I learn about people, the more afraid I am. I'm so afraid.

ME: I understand.

Jenny finally calls me on the phone to talk, and for the first five minutes, she cries into the phone, gulping and gasping for air: "Mom . . . Mommmmmmm. . . . Mom . . . Mommmmmmmmmmm. I am having a panic attack like I did when I was a very little girl. You thought I hated you. . . . I didn't. I longed for you so much, and the nannies used to prevent me from going to see you . . . They tackled me and barred me and said that you were studying, and I could not interrupt you. . . . So then later, when you finally came home to be with me . . . I did not know how to behave . . .

All that early blocking programming was there . . . And when you were with me, when you were working, you would say, 'It is my duty to educate you,' and you would teach me and spend your time doing class work with me and then go back to work. But, Mom, I never got the attention and love that I needed . . . I never got to play with you . . . I never got just to *be me* . . . just to *be* with you . . . enjoying each other's company with no pressure and just being loved for just being me and spending play time together. And that's why I acted out when I was a teenager . . . looking for that attention in all the wrong ways and all the wrong places . . . feeling so rejected by everyone but you in my family . . . bullied at school . . . and I knew you loved me, but you were never there . . . and I did not know how to interpret that because the bottom line was even though you had to go to work. . . . I needed you." I know it's true and that Jenny so needed to be able to say all of this.

Jenny is weeping profusely, and I am amazed at her insight and feel the depths of sorrow for all that she has suffered. That cannot be changed, but I am determined to strive for her substantial healing in the future, to give Jenny all the well-being that she deserves.

"You know, Mom. There is something out there. Something greater than us. You can feel it. Hope is fear in reverse. I want to help people. Truth just 'is'; there is no perception. Truth is just truth."

We continue talking about life and the world, and Jenny tells me two hours after calling that she is finally tired now and will try to sleep and that she loves me—that she always loved me so greatly, so intensely, so much.

Rebirth

It is July 2017, and Jenny and I are still a work in progress, but our relationship has come a very long way. I, myself, have undergone changes through the exceptional struggles borne to save Jenny. We are not the people we were seven years ago, or even a lifetime ago. We are transformed, we are becoming the people who we were always meant to be, and we have a close and caring bond.

Jenny is mostly thoughtful, empathic, and loving. On my birthday, Jenny writes me a beautiful card: "You are the sweetest mother a daughter could ever hope for. You've never given up on me and always picked me up when I fell. You are a soldier in the front line of my army and my hero. You are my angel, my protector, my leader, and my light in a dark room. I love you so much. Thank you for being you, so I can be me."

I feel that my heart will burst with love and gratitude, and I also feel humbled before the profoundly good and forgiving person Jenny is and so proud of her for all that she has come through with such great courage. I am so deeply indebted to God for never leaving us because I know there is no way we came through this on our own.

Jenny has goals and is working in the hope of achieving them, at her own pace, and with authenticity and passion. And we both acknowledge that finding our faith in a loving creator, and the power of prayer, has made all this possible. We also know that Jenny, as she moves forward, will become more self-sufficient, autonomous, and independent of me. That will happen as well, as it should.

Being realistic, I know that one can expect regressive trends in life, but if one should occur, I am confident that we will overcome it again, with the help of God.

BIBLIOGRAPHY

Alcoholics Anonymous World Services Inc. *Alcoholics Anonymous: The Story of How Many Thousands of Men and Women Have Recovered from Alcoholism*. New York: Alcoholics Anonymous World Services Inc., 2001.

Amorth, Gabriele. *An Exorcist Explains the Demonic*. Manchester, NH: Sophia Institute Press, 2016.

Andreasen, N. C. "Body and Soul." *American Journal of Psychiatry* 153, no. 5 (1996): 589–90.

Anzieu, Didier. *The Skin Ego: A Psychoanalytic Approach to the Self.* New Haven: Yale University Press, 1989.

Armstrong, David, and Evan Allen. "The Addict Brokers: Middlemen Profit as Desperate Patients Are Treated Like Paychecks." *Boston Globe*, May 28, 2017.

Armstrong, Doree, and Micelle Ma. "Researcher Controls Colleague's Motions in 1st Human Brain-to-Brain Interface." *UW News*, August 27, 2013.

Bach, Sheldon. *Narcissistic States and the Therapeutic Process*. New York: Jason Aronson, 1977.

Barker, Kim. "The Choice for Recovering Addicts: Relapse or Homelessness." *New York Times*, May 31, 2015.

Beasley, Violet E. *The Role of Memory in the Poetry of Alfred Lord Tennyson*. Simcoe, ON: Davus, 2010.

Beller, Hava Kohav, dir. *The Restless Conscience* (film). Santa Monica, CA: Docurama, 1993.

Brand, Russell. *Recovery: Freedom from Our Addictions*. New York: Henry Holt, 2017.

Brooks, David. "If It Feels Right." *New York Times*, September 12, 2011.

Buckholtz, Allison. “Help from Above: In Times of Trouble, Growing Numbers of People Take Comfort in Faith-Based Therapy.” *Washington Post*, December 6, 2005.

Cidambi, Indra. “Actual Cost of Drug Abuse in the U.S. Tops $1 Trillion Annually.” PsychologyToday.com, August 10, 2017. https://www.psychologytoday.com/us/blog/sure-recovery/201708/actual-cost-drug-abuse-in-us-tops-1-trillion-annually.

Clegg, Bill. *Portrait of an Addict as a Young Man: A Memoir*. New York: Back Bay Books, 2011.

Culliford, Larry. “Spirituality for Beginners 8: Soul and Spirit.” PsychologyToday.com, June 14, 2012. https://www.psychologytoday.com/blog/spiritual-wisdom-secular-times/201206/spirituality-beginners-8-soul-and-spirit.

Davidowitz, Seth Stephen. “How Googling Unmasks Child Abuse.” *New York Times*, July 13, 2013.

Day, Franklin. “The Future of Psychoanalysis and Religion.” *Psychoanalytic Quarterly* 13 (1944): 84–92.

Debbarma, Mohan. “Importance of Human Values in the Society.” *IJELIH: International Journal of English Language, Literature and Humanities* 2, no. 1 (April 2014): 181–95.

De Forest, Izette. “The Therapeutic Technique of Sandor Ferenczi.” *International Journal of Psychoanalysis* 23 (1942): 120–39.

deMause, Lloyd. “The History of Child Abuse.” *Journal of Psychohistory* 25, no. 3 (Winter 1998): 216–36.

de Tocqueville, Alexis. *Democracy in America: The Complete and Unabridged Volumes I and II.* New York: Bantam Dell, 2002.

Dwyer, Collin. “Ohio Sues 5 Major Drug Companies for ‘Fueling Opioid Epidemic.’” The Two-Way, National Public Radio, May 31, 2017.

Engle, Jonah. “Merchants of Meth: How Big Pharma Keeps the Cooks in Business.” *Mother Jones*, July/August 2013.

Erickson, Erik H. *Childhood and Society*. New York: W. W. Norton, 1993.

Euripides. *Hecuba*. Trans. Edward P. Coleridge. Great Books of the Western World. Chicago: Encyclopedia Britannica, 1952.

Fagan, Patrick. "Why Religion Matters: The Impact of Religious Practice on Social Stability." The Heritage Foundation, January 25, 1996. http://www.heritage.org/civil-society/report/why-religion-matters-the-impact-religious-practice-social-stability.

Feldman, Brian. "Do I Dare to Eat a Tide Pod?" NYMag.com, January 19, 2018. http://nymag.com/selectall/2018/01/why-are-people-eating-tide-pods.html.

Fenichel, Otto. *The Psychoanalytic Theory of Neurosis*. New York: W. W. Norton, 1945.

Ferenczi, Sandor. "Confusion of Tongues between Adult and the Child: The Language of Tenderness and of Passion." *International Journal of Psychoanalysis* 30 (1949): 196–206.

Field, Tim. *Bully in Sight: Overcoming the Silence and Denial by which Abuse Thrives*. London: Bantam Press, 1994.

Florida, Richard. "The Geography of Middle Class Decline." Citylab.com, November 15, 2016. https://www.citylab.com/life/2016/11/the-geography-of-middle-class-decline/505769/.

Forman, Mark D. *A Guide to Integral Psychotherapy: Complexity, Integration and Spirituality in Practice*. Albany: State University of New York Press, 2010.

Freud, Sigmund. *The Aetiology of Hysteria*. In *Collected Papers*, vol. 1, pp. 182–219. London: Hogarth Press, 1948.

———. *Beyond the Pleasure Principle*. In *The Standard Edition of the Complete Psychological Works of Sigmund Freud*, vol. 18, pp. 3–64. London: Hogarth Press, 1955.

———. *The Future of an Illusion*. In *The Standard Edition of the Complete Psychological Works of Sigmund Freud*, vol. 21, pp. 5–56. London: Hogarth Press, 1961.

Friedman, Dan. "Obama Official Unveils Plan to Fight Heroin Use." *New York Daily News*, August 17, 2015.

Fromm, Erich. *The Anatomy of Human Destructiveness*. New York: Holt, 1992.

Galanter, Marc, Zoran Josipovic, Helen Dermatis, Jochen Weber, and Mary-Alice Millard. "An Initial fMRI Study on Neural

Correlates of Prayer in Members of Alcoholics Anonymous." *American Journal of Drug and Alcohol Abuse* 43, no. 1 (March 25, 2016): 44–54. doi:10.3109/00952990.2016.1141912.

Garnier, Terace. "South Carolina Church Uses Bible and Prayer to Help Faithful Fight Opioid Addiction." *Fox News*, November 14, 2017.

Gandhi, Mohandas K. *Autobiography: The Story of My Experiments with Truth*. Mineola, NY: Dover Publications, 1983.

Gilbert, Martin. *Churchill: A Life*. New York: Henry Holt, 1991.

Gold, Jenny. "Health Insurers Are Still Skimping on Mental Health Coverage." NPR.org, November 30, 2017. https://www.npr.org/sections/health-shots/2017/11/29/567264925/health-insurers-are-still-skimping-on-mental-health-coverage.

Gruppo di Preghiera Padre Pio. "A Thought for Each Day of the Year—November." Evangelizzare.org, November 2, 2010. http://www.evangelizzare.org/2010/11/a-thought-for-each-day-of-the-year-november/.

Hatton, Celia. "The Ketamine Connection." BBC.co.uk, July 10, 2015. http://www.bbc.co.uk/news/resources/idt-bc7d54e7-88f6-4026-9faa-2a36d3359bb0.

Herman, Judith. *Trauma and Recovery: The Aftermath of Violence—from Domestic Abuse to Political Terror*. New York: Basic Books, 1992.

Hoffman, Peter. "The Last Days of Tennessee Williams." *New York Magazine*, July 1983.

"How Many People Are Watching Porn Right Now? (Hint: It's a Lot)." fightthenewdrug.org, September 11, 2017. https://fightthenewdrug.org/by-the-numbers-see-how-many-people-are-watching-porn-today/.

Human Unlimited. "Gandhi's 7 Dangers to Human Virtue." October 18, 2015. https://www.humanunlimited.com/blogs/blog/71610627-gandhi-s-7-dangers-to-human-virtue.

Johnson, Judith. "Teens Addicted to Social Media." HuffPost blog, April 15, 2016. https://www.huffingtonpost.com/judith-johnson/teens-addicted-to-social-_b_9696378.html.

Jula, Megan. "How Staten Island's Drug Problem Made It a Target for Poaching Patients," *New York Times*, August 23, 2016.

Kaysen, Susanna. *Girl, Interrupted*. New York: Vintage, 1994.

Kelley, John. "Antidepressants: Do They 'Work' or Don't They?" *Scientific American*, March 2, 2010. https://www.scientificamerican.com/article/antidepressants-do-they-work-or-dont-they/.

Kim, Victoria. "China Wants to Ban Ketamine, World Health Organization Disagrees." TheFix.com, March 18, 2015. https://www.thefix.com/content/china-wants-ban-ketamine-world-health-organization-disagrees.

Koenig, Harold G. "Science Proves the Healing Power of Prayer." *NewsmaxHealth*, March 31, 2015. https://www.newsmax.com/t/health/article/635623.

Kramer, Stanley, dir. *Judgment at Nuremberg* (film). USA: Roxlom Films, 1961.

Kubler-Ross, Elisabeth, and David Kessler. *On Grief and Grieving*. New York: Scribner, 2005.

Lavitt, John. "No Profit in Junkies New Heroin Vaccine Ignored." TheFix.com, June 2, 2014. https://www.thefix.com/content/no-human-trials-damn-junkies-story-promising-heroin-vaccine-ignored?page=all.

Leonard, Kimberly. "Study: Most Antidepressants Don't Work on Teens or Kids." USNews.com, June 8, 2016. https://www.usnews.com/news/articles/2016-06-08/study-most-antidepressants-dont-work-on-kids-or-teens.

Levine, Howard B., ed. *Adult Analysis and Childhood Sexual Abuse*. Hillsdale, NJ: Analytic Press, 1990.

Lewis, C. S. *The Lion, the Witch and the Wardrobe*. New York: HarperCollins, 2008.

———. *Mere Christianity*. London: Collins, 1952. Reprint, New York: HarperCollins, 2001.

———. *The Screwtape Letters: A Devil's Diabolical Advice for the Capturing of the Human Heart*. New York: HarperOne, 2015.

Linehan, M. M. *Skills Training Manual for Treating Borderline Personality Disorder*. New York: Guildford, 1993.

Lisle, McIntire William. *The Evolution of Spiritual Man*. Boston: Silver, Burdett, 1894.

Livingston, Gretchen. "Fewer Than Half of U.S. Kids Today Live in a 'Traditional' Family." *Pew Research Center*, Fact Tank Blog, 2015. http://www.pewresearch.org/fact-tank/2014/12/22/less-than-half-of-u-s-kids-today-live-in-a-traditional-family/.

Lorentz, Konrad. *The Waning of Humaneness*. Boston: Little, Brown, 1987.

Mack, John E., and Steven L. Ablon, eds. *The Development and Sustaining of Self Esteem in Childhood*. New York: International Universities Press, 1983.

Mahler, Margaret S., Fred Pine, and Anni Bergman. *The Psychological Birth of the Human Infant: Symbiosis and Individuation*. New York: Basic Books, 1975.

Masson, Jeffrey Moussiaef, trans. and ed. *The Complete Letters of Sigmund Freud to Wilhelm Fliess, 1887–1904*. Cambridge, MA: Belknap Press, 1985.

Masterson, James F. *The Search for the Real Self: Unmasking the Personality Disorders of Our Age*. New York: Free Press, 1988.

Maté, Gabor. *Scattered: How Attention Deficit Disorder Originates and What You Can Do About It*. New York: Plume, 2000.

Mattoon, Mary Ann. *Jungian Psychology in Perspective*. New York: Free Press, 1985.

Mayo Clinic Staff. "Forgiveness: Letting Go of Grudges and Bitterness." Mayo Clinic Healthy Lifestyle: Adult Health, November 4, 2017. https://www.mayoclinic.org/healthy-lifestyle/adult-health/in-depth/forgiveness/art-20047692.

McDonald, Dale, and Margaret Schultz. *United States Catholic Elementary and Secondary Schools 2016-2017: The Annual Statistical Report on Schools, Enrollment, and Staffing*. Arlington, VA: National Catholic Education Association, March 9, 2017.

Miller, Alice. *Thou Shalt Not Be Aware*. New York: Farrar, Straus & Giroux, 1984.

Milton, John. *Paradise Lost*. New York: Oxford University Press, 2008.

———. Paradise Regained *and* Samson Agonistes *and the Complete Shorter Poems*. New York: Modern Library, 2012.

National Institute of Mental Health. "Antidepressant Medications for Children and Adolescents: Information for Parents and Caregivers." Washington, DC, n.d. Accessed January 8, 2018. https://www.nimh.nih.gov/health/topics/child-and-adolescent-mental-health/antidepressant-medications-for-children-and-adolescents-information-for-parents-and-caregivers.shtml.

Nussbaum, Martha C. *The Fragility of Goodness, Luck and Ethics in Greek Tragedy and Philosophy*. Cambridge: Cambridge University Press, 1986.

Ollove, Michael. "In Rural States 'Pastoral Counselors' Help Fill Mental Health Gap." *Stateline*, Pew Charitable Trusts, August 20, 2014. http://www.pewtrusts.org/en/research-and-analysis/blogs/stateline/2014/08/20/in-rural-states-pastoral-counselors-help-fill-mental-health-gap.

"Opioid Crisis Linked to Two-Year Drop in US Life Expectancy." *BBC News*, December 22, 2017. http://www.bbc.com/news/world-us-canada-42452733.

Pew Research Center. "The American Middle Class Is Losing Ground." Washington, DC, December 9, 2015. http://www.pewsocialtrends.org/2015/12/09/the-american-middle-class-is-losing-ground/.

Prager, Dennis. "How Do You Know What's Right and Wrong?" *The Dennis Prager Show*, August 18, 2015. http://www.dennisprager.com/how-do-you-know-whats-right-and-wrong-left-right-differences-part-vii/.

Qiu, Linda. "CNN Legal Analyst: By 18, Kids Have Killed Over 100,000 People in Games." *Politifact*, July 21, 2014.

Rickman, Dina. "Ketamine Reality." *The Guardian*, April 1, 2010.

Riley, Naomi Schaefer. "Can a New Religious Movement Save America from Drug Addiction?" *New York Post*, June 17, 2017.

Roheim, Geza. "The Evil Eye." *Yearbook of Psychoanalysis* 9 (1953).

Sanders, Katie. "Bernie Sanders Says 99 Percent of 'New' Income Is Going to the Top 1 Percent." *Politifact*, April 19, 2015.

Sandys, Celia, and Jonathan Littman. *We Shall Not Fail: The Inspiring Leadership of Winston Churchill*. New York: Portfolio, 2003.

Savedow, Steve, ed. and trans. *Sepher Rezial Hemelach: The Book of the Angel Rezial*. York Beach, ME: Samuel Weiser, 2000.

Scott, Gale. "Verghese: Patients Have Two Hearts," MDmag.com, March 14, 2015. http://www.mdmag.com/conference-coverage/acc-2015/verghese-patients-have-two-hearts.

"Selective Serotonin Reuptake Inhibitors (SSRI's) for Depression in Children and Teens." WebMD, accessed January 8, 2018. https://www.webmd.com/depression/selective-serotonin-reuptake-inhibitors-ssris-for-childhood-and-adolescent-depression.

Shengold, Leonard. *Soul Murder, the Effects of Childhood Abuse and Deprivation*. New Haven, CT: Yale University Press, 1989.

Siegel, Daniel J., and Mary Hartzell. *Parenting from the Inside Out: How a Deeper Self-Understanding Can Help You Raise Children Who Thrive*. New York: Penguin, 2005.

Simons, Peter. "New Data Show Lack of Efficacy for Antidepressants." Mad in America, February 27, 2017. https://www.madinamerica.com/2017/02/new-data-showslack-efficacy-antidepressants/.

Smith, Michelle, and Lawrence Pazder. *Michelle Remembers*. New York: Pocket Books, 1980.

Smith, Shane, series founder and correspondent. *VICE*. Season 3, episode 15, "Fixing the System." Aired September 27, 2015, on HBO.

Solomon, Dave. "Firefighters Reach Out to Addicts with 'Safe Station.'" *New Hampshire Union Leader*, May 4, 2016.

Sperling, Melitta. *Psychosomatic Disorders in Childhood*. New York: Jason Aaronson, 1978.

Spoto, Donald. *The Kindness of Strangers: The Life of Tennessee Williams*. New York: Da Capo Press, 1985.

Stewart, Will. "Inventor of Suicide Game Blue Whale 'Admits Inciting 16 Girls to Kill Themselves after Saying He's Cleansing Society.'" *The Mirror*, May 12, 2017.

Strauss, Elissa. "There's Not Even Close to Enough Child Care in the United States for All the Families That Need It," *Slate*, January 6, 2017. http://www.slate.com/blogs/xx_factor/2017/01/06/there_s_not_enough_child_care_in_the_u_s_for_all_the_families_that_need.html.

Sullivan, Erin M., Joseph L. Annest, Thomas R. Simon, Feijun Luo, and Linda L. Dahlberg. "Suicide Trends among Persons Aged 10–24 Years—United States, 1994–2012." Centers for Diseases Control and Prevention, March 6, 2015/64(08), 201–5.

"The Effects of Removing Prayer and the Bible from the Schools in 1962." Congressional Prayer Caucus Foundation, December 11, 2013. https://cpcfoundation.wordpress.com/2013/12/11/the-effects-of-removing-prayer-and-the-bible-from-the-schools-in-1962/.

Tyson, Peter. "The Hippocratic Oath Today." *NOVA*, March 27, 2001.

Van der Kolk, Besssel A., Alexander C. McFarlane, and Lars Weisaeth, eds. *Traumatic Stress: The Effects of Overwhelming Experience on Mind, Body, and Society*. New York: Guildford Press, 2007.

Van Gelder, Kiera. *The Buddha and the Borderline: My Recovery from Borderline Personality Disorder through Dialectical Behavior Therapy, Buddhism and Online Dating*. Oakland, CA: New Harbinger, 2010.

Verghese, Abraham. "Spirituality and Mental Health." *Indian Journal of Psychiatry* 50, no. 4 (October–December 2008): 233–37.

Weatherbe, Steven. "'Non-believer' Maté Helps Church Heal Addicts." *BC Christian News*, September 2010.

Weintraub, Karen. "Most Antidepressants Don't' Work on Kids and Teens, Study Finds." STATnews.com, June 8, 2016. https://www.statnews.com/2016/06/08/antidepressants-teens-kids/.

"White House Drug Policy Office Funds New Projects in High Intensity Drug Trafficking Areas." White House press release, August 17, 2015. https://obamawhitehouse.archives.gov/the-press-office/2015/08/17/white-house-drug-policy-office-funds-new-projects-high-intensity-drug.

Williams, Thomas D. "Professional Atheist Dawkins Says Christianity 'Bulwark against Something Worse.'" Breitbart.com, January 12, 2016. http://www.breitbart.com/national-security/2016/01/12/professional-atheist-dawkins-says-christianity-bulwark-against-something-worse/.

Wilson, Clare. "If Antidepressants Don't Work Well, Why Are They So Popular?" *New Scientist*, June 9, 2016. https://www.newscientist.com/article/2093239-if-antidepressants-dont-work-well-why-are-they-so-popular/.

Wilson, Giles. "Does Prayer Work?" *BBC News*, February 27, 2002. http://news.bbc.co.uk/2/hi/uk_news/1844076.stm.

Winnicott, D. W. *The Maturational Process and the Facilitating Environment*. London: Hogarth Press, 1965.

Zilboorg, Gregory. "The Future of Psychoanalysis and Religion—a Response." *Psychoanalytic Quarterly* 13 (1944): 93–100.

NOTES

INTRODUCTION

1 "Opioid Crisis Linked to Two-Year Drop in US Life Expectancy," *BBC News*, December 22, 2017, http://www.bbc.com/news/world-us-canada-42452733.

2 See Erin M. Sullivan, Joseph L. Annest, Thomas R. Simon, Feijun Luo, and Linda L. Dahlberg, "Suicide Trends among Persons Aged 10–24 Years—United States, 1994–2012." Centers for Diseases Control and Prevention, March 6, 2015/64(08), 201–5.

3 "Opioid Crisis Linked to Two-Year Drop in US Life Expectancy," *BBC News*, December 22, 2017, http://www.bbc.com/news/world-us-canada-42452733.

4 National Institute on Drug Abuse, "Principles of Drug Addiction Treatment: A Research-Based Guide," 3rd ed., "How Effective Is Drug Addiction Treatment?," last updated January 2018, http://www.drugabuse.gov.

5 David Armstrong and Evan Allen, "The Addict Brokers: Middlemen Profit as Desperate Patients Are Treated like Paychecks," *Boston Globe*, May 28, 2017.

CHAPTER 3

1 Megan Jula, "How Staten Island's Drug Problem Made It a Target for Poaching Patients," *New York Times*, August 23, 2016.

CHAPTER 5

1 Judith Herman, *Trauma and Recovery: The Aftermath of Violence—from Domestic Abuse to Political Terror* (New York: Basic Books, 1992), 145.

2 See Karen Weintraub, "Most Antidepressants Don't' Work on Kids and Teens, Study Finds." STATnews.com, June 8, 2016, https://www.statnews.com/2016/06/08/antidepressants-teens-kids/; Clare Wilson, "If Antidepressants Don't Work Well, Why Are They So Popular?," New Scientist, June 9, 2016, https://www.newscientist.com/article/2093239-if-antidepressants-dont-work-well-why-are-they-so-popular/; Peter Simons, "New Data Show Lack of Efficacy for Antidepressants," Mad in America, February 27, 2017, https://www.madinamerica.com/2017/02/new-data-showslack-efficacy-antidepressants; Kimberly Leonard, "Study: Most Antidepressants Don't Work on Teens or Kids," USNews.com, June 8, 2016, https://www.usnews.com/news/articles/2016-06-08/study-most-antidepressants-dont-work-on-kids-or-teens; John Kelley, "Antidepressants: Do They 'Work' or Don't They?," *Scientific American*, March 2, 2010, https://www.scientificamerican.com/article/antidepressants-do-they-work-or-dont-they/.

3 "Selective Serotonin Reuptake Inhibitors (SSRI's) for Depression in Children and Teens," WebMD, accessed January 8, 2018, https://www.webmd.com/depression/selective-serotonin-reuptake-inhibitors-ssris-for-childhood-and-adolescent-depression.

4 "Antidepressant Medications for Children and Adolescents: Information for Parents and Caregivers," National Institute of Mental Health, accessed January 8, 2018, https://www.nimh.nih.gov/health/topics/child-and-adolescent-mental-health/antidepressant-medications-for-children-and-adolescents-information-for-parents-and-caregivers.shtml.

5 Peter Tyson, "The Hippocratic Oath Today," *NOVA*, March 27, 2001.

Chapter 6

1 Dina Rickman, "Ketamine Reality," *The Guardian*, April 1, 2010.

2 Celia Hatton, "The Ketamine Connection," BBC.co.uk, July 10, 2015.

3 See Victoria Kim, "China Wants to Ban Ketamine, World Health Organization Disagrees,"TheFix.com, March 18, 2015, https://www.thefix.com/content/china-wants-ban-ketamine-world-health-organization-disagrees.

4 Doree Armstrong and Micelle Ma, "Researcher Controls Colleague's Motions in 1st Human Brain-to-Brain Interface," UW News, August 27, 2013.

5 See Jeffrey Moussiaef Masson, trans. and ed., *The Complete Letters of Sigmund Freud to Wilhelm Fliess, 1887–1904* (Cambridge, MA: Belknap Press, 1985).

Chapter 7

1 Alexis de Tocqueville, *Democracy in America: The Complete and Unabridged Volumes I and II,* trans. Henry Reeve (New York, Bantam Dell, 2002), 12.

2 Judith Herman, *Trauma and Recovery: The Aftermath of Violence—from Domestic Abuse to Political Terror* (New York: Basic Books, 1992), 67.

3 Ibid., 69.

Chapter 8

1 Brian Moore, "Reflecting on the Season of Advent," *Catholic Leader*, November 22, 2014, http://catholicleader.com.au/people/guest-writers/reflecting-on-the-season-of-advent.

2 Karen Weintraub, "Most Antidepressants Don't Work on Kids and Teens, Study Finds," STATnews.com, June 8, 2016, https://www.statnews.com/2016/06/08/antidepressants-teens-kids/. Emphasis mine.

3 Larry Culliford, "Spirituality for Beginners 8: Soul and Spirit," PsychologyToday.com, June 14, 2012, https://www.psychologytoday.com/blog/spiritual-wisdom-secular-times/201206/spirituality-beginners-8-soul-and-spirit.

4 Abraham Verghese, "Spirituality and Mental Health," *Indian Journal of Psychiatry* 50, no. 4 (October–December 2008): 233–37.

5 Nancy Coover Andreasen, "Body and Soul," *American Journal of Psychiatry* 153, no. 5 (1996): 589–90.

6 "President Trump Hosts an Opioid and Drug Abuse Listening Session," YouTube, White House, March 29, 2017. Emphasis mine.

7 Terace Garnier, "South Carolina Church Uses Bible and Prayer to Help Faithful Fight Opioid Addiction," *Fox News*, November 14, 2017.

8 Naomi Schaefer Riley, "Can a New Religious Movement Save America from Drug Addiction?," *New York Post*, June 17, 2017.

9 Ibid.

10 "The Effects of Removing Prayer and the Bible from the Schools in 1962," Congressional Prayer Caucus Foundation, December 11, 2013, https://cpcfoundation.wordpress.com/2013/12/11/the-effects-ofremoving-prayer-and-the-bible-from-the-schools-in-1962/.

11 Gretchen Livingston, "Fewer Than Half of U.S. Kids Today Live in a 'Traditional' Family," Pew Research Center, Fact Tank Blog, 2015, http://www.pewresearch.org/fact-tank/2014/12/22/less-than-half-of-u-s-kids-today-live-in-a-traditional-family/

12 Thomas D. Williams, "Professional Atheist Dawkins Says Christianity 'Bulwark against Something Worse,'" Breitbart.com, January 12, 2016, http://www.breitbart.com/national-security/2016/01/12/professional-atheist-dawkins-says-christianity-bulwark-against-something-worse/.

13 Judith Johnson, "Teens Addicted to Social Media," HuffPost blog, April 15, 2016, https://www.huffingtonpost.com/judith-johnson/teens-addicted-to-social-_b_9696378.html.

14 "How Many People Are Watching Porn Right Now? (Hint: It's a Lot)," fightthenewdrug.org, September 11, 2017, https://

fightthenewdrug.org/by-the-numbers-see-how-many-people-are-watching-porn-today/.

15 Johnson, "Teens Addicted."

16 Ibid.

17 Ibid.

18 Brian Feldman, "Do I Dare to Eat a Tide Pod?," NYMag.com, January 19, 2018, http://nymag.com/selectall/2018/01/why-are-people-eating-tide-pods.html.

19 Linda Qiu, "CNN Legal Analyst: By 18, Kids Have Killed Over 100,000 People in Games," *Politifact*, July 21, 2014.

20 Will Stewart, "Inventor of Suicide Game Blue Whale 'Admits Inciting 16 Girls to Kill Themselves after Saying He's Cleansing Society," *The Mirror*, May 12, 2017, https://www.mirror.co.uk/news/world-news/inventor-suicide-game-blue-whale-10394932.

21 Pew Research Center, "The American Middle Class Is Losing Ground," Washington, DC, December 9, 2015, http://www.pewsocialtrends.org/2015/12/09/the-american-middle-class-is-losing-ground/.

22 Richard Florida, "The Geography of Middle Class Decline," Citylab.com, November 15, 2016, https://www.citylab.com/life/2016/11/the-geography-of-middle-class-decline/505769.

23 Elissa Strauss, "There's Not Even Close to Enough Child Care in the United States for All the Families That Need It," *Slate*, January 6, 2017, http://www.slate.com/blogs/xx_factor/2017/01/06/there_s_not_enough_child_care_in_the_u_s_for_all_the_families_that_need.html.

24 Patrick Fagan, "Why Religion Matters: The Impact of Religious Practice on Social Stability," Heritage Foundation, January 25, 1996, https://www.heritage.org/civil-society/report/why-religion-matters-the-impact-religious-practice-social-stability.

25 Alexis de Tocqueville, *Democracy in America: The Complete and Unabridged Volumes I and II,* trans. Henry Reeve (New York, Bantam Dell, 2002), 13.

26 Carson Holloway, "Tocqueville on Christianity and American Democracy," The Heritage Foundation, March 7, 2016.

27 Katie Sanders, "Bernie Sanders Says 99 Percent of 'New' Income Is Going to the Top 1 Percent," *Politifact*, April 19, 2015, http://www.politifact.com/truth-o-meter/statements/2015/apr/19/bernie-s/bernie-sanders-says-99-percent-new-income-going-to.

28 Dennis Prager, "How Do You Know What's Right and Wrong?," *The Dennis Prager Show*, August 18, 2015, http://www.dennisprager.com/how-do-you-know-whats-right-and-wrong-left-right-differences-part-vii/.

29 de Tocqueville, *Democracy in America,* 357.

30 Ibid.

31 St. Augustine, *The City of God*, book 11, chapter 4.

32 Russell Brand, conversation with Dr. Drew Pinsky, Live Talks Los Angeles, October 11, 2017.

Chapter 9

1 Gabriele Amorth, *An Exorcist Explains the Demonic* (Manchester, NH: Sophia Institute Press, 2016), 94–95.

2 Judith Herman, *Trauma and Recovery: The Aftermath of Violence—from Domestic Abuse to Political Terror* (New York: Basic Books, 1992), 196.

3 Mahatma Gandhi, *The Story of My Experiments with Truth* (New York: Dover Publications, 1983), part 1, chapter 21.

4 Marc Galanter, Zoran Josipovic, Helen Dermatis, Jochen Weber, and Mary-Alice Millard, "An Initial fMRI Study on Neural Correlates of Prayer in Members of Alcoholics Anonymous," *American Journal of Drug and Alcohol Abuse* 43, no. 1 (March 25, 2016): 44–54.

5 Harold G. Koenig, "Science Proves the Healing Power of Prayer," *NewsmaxHealth*, March 31, 2015. https://www.newsmax.com/t/health/article/635623.

6 Ibid.

7 Giles Wilson, "Does Prayer Work?," *BBC News*, February, 27, 2002, http://news.bbc.co.uk/2/hi/uk_news/1844076.stm.

CHAPTER 10

1 Gruppo di Preghiera Padre Pio, "A Thought for Each Day of the Year—November," Evangelizzare.org, November 2, 2010, http://www.evangelizzare.org/2010/11/a-thought-for-each-day-of-the-year-november/.
2 Gale Scott, "Verghese: Patients Have Two Hearts," MDmag.com, March 14, 2015, http://www.mdmag.com/conference-coverage/acc-2015/verghese-patients-have-two-hearts.
3 Steven Weatherbe, "'Non-believer' Maté Helps Church Heal Addicts," *BC Christian News*, September 2010.
4 Mayo Clinic Staff, "Forgiveness: Letting Go of Grudges and Bitterness," Mayo Clinic Healthy Lifestyle: Adult Health, November 4, 2017, https://www.mayoclinic.org/healthy-lifestyle/adult-health/in-depth/forgiveness/art-20047692.
5 Michael Ollove, "In Rural States 'Pastoral Counselors' Help Fill Mental Health Gap," *Stateline*, Pew Charitable Trusts, August 20, 2014, http://www.pewtrusts.org/en/research-and-analysis/blogs/stateline/2014/08/20/in-rural-states-pastoral-counselors-help-fill-mental-health-gap.
6 Allison Buckholtz, "Help from Above: In Times of Trouble, Growing Numbers of People Take Comfort in Faith-Based Therapy," *Washington Post*, December 6, 2005.

CHAPTER 11

1 "White House Drug Policy Office Funds New Projects in High Intensity Drug Trafficking Areas," White House press release, August 17, 2015, https://obamawhitehouse.archives.gov/the-press-office/2015/08/17/white-house-drug-policy-office-funds-new-projects-high-intensity-drug.
2 Dave Solomon, "Firefighters Reach Out to Addicts with 'Safe Station,'" *New Hampshire Union Leader*, May 4, 2106.

3 Indra Cidambi, "Actual Cost of Drug Abuse in the U.S. Tops $1 Trillion Annually," *Psychology Today*, August 10, 2017, https://www.psychologytoday.com/us/blog/sure-recovery/201708/actual-cost-drug-abuse-in-us-tops-1-trillion-annually.

4 Mohan Debbarma, "Importance of Human Values in the Society," *IJELIH: International Journal of English Language, Literature and Humanities* 2, no. 1 (April 2014): 181–95.

5 Ibid.

6 From an article in *Young India*, October 22, 1925, listed in Human Unlimited. "Gandhi's 7 Dangers to Human Virtue," October 18, 2015, https://www.humanunlimited.com/blogs/blog/71610627-gandhi-s-7-dangers-to-human-virtue.

7 Jenny Gold, "Health Insurers Are Still Skimping on Mental Health Coverage," NPR.org, November 30, 2017, https://www.npr.org/sections/health-shots/2017/11/29/567264925/health-insurers-are-still-skimping-on-mental-health-coverage.

8 Kim Barker, "A Choice for Recovering Addicts: Relapse or Homelessness," *New York Times*, May 31, 2015.

9 John Lavitt, "No Profit in Junkies New Heroin Vaccine Ignored," TheFix.com, June 2, 2014, https://www.thefix.com/content/no-human-trials-damn-junkies-story-promising-heroin-vaccine-ignored?page=all.

10 Collin Dwyer, "Ohio Sues 5 Major Drug Companies for 'Fueling Opioid Epidemic,'" The Two-Way, National Public Radio, May 31, 2017.

11 David Brooks, "If It Feels Right," *New York Times*, September 12, 2011.

12 Dale McDonald and Margaret Schultz, *United States Catholic Elementary and Secondary Schools 2016–2017: The Annual Statistical Report on Schools, Enrollment, and Staffing* (Arlington, VA: National Catholic Education Association, March 9, 2017).